The Best of
Imprimis
1972–2002

Educating for Liberty

The Best of *Imprimis* 1972–2002

Edited by Douglas A. Jeffrey

Hillsdale College Press   Hillsdale, Michigan 49242

© 2002 Hillsdale College Press

Published by Hillsdale College Press
33 East College Street, Hillsdale, Michigan 49242
517.437.7341 phone   517.437.3923 fax
www.hillsdale.edu

05   04   03   02   4   3   2   1

Library of Congress Control Number 2002103896

ISBN 0-916308-55-3

The opinions expressed in IMPRIMIS are not necessarily the views
of Hillsdale College.

Manufactured in the United States of America

Printed and bound by Edwards Brothers, Ann Arbor, Michigan

Cover design by Hesseltine & DeMason, Ann Arbor, Michigan

Contents

v

CULTURE

INTERNATIONAL RELATIONS

Foreword

IMPRIMIS is a national monthly speech digest published by Hillsdale College. It was launched thirty years ago with a circulation of only a few thousand. Ten years ago, upon the publication of In the First Place—a collection of the best of IMPRIMIS's first twenty years—its circulation had grown to 335,000. Today its circulation is well over 1,000,000—and growing. It is sent free of charge to anyone who wishes to receive it.

We are often asked about our reasons for sending IMPRIMIS to so many people each and every month. There are two main answers to this question, each connected to the unique history of Hillsdale College.

The first answer is connected to Hillsdale's recent history. It was in the 1970s that the federal government sought to force the College to "count by race" in its admissions and hiring policies. This was especially galling to a college that had opened its doors to blacks and women long before the Civil War. Besides being galling, it was wrong. Racial quotas violate the principle of equal rights that forms the basis of justice and concord in a free society. And besides being wrong, this interference with a private college's internal affairs violated the principle of limited government that is at the heart of American constitutionalism.

Hillsdale refused to comply. And as the battle wound its way through the courts, the College—which had never itself accepted federal taxpayer funds—was forced to go even further to maintain its independence. It was forced to tell its students and their parents that they could no longer accept federal taxpayer-subsidized grants and loans. Then, to stay competitive, Hillsdale had to replace that financial aid for its students and their parents with private contributions. To do this it needed a lot of friends, and IMPRIMIS proved to be an effective vehicle for making them.

The second reason for publishing IMPRIMIS is connected to the College's older history. Over 150 years ago, Hillsdale's founders linked its educational mission to perpetuating the founding principles of America. This idea of the College's duty to the nation has remained strong, even as other colleges and universities have fallen prey to the mind-numbing doctrines of moral and cultural relativism and the dispiriting oppression of "political correctness."

Maintaining the College's independence, then, is inseparable from defending the Constitution, and the principles of civil and religious liberty that underlie it. This means promoting the ideas of limited government, free enterprise, individual rights, personal responsibility, and strong national defense. In promoting these ideas nationwide through IMPRIMIS—particularly when they are under fierce assault from almost every other quarter in academia—Hillsdale College is simply and doggedly carrying out its original mission.

That mission will continue to guide Hillsdale College and IMPRIMIS as we head into our fourth decade of publication.

DOUGLAS A. JEFFREY
Vice President for External Affairs
Editor, IMPRIMIS
Hillsdale College

May 2002

EDUCATION

❑ ❑ ❑

Hillsdale and America

Larry P. Arnn

June 2000

Dr. Arnn delivered this speech at a Hillsdale College seminar, "Heroes for a New Generation and a New Century," in Dallas, Texas.

❏ ❏ ❏

In this and like communities, public sentiment is everything. With public sentiment, nothing can fail; without it nothing can succeed. Consequently he who moulds public sentiment, goes deeper than he who enacts statutes or pronounces decisions. He makes statutes and decisions possible or impossible to be executed. —Abraham Lincoln, August 21, 1858

Hillsdale College is two things. It is first a small liberal arts college in southern Michigan boasting an old history full of struggle and distinction. It is second a national institution, known in every corner of the land. It has been both things for a long time.

The combination of these things is unusual. There are many liberal arts colleges that are the size of Hillsdale or larger. A few are just as old or older. For some reason Hillsdale has become one of the best-known colleges in the nation. Why is that?

3

The importance and the fame of Hillsdale College are not accidental. The cause is something old, something high and fundamental. It is the mission of Hillsdale. It is the relationship of that mission to the principles and heritage of our country. It is the fact that the mission, those principles, and that heritage have become controversial.

To see why Hillsdale is both famous and important, we need to understand the liberal arts and how they relate to free government. We need to see what has happened to the liberal arts in most places where they are studied. We need to see in what way Hillsdale is exceptional in the pursuit of the liberal arts.

What the Liberal Arts Are Not

The relationship between the liberal arts and government is shown immediately by their current state. Certain new principles have in the last generation become authoritative in our land. First these principles became entrenched in the academy, where the liberal arts are supposed to live. Consequently they became authoritative in the government, and because of this the government is much changed.

Think first of the changes in the study of the liberal arts. Princeton University, one of the great universities of the world, has lately appointed a professor who believes that middle-class families in the United States have a moral obligation to pay 33 percent of the first $30,000 they make to combat poverty around the globe. After that, they should pay 100 percent. He explicitly rejects the theory of property rights as an "unacceptable ethical view." The New Yorker calls this man, Peter Singer, "the most influential living philosopher." Along with his depreciation of the rights of free labor, he argues that certain animals are persons having "the same special claim to be protected" as humans. With an eerie consistency, he also argues that euthanasia and infanticide are in some cases morally obligatory. Perhaps then it is not only that cows are to be treated like people; also people are to be treated like cows.

Over at Yale, one of the oldest institutions of higher learning in the New World, the college has returned an endowment gift of $20 million for the study of Western civilization. Yale went more than three years without implementing the program. There was controversy about it on the faculty. When he became aware of the controversy, the donor asked for the authority to approve faculty members appointed to teach in the program. This gave Yale an out, and it returned the money in the name of academic freedom. A brilliant opportunity was thereby squandered. Not long after at Stanford, the chant was heard: "Hey, hey, ho, ho, Western Civ has got to go."

At the 1984 convention of the American Political Science Association, a straw poll was taken to see how the assembled doctors of political science would vote in the presidential race between Ronald Reagan and Walter Mondale. You may recall that Reagan won that election with almost 60 percent of the vote. Among the political scientists, however, Mondale topped 90 percent of the vote, and much of the remaining 10 percent did not go to Reagan, but rather to someone to the left even of Mondale. This is the phenomenon we call diversity in the modern academy.

Professor Singer and his many like-minded colleagues epitomize something fundamental and new. His views speak in direct contradiction to the distinctions that underlay the American Revolution, distinctions fundamental to the meaning of "liberal" in both "liberal democracy" and "liberal arts." The Declaration of Independence proclaims that "all men are created equal." Of course the obvious thing about human beings is that they are not equal. Some are tall, and others short. Some are pale, and others dark. Some are male, and others female. Some are active, and others less so.

What can it mean, then, that human beings are "created equal"? In order to fathom the meaning of this principle, we must expand our view. It is in relation to other creatures that the equality of human beings becomes obvious. Up close, the trees in a forest look different from one another; from a distance, or compared to a sand dune, they look alike.

In *The Federalist*, for example, there is the famous statement by James Madison: ". . . what is government itself but the greatest of all reflections on human nature? If men were angels, no government would be necessary. If angels were to govern men, neither external nor internal controls on government would be necessary."

Human beings are less than angels. This distinction echoes the Declaration itself, in which God appears four times. He is named as the Creator ("endowed by their Creator with certain inalienable rights"); as the legislator (the author of the "laws of nature and of nature's God"); as the executive ("Divine Providence"); and as the judicial officer ("the Supreme Judge of the World"). The implication is clear: In His hands alone would it be safe to combine all the powers of government. When government is to be run by human beings, it is important that the powers of government be separated. Both "external and internal controls on government" are nothing less than essential.

If man is below the angels, he is also above the beasts. In the last letter that he ever wrote, Thomas Jefferson addressed with poetic justice one aspect of the meaning of the Declaration of Independence. Writing to Roger Weightman on June 24, 1826, just ten days before he died (on the Fourth of July!) and just eighteen years before the founding of Hillsdale College, Jefferson said: ". . . the mass of mankind has not been born with saddles on their backs, nor a favored few booted and spurred, ready to ride them legitimately, by the grace of God." If men are not angels, so also are they not horses. They are something else, something in between.

The distinction between men and beasts, on the one hand, and men and God, on the other, gives perspective and definition to the statement that "all men are created equal." In light of that distinction, the rights of man become clear. No man should be trusted with the power of God. Government must be limited. No man may rule another as any man may rule a cow, a dog, or a horse. We do not ask our horses' permission before we hitch them to the buggy. We do not ask our dogs' permission before we put them on the leash. But government of human beings is different; it must be based upon the consent of the governed.

It can be protested that Professor Singer of Princeton is not an owner of slaves, whereas Thomas Jefferson was. That is true. On the other hand, Thomas Jefferson was alive in his every fiber to the distinction between the human and the animal, and so he agonized over slavery. With his colleagues he brought principles into practice that secured both limited government and, ultimately, the abolition of slavery. Professor Singer seems less clear on this distinction. Nor is it a coincidence that, having blurred the line between humans and animals, he suggests that it is immoral for American families to keep more than $30,000 per year, regardless of how hard they work or how much good they do others by what they produce. It is a small and logical step from Professor Singer's ethics to coercive tax policies that begin to look quite a bit like slavery.

These changes in the academy have their echo in government as well. Over the past generation both the structure and the scope of the government have been revolutionized. Hillsdale College, like many institutions and many people, has been at odds with the government for much of its recent history because the government intrudes into every corner of private life. Hillsdale accepts no federal government support of any kind, even indirectly through aid to its students. Because of this it must replace the massive government aid that is available to other schools by appealing for private contributions, a huge effort requiring the generosity of tens of thousands of people. If Hillsdale did not make this effort, and if these people were not generous, then Hillsdale would be compelled to take race into account in its admissions and hiring policies.

This would be an abomination anywhere, but especially so in a college that was one of the first in American history to admit blacks as students, a college which proudly welcomed the great Frederick Douglass to speak on its campus, a college whose library is built around a massive gift by the anti-slavery statesman Edward Everett, who spoke before Lincoln at Gettysburg. Hillsdale has always boasted of the high proportion of its sons who gave their lives for the Union cause in the Civil War. From its beginning it has fought for freedom and equality. In its recent history one can see that the battle still rages today. Hillsdale, unlike most places, fights that battle. That is because it believes in the principles of liberty, which are implied in the pursuit of the liberal arts.

Nor is this the only sign of changes in the structure and scope of the government. Because legitimate government must be limited and based on consent, our Constitution was written upon the principle that powers not granted to the federal government explicitly are not available to it. It is a government of "enumerated powers." For this reason until the 1930s most government spending was accomplished by cities and towns, and they spent mostly money that they had collected within their own boundaries. Today their share of the government pie has eroded to less than 20 percent. Meanwhile the pie itself has expanded massively. At a time when the American economy has reached unprecedented size, still the government deploys nearly half of the gross domestic product of the land.

A State of the Union report by President George Washington would address seven or eight subjects. A modern president will propose several times that many new projects in a typical speech. President Clinton proposed dozens of new programs in his 1995 State of the Union Address, in which he said famously that "the era of big government is over." In truth, hardly anything appeared beyond his purview. He proposed federal programs to supervise children after school; federal programs to hire teachers and policemen; federal programs to subsidize private businesses of wide-ranging description.

Under the force of technology and innovation, the American economy is more productive, and the American people richer, than ever been. For this reason our citizens are not inclined right now to worry overmuch about the growth of government. But still it is true that unless men have become angels, it is dangerous to concentrate power in the hands of any of them. That fundamental fact will be true long after this economic boom is over and the next one has come and gone, too.

The situation is especially dangerous if government is animated by principles that undermine the citizen's claim to rights not given by government, but inherent in his nature. Another Princeton man, Woodrow Wilson, was the first president of the United States to hold the Doctor of Philosophy degree. He, like Professor Singer, was impatient with the distinctions that underlay the limitation of government and the separation of powers.

In one of his academic writings, an essay titled "What Is Progress?," Wilson writes:

> Jefferson wrote of the "laws of Nature,"—and then by way of afterthought,—"and of Nature's God." And they constructed a government as they would have constructed an orrery [a mechanical model of the solar system],—to display the laws of nature. Politics in their thought was a variety of mechanics. The Constitution was founded on the law of gravitation. The government was to exist and move by virtue of the efficacy of checks and balances.

> The trouble with the theory is that government is not a machine, but a living thing. It falls, not under the theory of the universe, but under the theory of organic life. It is accountable to Darwin,

not to Newton. It is modified by its environment, necessitated
by its tasks, shaped to its functions by the sheer pressure of life.

This sentiment did not bode well for the separation of powers, or for
the doctrine of limited and enumerated powers of government. This rejection of the ground of American constitutionalism prepared the way for a
rejection of the ground of rights, as they were understood in the institutions of America. Never mind that Wilson distorted the basis of those rights,
which are grounded not as he said in mechanics, but rather in the natural
distinctions between man and God on the one hand, and man and beast
on the other, that are obvious to the liberally educated. Once his views
became established, then the way was prepared for what Franklin Roosevelt
would call in a 1944 speech "new self-evident truths" that justify the writing of a "new Bill of Rights." This new Bill of Rights undermines the old; in
particular it replaces natural rights with entitlements. By this means the
government of human beings is replaced with the administration of things.

This development constitutes the supreme challenge to the American people in our time. At bottom it calls forth a debate about the meaning of the human being and his status before the law. It is a subject to be
taken up most profoundly in the institutions that pursue the liberal arts.
That brings us finally to the mission of Hillsdale College.

The Liberal Arts and Free Government

Just as our nation was built upon certain principles of government, so it
was built with a certain view of the liberal arts. Toward the end of their lives,
when Thomas Jefferson was eighty-two and James Madison was seventy-
four, they struck up a correspondence about how to teach the law. These
two men were the most distinguished living Americans. A generation before, Jefferson had been the foremost author of the Declaration of Independence, and Madison the foremost author of the Constitution of the
United States. Both had been legislators. Both had been president. Together they had founded the dominant political party in the land. Now as
the evening came upon them, they were thinking of the preservation of all
they had built. This discussion of teaching the law expanded into a discussion of preserving the Republic.

Jefferson proposed that some sort of textbook be created or adopted. Madison replied that this would be difficult. Of course the Declaration of Independence, wrote Madison, says "everything that could be said in the same number of words." Of course *The Federalist* is the most "authentic exposition of the text of the Constitution." Locke and Sidney, and the Inaugural and Farewell addresses of George Washington are most useful, even essential readings for any student of the law in this free country. And yet, useful though these documents are, still Madison writes that it is hard to define any set of "books that will be both guides & guards for the purpose."

Madison concludes: ". . . after all, the most effectual safeguard against heretical intrusions into the School of Politics, will be an Able & Orthodox Professor, whose course of instruction will be an example to his successors. . . ."

From discussion about a school of law, a School of Politics is born. From a discussion about which books to read, an institution is born. It is not enough to have a course of study; there must be a place of study. It is not enough to have materials to read; there must be teachers to show the meaning of what is read. The preservation of the political institutions of liberty requires an institution of a different type. This is no merely individual effort. The young cannot be trained by books alone, by documents alone, or by laws alone. They must be trained by teachers, who must themselves be trained by teachers. This is what happens in colleges. Colleges of a certain type are necessary to the preservation of liberty. They are necessary to the making of good laws. Without them the laws will lose the spirit of freedom, and then freedom itself will soon be gone.

It may seem strange that private institutions are seen as vital to the preservation of public institutions, but this is characteristic of the American constitutional system. For example, the founding of America is replete with statements that neither liberty nor justice can survive without religion; yet religion is not to be controlled by the government. The founding of America is replete with statements that neither liberty nor justice can survive without strong and well-functioning families; yet the family is to remain a private, a sacredly private institution, protected but not controlled by the power of the law.

This is the theme and the paradox of the American Revolution. Public institutions are necessary to the preservation of private rights. And so the government and the people, the public and the private, live in a tight relationship with each other, each dependent upon the other, each benefiting from the other.

Liberal education, like religion and family, has then a sort of public standing in America. In its original sense, in the sense in which it has been practiced at Hillsdale College for over a century and a half, it operates within, it is sanctioned by, the principles of the nation just as much as is the government itself.

Hillsdale College Was Built According to This Understanding

What is the substance of this liberal education that is necessary to the preservation of freedom? We can find some information about this in the first documents of Hillsdale College.

The Articles of Incorporation of Hillsdale College date from March 1855. Their preamble states:

> Whereas the denomination of Christians, Known as Free-Will-Baptists, with other friends of education, grateful to God for the inestimable blessings resulting from the prevalence of civil and religious Liberty and intelligent piety in the land, and believing that the diffusion of sound learning is essential to the perpetuity of these blessings, have founded and endowed a college at Hillsdale. . . .

These "Free-Will-Baptists" believed with Thomas Jefferson that "Almighty God hath created the mind free." They saw the human being as responsible for his actions, responsible specifically to a standard established in the divine and natural order of the universe and perceivable by human reason. Because of this, the human being is naturally entitled to "civil and religious liberty." Because of this, the human being is naturally capable of an "intelligent piety." Because of this, "sound learning" is essential to the perpetuity of human freedom and morality. Because of this, the citizen educated for liberty must explore the meaning of those "laws of nature and of nature's God."

Although these are wonderful doctrines, put into practice for the first time by the birth of the American Republic, they are nothing unusual for an American college in 1855. Similar words can be found in the preamble to the Michigan Constitution today. Similar words can be found in the preambles of forty-six of the fifty state constitutions and in the religious freedom clauses of all fifty.

Like the Articles of Incorporation of Hillsdale, all of these documents group together certain things that we today often think are opposed. In the American heritage, reason and revelation go together in support of freedom and morality, which means that freedom and morality go together, too. This is the characteristically American teaching. The Declaration of Independence talks very much of freedom and government by consent, but it justifies these on the ground of the "laws of nature and of nature's God." The Northwest Ordinance of 1787, under which Michigan came into the Union, states in Article III: "Religion, morality, and knowledge being necessary to good government and the happiness of mankind, schools and the means of education shall forever be encouraged."

Hillsdale College was then founded according to the same principles that gave rise to the American Union itself. From the first days it built a faculty of people inspired by these principles and ready to sacrifice for them. It has just such a faculty even today. The College has grown directly from the third of the four fundamental laws of the nation. It set out from the beginning to fulfill the need elaborated by Madison in his letter to Jefferson. It pursues that noble goal still.

Little wonder, with such a beginning, that Hillsdale should be among the first colleges in America to admit blacks into its student body. Little wonder that it should be among the first to give the same benefit to women. Little wonder that the College would be proud of the high percentage of its graduates who would give their lives to the cause of the Union and of liberty in the Civil War. Hillsdale was not, by any means, the only college built before the Civil War with these principles. But it shows from the first day a particular devotion to them. If in later days Hillsdale has demonstrated the spirit of independence to a unique degree, that fact is but the flower of a planting made generations before in the first soil of the Republic.

Conclusion

It is then no accident that Hillsdale has run afoul of the federal government. That government has today assumed a new form, the form of a modern centralized administrative state, because it is devoted to a new purpose. This new purpose is built upon principles incompatible with the first principles of our nation, to which Hillsdale remains devoted.

We at Hillsdale are not likely to be able perfectly to meet the high standards laid down by the principles of the College, which are also the first and greatest principles of the nation in which we live. But although we will likely fall short, we will hold up those standards, and we will be ready to be judged by them. In so doing we will prepare our students to live up to them, too, insofar as it is possible for human beings to do so.

In this respect Hillsdale College is unique. It pursues the liberal arts first and foremost as an academic task. It pursues them with rigor, with love, and with devotion. Because of that it is at the same time something more than an academic institution. It is an institution of freedom, of just the kind that our Fathers believed would be necessary to the preservation of freedom. To fulfilling that duty, we at Hillsdale will continue our devotion. In that task we act at once as seekers of the truth, as creatures of the Almighty, and as citizens of the greatest Republic ever built.

❑   ❑   ❑

LARRY P. ARNN is the twelfth president of Hillsdale College. From 1985 to 2000, he was president of The Claremont Institute, a California-based organization that studies and promotes America's founding principles. In 1996 he was the founding chairman of the California Civil Rights Initiative, the successful ballot measure to eliminate racial preferences in state employment, admissions, and contracting policy. He is a member of the board of trustees of the Heritage Foundation, and of the boards of directors of The Claremont Institute, the Henry Salvatori Center at Claremont McKenna College, and the Center for Individual Rights. Previously, he served as director of research for Martin Gilbert, now Sir Martin, the official bio-grapher of Winston Churchill. A graduate of Arkansas State University with master's and doctoral degrees from the Claremont Graduate School, Dr. Arnn has also studied at the London School of Economics and at Wor-chester College, Oxford University.

Decadence and Recovery in American Education

Russell Kirk

May 1973

Dr. Kirk delivered this speech at a Hillsdale College seminar, "Education in America: Democratic Triumph or Egalitarian Disaster?," on the Hillsdale campus

❏ ❏ ❏

A few years ago, a Scottish girl visiting these United States remarked to me that American attitudes toward educational discontents are very like the American attitudes toward the problem of being overweight: Everyone talks about such things, but no one does anything about them. For a quarter of a century, books about the failure of American education have been pouring from the presses; yet one encounters few signs that all this protest has compelled substantial improvement.

As Plato wrote, education is meant to develop wisdom and virtue. But American educational establishments, in general, appear to have forgotten about those ends: Instead, they offer chiefly the pursuit of sociability and of material success. In the definition of C. E. M. Joad, "decadence" is the loss of an object: Joad meant that we fall into decadence when we forget or ignore aim or purpose in existence. By this definition, American education—from kindergarten through graduate school—is decadent. The search for wisdom and virtue has been abandoned.

Formal schooling is not the only aspect of modern culture that exhibits symptoms of decadence; and we are not to expect that schools and

15

colleges and universities, by an effort wholly their own, can renew modern civilization. As my colleague Dr. Ernest van den Haag has written, faith in education is the Pelagian heresy of modern America. Old Pelagius, in the fourth century of the Christian era, declared that the souls of all men would be saved eventually, through the natural goodness of humankind, without need for divine grace. In our time, the typical American believes that the souls of all men will be saved through education—without need for thought.

But it is not so, and the evidences of this theory's failure lie all about us. We cannot redeem the human condition through free and compulsory schooling alone. Nevertheless, one must begin a work of regeneration somewhere, and schooling remains one of the more important means for a renewed apprehension of wisdom and virtue. Is it possible for us to recover from fad and foible, from boredom and violence?

To answer that question, first we must diagnose our afflictions in the realm of education. We have been suffering, I believe, from two diseases: one a sickness of understanding among the general public, the other a malady among many of our educators.

First, the American public, taken as a whole, has forgotten—or else never knew—that the ends of education are wisdom and virtue. The typical parent looks upon education as a means to material ends: the way to practical success, social advancement of a private character, and general jolliness. Although these may be desirable goals, they are not the true ends of genuine education. They may be achieved through *training* (as distinguished from *education*), through personal endeavor of a kind not scholastic, and through a state of mind, perhaps, like that of Democritus, the laughing philosopher. But these goals are not the primary concern of real schools, colleges, and universities.

Once I undertook my private survey of the opinions of children, and of the opinions of school-board members, in my part of Michigan. I asked a good many such people what they considered the most important function of their schools. Why did they support those schools? What activity in those schools did they find most interesting?

One response, it turned out, was more general than was any other answer. What did these people, these adult products of the American educational apparatus, believe to be the most worthy achievement of their schools? Why, the basketball games. When pressed for a reason, those who responded informed me that games were good for the health of young people—or of those permitted to play on the teams, anyway; and besides, the night games supplied free entertainment for the local public.

You may perceive here what I mean by "decadence," the loss of an object. Almost nobody with whom I conversed mentioned wisdom and virtue as objects of public instruction. Yet perhaps we are just beginning to recover from this delusion that formal education means fun and games; perhaps the public grows vaguely aware that something has gone wrong with the moral and the intellectual order of our culture, and that there ought to be more to education than games and sociability.

If one wishes to defend the general public's indifference toward the true ends of learning, in may be argued that the average American parent is a hungry sheep—or a sheep, anyway—who looks up and is not fed. If we are to take professors of education for the shepherds of this sheepwalk, surely those gentlemen and scholars, as a breed, have offered little imaginative guidance. And this observation leads us to the second form of sickness in the realm of education: to the disease of theory.

The Americans, says Alexis de Tocqueville, tend always to neglect the general for the particular: that is, they shy away from theory. A pragmatic attitude dominated the United States before the term "pragmatism" was coined among us. When a nation achieves great power and corresponding responsibilities nevertheless, sometimes people must refer to first principles. In no other aspect of life has a vulgarized pragmatism— raised to an orthodoxy in education by certain disciples of John Dewey— accomplished more damage to thought and action than in the domain of American schooling.

We have with us Professor Sidney Hook, the stoutest defender of Dewey's thought. But Dr. Hook mordantly criticizes the excesses or misunderstandings of many educationalists who consider themselves Dewey's inheritors. Often Dewey the innovator has become Dewey the dead hand, lying heavy upon the lower learning and the higher. In Dewey's name, at any rate, notions of "socialization," "life adjustment," "permissive approaches," and the like have done much to break down intellectual and ethical disciplines.

But cheerfulness will keep breaking in. No longer do all Americans take for a sign of health the passion for compelling young people to "adjust" to modern society; indeed, the revolt of the young against such "adjustment" strongly suggests that such theories work their own ruin. If the time is out of joint, conformity to vulgar errors is sin and shame.

The aim of the "life adjustment" enthusiasts—as summarized ironically by a disgruntled superintendent of schools whom I know—has been to subject all young people to a uniform (although nearly formless) curriculum of "socialization," and thus to turn out a standard product—The American, who will be cooperative in a new society of Togetherness. Mixed up with this scheme has been the trauma of the Natural Goodness of Man, or Perfectibility.

Confronted by hot criticism, the masters of the American public-school apparatus have made some gestures of appeasement to "traditionalists" on the one hand, and to "radicals" on the other. Holding office, these masters are difficult to move greatly. Here and there concessions have been made by them, tardily, to permit special treatment for the "gifted child," though they remain fonder far of special treatment for the "culturally disadvantaged." They continue to mutter their familiar incantations: preparation for a changing world, education for leisure, reconstruction of society through new schools for better learning, the forming of The American, shaping "patterns for democratic society," and all the rest.

Many members of the American educationist establishment, and their counterparts in other quarters of the world, do not seem to be thinking of our present troubled year when they talk of adjustment: They are thinking of 1900, or 1910. At best, they think of those glorious days when they became doctors of education. Dewey's instrumentalism remains their ideology; but they fail to apply the pragmatic test to their own lives and careers. For such dull dreamers, the reluctant taxpayer is the chief remaining obstacle to perfection through Holy Education. In a time when (in Yeats' phrase) "the worst are full of passionate intensity," when schools are tormented by arsonists, narcotics peddlers, and violent ideologues, these gentlemen go on recommending that we settle snugly into the warm collectivity of modern existence. To read the books and articles of many of them, even today, one might not guess that the world has been falling apart ever since 1914.

This is a dreary failure of imagination. Any society depends for the mere mechanics of its functioning—and for much else—upon the maintenance of a certain level of imagination and integrity among the people who make decisions, great or small. And any society depends for the foundation and scaffolding of its intellectual life—and for much else—upon the accumulated wisdom of our intellectual and moral patrimony. It may tickle an educationist's fancy to pose as an omniscient director of politics, morals, and metaphysics. But then, as during the past decade, up starts Sansculotte, "many-headed, fire-breathing, crying 'What think ye of me?'"

At the beginning of our century, in his first book, Irving Babbitt foresaw what was to happen upon every level of American education in the dawning age:

> The firmness of the American's faith in the blessings of education is equaled only by the vagueness of his ideas as to the kind of education to which these blessings are annexed. One can hardly consider the tremendous stir we have been making about education, the time and energy and enthusiasm we are ready to lavish on educational undertakings, without being reminded of the words of Sir Joshua Reynolds: "A provision of endless apparatus, a bustle of infinite inquiry and research, may be employed to evade and shuffle off real labor—the real labor of thinking."

What Babbitt predicted then is upon us now. Perhaps a grand act of will—or rather, a series of such acts, preceded by serious reflection, on the part of many of us—may yet redeem modern education. Some people suggest that we may have to abandon established "Education," as a kind of quasi-religion or mass-production business offering next to nothing for mind and conscience. Let the usurpers have it, these writers say. The awakening of imagination, by the discipline of intellect, may have to be undertaken by new voluntary associations, in defiance of the Educational Establishment.

Aye, this may be so; or possibly there remains to us hope for reformation of school, college, and university. So turn we now to restoration. My time being limited, let me confine myself here to recovery of reason and imagination in social studies.

We have seen during the past decade a violent rebellion of many among the rising generation against the regime of dullness and complacency that long dominated American schooling, and which is little reformed today. The young rebels were bored with what they had been taught; they embraced shallow ideology as a relief from boredom. For the most part, the violence has subsided for the present. But unless we offer the rising generation something more satisfying than the typical "social stew" curriculum, once more external events may set fire to ideological impulses.

School, college, and university, for several decades, have been ineffectual in preparing their students for making considered judgments upon public concerns. At the school level—and even in many college textbooks and classes—political socialization too often has amounted to little more than the imparting of a kind of ethos of sociability, with a faint aroma of *Animal Farm*. The rising generation has been assured, for instance, that there is but one tolerable form of government anywhere, democracy (most vaguely defined or described); that practically anything ever done by "we Americans" has been wise and blameless, except for minor activities by isolated robber-barons and ephemeral crypto-imperialists; that American "problems" are mostly of a material sort, to be solved by positive legislation; that in foreign affairs, little is necessary but to trust in the omnicompetence of the United Nations. Such, at any rate, was the character of this instruction until Sansculotte took a hand. It was small wonder that students grew bored or resentful at this bland intellectual diet. Abandoning this form of unreality, many of them embraced another form of unreality—fanatic ideology.

So of the many programs of reform which ought to be commenced, I think it especially important to reunite the ethical understanding with the study of society. Economics moves upward into politics, politics upward into ethics. A political structure without discernible ethical foundation will attract little interest or loyalty among young people; students in both college and high school are starved for first principles today—and many of them know it. It will not do to talk windily of "the essential rightness of democracy" or of "the religion of democracy," as platitudinous substitutes for political philosophy, historical consciousness, and clear knowledge of social institutions.

It does not follow that such introduction to the principles of order—the inner order of the soul, and the outer order of the commonwealth—need to be abstract. The ethical imagination may be moved, particularly in early life, through the instrument of biography—by which I do *not* mean simple panegyric. And a thoroughgoing course in the history of ideas, at the high school level, would be preferable to the repetitious "civics" and "problems of democracy" courses now prevalent. As a survey a few years ago by Mr. Kenneth P. Langston and Mr. M. Kent Jennings indicated, juniors and seniors in the typical high school have been acquiring next to no additional knowledge of social concerns through the usual courses in American government and history, and the like; nor have they been acquiring any additional interest in public affairs. A quite different approach appears to be required at this level—in part because the same thing already has been done in earlier grades.

We may need a study of moral philosophy, if you will, as related to social institutions. I confess that we stand ill-prepared for such a recovery. Among political scientists and sociologists and even professors of history, the dominant modes of thought are behavioristic and institutional; this intellectual climate of opinion therefore overshadows the teachers' colleges and the secondary schools, too. Behaviorism amounts to little more (except for the half-unconscious prejudices of its practitioners) than a cataloguing of opinion and phenomena; institutionalism often has declined into dry recitation. Little place remains for philosophy, and for the moral imagination. Even should we commence today, our results would not be apparent in colleges for some years, and in high schools no sooner. Such a reform will not much affect the immediate conduct of American foreign policy, say, and so will not satisfy the votaries of "relevance." But there always will be wars and rumors of wars, and the high and grim decisions which the American republic must make will not diminish with the elapse of decades.

Along with the reinvigoration of programs of social studies, we must much improve the education of teachers in such disciplines. We must have fewer courses in educational techniques, and more and better courses in genuine history, genuine politics, and genuine philosophy. There must be less reliance upon the crib, by teacher and by student.

Politics, after all, is the application of ethics to the concerns of the commonwealth. Politics cannot be apprehended properly without reference to biographical and historical models for order, justice, and freedom; nor without reference to theory. Any community, great or small, is knit together by belief in certain enduring norms or principles. When knowledge of those norms dwindles, the fabric of society wears thin. Lacking a knowledge of the permanent things, a people become interested chiefly in immediate self-interest; and "good natured, unambitious men," as George Bernard Shaw put it, "stand by in helpless horror" at the consequences of this triumph of the ravenous ego.

Here I have suggested only the bare bones of a reform in the teaching of social studies; other disciplines require a parallel regeneration. Decadence never is inevitable, so long as a tolerable number of people retain the elements of right reason, and a will to survive. The need for reinvigoration of the discipline of humane letters is at least as urgent as that need in the social studies.

University, college, and high school all suffered from far too much impulsive action during the past decade: anti-intellectual action. The highest sort of action, as Aristotle suggests, is intellectual action. We cannot repeat too often the admonition of Demosthenes to the Athenians, then about to dash into violent action: "In the name of God, I beg you to *think!*" That is what education is all about—thinking, which may lead toward wisdom and virtue.

Has education in America been a democratic triumph or an egalitarian disaster? Neither, as yet—although we have been sliding in recent years toward the latter. Education, I suggest, ought not, *per se*, to be "democratic" or "aristocratic": that would be to impose political forms and slogans upon the ordering of intellect and character. Educate the rising generation well in politics, and the political institutions of any people will benefit—whether those institutions are democratic or not. Educate the rising generation well ethically, and political forms may matter comparatively little.

Democracy may be improved by genuine education, but education will not be improved by forcing it into a political mold; we have had far too much politicizing of schools already. And intellectual talents and appetites being unequal, we fall into grave error if we attempt to make schools and colleges a kind of cauldron for brewing equality of condition; this point has been put ably by Dr. Christopher Jencks recently. Genuine education is the advancement of right reason, for reason's sake. If the choice had to be made, T. S. Eliot wrote once, it would be better to educate well a comparatively few people than to educate everybody shoddily; for in the former circumstances, at least we would enjoy some competent leadership. An egalitarian disaster has not yet occurred in this country, because in fact we have not yet altogether abandoned the older understanding of education as an intellectual means to an ethical end. Once we systematically and deliberately convert schooling into a means for achieving equality of condition—which seems to be the object of the federal judge at Denver in the Denver "busing" decision, now appealed to the Supreme Court—we will achieve, in fact, only mediocrity of mind and character. And no democracy can endure if it rests upon intellectual apathy and indifference.

We have succeeded in schooling a great many people—too many, at college and university levels, because neither their own interests nor the employment market justify today so grand a production of people with academic degrees. We have not yet succeeded in educating a great many people—for which sorry fact the declining sales of serious books are some evidence. We have not developed so successful a system of popular instruction as Switzerland has, nor yet so admirable a system of higher education as Britain used to have. The typical product of our schools and colleges is mediocre intellectually—no triumph, no disaster.

But the times demand more than mediocrity. Our failure to quicken imagination accounts, in large part, for our national difficulties, now formidable. Our public men tend to lack moral imagination and strength of will; our communities grow ugly and violent because vision and courage are wanting. Mediocrity in a pattern of education may not be disastrous in itself, and yet it may contribute gradually to private and public decadence. Mediocre appeals for "excellence" will not suffice, in the absence of real educational reform. Who at P.S. 137 really aspires to impart wisdom and virtue? Who at Behemoth University has any time for such abstract ends? And yet if those with power in the educational establishment remain unconcerned with wisdom and virtue, the ethos of sociability and material success will evaporate gradually, or perhaps swiftly—leaving a vacuum, possibly to be filled by force and a master.

❏   ❏   ❏

RUSSELL KIRK was born in Plymouth, Michigan, in 1918. He received his B.A. from Michigan State University, his M.A. from Duke University, and his Doctor of Letters from St. Andrews in Scotland. He was the author of several books, including the classic *The Conservative Mind* (1953), edited the educational quarterly *The University Bookman*, and was founder and first editor of the quarterly *Modern Age*. In addition to a nationally syndicated newspaper column, Dr. Kirk contributed to numerous publications, including *National Review, Yale Review, Fortune, Humanitas,* and *Commonweal.* He was a Guggenheim Fellow, a senior fellow of the American Council of Learned Societies, and a Constitutional Fellow of the National Endowment for the Humanities. Among his several awards were the Ann Radcliffe Award of the Count Dracula Society for his gothic fiction, the Weaver Award of the Ingersoll Prizes for his scholarly writing, and the Salvatori Prize for historical writing. In 1989 President Reagan conferred on him the Presidential Citizens Medal. Dr. Kirk passed away in 1994.

Why We Need a Core Curriculum for College Students

Lynne V. Cheney

May 1990

The following is excerpted from Dr. Cheney's 1988 National Endowment for the Humanities report, "50 Hours: A Core Curriculum for College Students," which she discussed at Hillsdale College.

❏   ❏   ❏

Reporting about curricula, Professor Rudolph once observed, is hardly the same as writing about the winning of the West or the collapse of the Old South. The word curriculum is, for many, almost pure denotation, almost pristine in the way it refuses to call up images that compel interest. It is a dull word, dry and dusty, and yet it goes to the heart of formal learning. It is through the curriculum that college and university faculties establish a design for education. It is through the curriculum that they communicate what it is an educated person should know.

While the matter of what should be taught and learned is hardly one on which we should expect easy agreement, the confusion about it on many campuses has seemed extraordinary in recent years. Entering students often find few requirements in place and a plethora of offerings. There are hundreds of courses to choose from, a multitude of ways to combine them to earn a bachelor's degree, and a minimum of direction. In the absence of an ordered plan of study, some undergraduates manage to put together coherent and substantive programs, but others move through

25

college years with little rationale. All too often, as "Humanities in America," a 1988 report from the National Endowment for the Humanities, noted, it is "luck or accident or uninformed intuition that determines what students do and do not learn."

The Endowment's report was by no means the first to make such observations. Indeed, throughout the 1980s there has been growing concern about the fragmented state of curricula. In reports, books, and conferences, educators have talked about the need for greater structure and coherence—particularly in the area of college study known as "general education." It is here, outside the major, where students can gain insights into areas of human thought that are not their specialties. In general education, as the Harvard "Redbook," a classic study of curriculum, noted, the primary focus can be on the student's life "as a responsible human being and citizen."

But recognition of the importance of reforming general education has far outpaced actual reform. A recent survey funded by the National Endowment for the Humanities showed that in 1988–1989 general education requirements were still so loosely structured that it was possible to graduate from:

- 78 percent of the nation's colleges and universities without ever taking a course in the history of Western civilization;
- 38 percent without taking any course in history at all;
- 45 percent without taking a course in American or English literature;
- 77 percent without studying a foreign language;
- 41 percent without studying mathematics;
- 33 percent without studying natural and physical sciences.

Explanations abound for the slow pace of reform. A contributing factor may well be the highly general nature of national discussions. Wise commentaries set forth important aims for undergraduate education, affirming, for example, that students should learn about science and history, understand institutions and symbols, and be able to think critically. But exactly how these ends might be accomplished has been a subject of less attention—and for understandable reasons.

There are, first of all, many possible ways to organize a curriculum to achieve agreed-upon goals. Indeed, the variety of options is part of the intellectual challenge of reorganizing undergraduate study. Even more important is the diversity of American colleges and universities. Student bodies and faculties differ, as do resources and missions. As Edwin J. Delattre notes in *Education and the Public Trust*, each institution must ask itself: "What should be the curriculum *here*, in this school, college, university? Why should *we* and *our* students study this curriculum?"

Nevertheless, different institutions can learn from one another, can profit by seeing how other colleges and universities have solved problems with which they are wrestling. Curriculum reform that proceeds in awareness of what is happening elsewhere is likely to move at a faster pace.

The NEH report, "50 Hours," is a way of informing colleges engaged in curricular reform about how other schools are managing the task. Its aim is to be specific; its central device for organizing details is an imagined core of studies—fifty semester hours—that would encourage coherent and substantive learning in essential areas of knowledge.

So far as I know, this particular core curriculum does not exist anywhere. Parts of it can be found at different colleges and universities; so can alternatives to both the parts and the whole. Many alternatives are described in this report in order to call attention to the variety of ways in which substantive and coherent learning can be achieved.

Because it is not the proper role of government to determine a nationwide curriculum, it needs to be emphasized that "50 Hours" is not offered as a single prototype. Instead, it is a way of providing information about various models to individual faculties that must decide the undergraduate course of study. "50 Hours" is intended as a resource for the many dedicated and thoughtful men and women across the country who are working to improve undergraduate education. It is meant to support them by placing their individual efforts into a larger context of national questions and concerns.

Administrators, as well as faculty members, often initiate discussions about reform; and this report is also intended for them. Governing boards, too, sometimes encourage reform: In 1986 the Louisiana Board of Regents mandated general education requirements for state colleges and universities in order to ensure study of essential areas of knowledge; in 1989 the Massachusetts Board of Regents called on the state's public colleges and universities to revise general education with the aim of developing in students a broad range of abilities and knowledge.

Why is a Core Important?

A 1989 survey funded by the National Endowment for the Humanities and conducted by the Gallup Organization showed 25 percent of the nation's college seniors unable to locate Columbus's voyage within the correct half-century. About the same percentage could not distinguish Churchill's words from Stalin's, or Karl Marx's thoughts from the ideas of the U.S. Constitution. More than 40 percent could not identify when the Civil War occurred. Most could not identify the Magna Carta, the Missouri Compromise, or Reconstruction. Most could not link major works by Plato, Dante, Shakespeare, and Milton with their authors. To the majority of college students, Jane Austen's *Pride and Prejudice*, Dostoyevsky's *Crime and Punishment*, and Martin Luther King, Jr.'s "Letter from the Birmingham Jail" were clearly unfamiliar.

Education aims at more than acquaintance with dates and places, names and titles. Students should not only know when Columbus sailed but also perceive the world-altering shock of his voyage. They should not only know what Plato wrote but also understand the allegory of the cave. When education is rightly conceived, events and ideas become, in philosopher Michael Oakeshott's words, "invitations to look, to listen and to reflect." But students who approach the end of their college years without knowing basic landmarks of history and thought are unlikely to have reflected on their meaning.

A required course of studies—a core of learning—can ensure that students have opportunities to know the literature, philosophy, institutions, and art of our own and other cultures. A core of learning can also encourage understanding of mathematics and science, and "50 Hours" includes these fields of inquiry. The National Endowment for the Humanities must be concerned with the literature major who has no understanding of physics as well as with the engineer who graduates without studying history. Both are less prepared than they should be to make the subtle and complex choices today's life demands. Both bring limited perspective to enduring human questions: Where have we come from? Who are we? What is our destiny? Kant struggled for answers in his study; Boyle, in his laboratory. Thoreau, Gauguin, and Einstein took up these questions, approaching them in different ways, but sharing a common goal. All the various branches of human knowledge, as physicist Erwin Schrodinger once observed, have the same objective: "It is to obey the command of the Delphic deity," to honor the ancient injunction, "Know thyself."

To the task of learning about oneself and the world, a required course of studies can bring needed order and coherence. At one Midwestern university where there is no core: Students choose from almost 900 courses, with topics ranging from the history of foreign labor movements to the analysis of daytime soap operas. The result is all too often "a meaningless mosaic of fragments," in naturalist Loren Eiseley's words. "From ape skull to Mayan temple," he wrote, "we contemplate the miscellaneous debris of time like sightseers to whom these mighty fragments, fallen gateways, and sunken galleys convey no present instruction." A core of learning shows the patterns of the mosaic. It provides a context for forming the parts of education into a whole.

A core of learning also encourages community, whether we conceive community small or large. Having some learning in common draws students together—and faculty members as well. When the common learning engages students with their democratic heritage, it invites informed participation in our ongoing national conversation: What should a free people value? What should they resist? What are the limits to freedom, and how are they to be decided?

When students are encouraged to explore the history and the thought of cultures different from their own, they gain insight into others with whom they share the earth. They come to understand unfamiliar ideals and traditions—and to see more clearly the characteristics that define their own particular journey.

Is There Time in the Curriculum for a Core?

Almost all colleges and universities have requirements in "general education"—a part of the curriculum that is specified for all undergraduates, regardless of major. The hours set aside for general education are the hours from which a core of learning can be constructed. The larger and more complex the educational institution, the more difficult it is to commit hours to general education. A school that offers an accredited engineering program has to recognize that few engineering students will be able to graduate in four years if they devote much more than a semester to the humanities and social sciences. Schools offering a bachelor's degree in music must face the demands of the National Association of Schools of Music, an accrediting association that expects students to devote 65 percent of their coursework to studying music.

Nevertheless, even doctorate-granting universities, the most complex institutions of higher education, require, on the average, more than thirty-seven semester hours in general education. For all four-year institutions, the average requirement in general education is fifty-two semester hours. There is time in most schools for a significant core of learning.

As it is now, however, these hours that could be devoted to a core are all too often organized instead into loosely stated "distribution requirements"—mandates that students take some courses in certain areas and some in others. Long lists of acceptable choices are set out in catalogs. Specialized offerings for the most part, they often have little to do with the broadly conceived learning that should be at the heart of general education. Indeed, some courses seem to have little to do with the areas of human knowledge they are supposed to elucidate. At a public university in the West, it is possible to fulfill humanities requirements with courses in interior design. In 1988–1989 at a private university in the East, one could fulfill part of the social science distribution requirement by taking "Lifetime Fitness."

Some core programs do offer choices: Alternative possibilities for mathematics and science are almost universal. Choice within a core can work well, so long as each of the choices fits within a carefully defined framework and aims at broad and integrated learning. The University of Denver's core, for example, offers five, year-long options in the arts and humanities. In one course, "The Making of the Modern Mind," philosophy, literature, music, and art are studied from the Enlightenment to the present. A second course, "Commercial Civilization," emphasizes history, political thought and institutions, and classical economic theory from the origins of capitalism to contemporary times.

Is a Core Too Hard for Some Students?
Too Easy for Others?

The 1983 report, "A Nation at Risk," recommended that college-bound high school students take four years of English, three of social studies, science, and mathematics, and two years of foreign language. Students who have completed such a course of studies should be ready to undertake the work required by a program like "50 Hours." Entering students who lack necessary verbal and mathematical skills should prepare for core work by taking remedial courses. Such a plan benefits the core and can be of value to remedial programs as well as providing a well-defined goal for teaching and learning. The faculty of the remedial and developmental programs of Brooklyn College of the City University of New York recently dedicated a conference to Brooklyn's core curriculum to recognize its importance for their work.

In "50 Hours," students are expected to write papers of varying length in every course, including those in science and mathematics. The practice of organizing ideas and presenting them coherently is a useful tool for learning in all subjects. Students who write in every course also come to understand that clear and graceful expression is universally valuable, not merely an arbitrary preoccupation of English departments. Some students who are prepared for core work may still need extra practice in composition. For them, writing-intensive sections of required courses can be designated— as they are at Brandeis and Vanderbilt universities.

Students who come to college well-prepared may have read some of the works assigned in the core. But so long as those works are profound, provocative, and revealing, these students will again be challenged. Indeed, a criterion for choosing works for the core should be that they repay many readings. They should be books that remain fresh, full of power to quicken thought and feeling, no matter how many times we open their pages.

Why Is Establishing a Core So Difficult?

Curricular change has never been easy: Henry Bragdon, writing about Woodrow Wilson's years at Princeton, called it "harder than moving a graveyard." And the way in which higher education has evolved over the last century has complicated the task.

The forces that have come to dominate higher education are centrifugal rather than centripetal, weakening the ties that individual faculty members have to their institutions. As professional advancement has come increasingly to depend on the esteem of other specialists on other campuses, there has been less and less incentive for scholars at any single college or university to identify fully with that institution and the shared efforts unnecessary for a complicated task like curricular reform.

At the same time, faculty responsibility for the curriculum has grown. If it is to change, the faculty must come together and act for the common purpose of changing it. "We have a paradox," Professor James Q. Wilson observed after curriculum reform at Harvard. "The faculty is supposed to govern collegially, but it is not a collegium."

The increasingly specialized nature of graduate study is also an impediment. Many Ph.D.'s do not receive the broad preparation necessary to teach courses in general education. Even those who do often step uneasily outside their specialties are concerned that it is unprofessional to teach Dante when one's expertise is Donne. They perceive hours spent teaching in general education—and days consumed devising its courses and curricula—as time away from the labor that the academic system most rewards: research and publication. One young professor called curriculum reform "a black hole," and the time and energy it absorbs are seldom professionally recognized.

Crucial to establishing a core of learning is administrative leadership: college presidents who make general education a priority by putting institutional resources behind it; deans who support those faculty members who are willing to invest the time necessary to develop coherent requirements and seek consensus for them. A recent survey by the American Council on Education suggests that students, parents, alumni, and trustees can also play an important role in encouraging curricular reform: Thirty percent of doctorate-granting institutions that were revising general education requirements reported that the initiators of reform were people other than faculty or administration members.

Successfully establishing and sustaining a core may well require efforts aimed at encouraging intellectual community. Seminars in which faculty members read together the works to be taught in core courses can create common understandings, while at the same time providing background for teaching. At Rice University in Houston, where extensive curricular reform is underway, faculty members met in day-long sessions for two weeks to discuss works to be taught in the humanities foundation course. A classicist led discussion of the *Iliad*; a philosopher, of Plato's *Republic*; a professor of music, of Mozart's *Marriage of Figaro*.

How Should Courses in the Core Be Taught?

"The two great points to be gained in intellectual culture," an 1828 report from Yale University noted, "are the *discipline* and the *furniture* of the mind; expanding its powers, and storing it with knowledge." For a core of learning to encourage intellectual discipline as well as the acquisition of knowledge, some small classes are essential. Students must have opportunities to participate in discussion and to be encouraged by teachers and peers to think critically about concepts and ideas.

Every course in the core should be taught with other core courses in mind. Students reading Descartes' philosophy in a Western civilization course should be reminded of his contributions to mathematics. Students reading Darwin in a science class should be encouraged to explore in their social science and humanities courses the ways in which evolutionary theory affected social thought and literature. Such connections help demonstrate that human knowledge is not a disconnected series of specialized subjects but interrelated domains of thought.

An institution's most distinguished faculty should teach in the core. Philosopher Charles Frankel once reported that Philipp Frank, Einstein's biographer and collaborator, expressed surprise on learning that in the United States he would not be allowed to teach elementary courses. In Vienna, where Frank had previously taught, beginning courses were considered the greatest honor—one to be bestowed on only those who had mastered their fields sufficiently to be able to generalize. "But in America," Frankel noted, "we thought that was for fellows who know less. Frank believed not—you had to know more and in fact you had to have lived your field and felt the passion of it . . . to communicate it."

Graduate assistants and nontenured faculty, to whom much of the responsibility for undergraduate teaching falls today, are often fine instructors. But the stature of general education is diminished when a college or university's most distinguished faculty do not teach in it. The quality of instruction is diminished when they do not bring their learning and experience to it.

Good teaching is crucial to the success of any curriculum, and it can take a multitude of forms. But teachers who inspire their students to intellectual engagement are themselves always engaged. They do not agree with every book or idea they discuss, but they approach them generously, demonstrating that neither agreement nor disagreement is possible until there has been the hard work of understanding. Learning is not a game for them, not simply an intellectual exercise, but an undertaking that compels mind and heart. Recalling his great teachers, Leo Raditsa of St. John's College in Maryland recently described I. A. Richards. "He conceived reading as the cure of souls. . . ." Raditsa wrote. "And he included his own soul."

In the core, as throughout the curriculum, courses should be taught by men and women who, though deeply knowledgeable, remain eager to learn.

❏ ❏ ❏

LYNNE V. CHENEY, a senior fellow at the American Enterprise Institute, earned her B.A. from Colorado College, her M.A. from the University of Colorado, and her Ph.D. with a specialization in British literature from the University of Wisconsin. From 1986 to 1993 she served as chairman of the National Endowment for the Humanities, where she published "American Memory," a report that warned about the failure of schools to transmit knowledge of history. She is author or co-author of five books, including *Kings of the Hill* (1996) and *Telling the Truth* (1996). Dr. Cheney is currently completing *America: A Patriotic Primer*, an alphabet book intended for elementary school children and their families. She serves as a director of the Reader's Digest Association and American Express Funds, and is the recipient of numerous awards and honorary degrees. In 2001, Dr. Cheney became Second Lady when her husband of thirty-seven years, Richard B. Cheney, was sworn in as Vice President of the United States.

Education: The Second Door to Freedom

Clarence Thomas

June 1994

Justice Thomas delivered the following speech at Hillsdale College's 1994 Spring Convocation.

❑ ❑ ❑

Recently, while speaking to a group of law students, I was asked what the difference was between the youthful Clarence Thomas and Clarence Thomas the judge. There is much that is different and much that is the same. Over time, the depth of one's faith and experience is bound to increase. Mine certainly did. But there was a real change of direction in life that occurred during my college years. It is my sincere hope that my discussion of this change will be helpful to at least one of you.

When I began at the College of the Holy Cross in the fall of 1968, as a transfer student from Immaculate Conception Seminary, I was confused and intimidated as were so many of my fellow students. It was a time of turmoil and challenge to authority and to those in authority. In fact, it was a time of rudeness and poor manners, no matter how conveniently history is today revised. Although much of our conduct was for what we considered good and noble reasons, we still conducted ourselves in an ill-mannered and reprehensible way. That is both regretable and unfortunate. But more on that later.

The College of the Holy Cross was the only true opportunity that I had to leave Savannah for college. And this opportunity only came about as a result of the dedication and kindness of my high school chemistry teacher and a classmate from parochial school, who was a student there. But college gave me the opportunity to take on the challenges of education during a most critical time in my life. And, as is true for so many in this country, education was the only available opportunity to escape a life that seemed predetermined for me. Having lived to see the official end of segregation, education was now the second door of freedom.

What Education Provides

I must first admit that I am somewhat old-fashioned about education. I opposed the move away from the old core requirements and traditional liberal arts education, and I still hold tenaciously to that position. Perhaps it is in some small measure due to my misfortune of having been subjected to "new math" in the ninth and tenth grades. The traditional liberal arts education was a way of showing us that we were to discipline, train, and expand our minds. It provided fewer opportunities to justify intellectual laziness and almost no opportunity to avoid some of the more difficult and exacting courses. Certainly, there were very few of us, who, were it left to us, would choose to study metaphysics or classics.

Of course, it would be a fair question to ask why anyone would want to put that kind of stress on himself or herself. To respond to this inquiry requires that I set out what, in retrospect, I see that education provides. Since I am not an educator, I must rely quite heavily on my own experiences.

My first days of school started in a rather inauspiciously routine manner, a fun trek down Pinpoint Road to catch the school bus for Haven Home School. That was exciting for about a week. Then, I was quite prepared to get back to catching minnows in the creek and tracking down fiddler crabs in the marshes. There seemed to be no reprieve in sight, since those in charge seemed more interested in my going to school than I was. But thanks to the fine mischief of my brother and our cousin, Little Richard (no relation to the entertainer), an opportunity presented itself. You see, they burnt down the house in Pinpoint, forcing my brother and me to go to Savannah to live with our mother. As good fortune would have it, I was left unsupervised, since my mother worked, and school for me at Florance Street School did not start until the afternoon. Under this arrangement, I found ample opportunity to wander through the streets, quite often to the exclusion of school. But it seems that all good things must come to an end; my brother and I went to live with my grandparents. There, the law was laid down: School came before all else. The nuns were always right, and any complaints about them at home would result in nothing more than additional punishment. It did not take a genius or legal scholar to see that this right of appeal was nothing more than mere formality with significant adverse consequences and no possible benefits.

Suddenly, education was paramount. Because they did not have the benefit of education or freedom, my grandparents treasured them both. Freedom they felt would come, so we had to be prepared to take advantage of it. And, even if it didn't, they felt that we would be better off educated. Suddenly, our lives revolved around education. Under no circumstances were we to miss a day of school. Thus, we were required to eat properly, get plenty of sleep, and take regular doses of castor and cod liver oils to avoid any illnesses that could potentially lead to absences. Then there was the warning that no excuses would be accepted and all illnesses would be presumed to be feigned. Indeed, my grandfather announced that if we died, he would take us to school for three consecutive days to make sure that we were not faking. Not a day passed that we did not receive a lecture on the importance of education. And time not spent on our education was to be spent working.

This attitude toward education and work was constantly reinforced by family members and neighbors. From my perspective, things did not look good. There seemed to be little hope that I would be allowed to become the next Bob Cousy or Jim Brown, since I could only pilfer tiny morsels of time to pursue my dreams of athletic stardom.

But education was the road to freedom and independence. It was the promise of possibilities beyond the cramped oppressive worlds of segregation and ignorance. It was the way to a better life and a bigger world.

I can still remember and reflect on the wonderful, wonderful hours I spent at the local Negro library, the Carnegie Library. That small library took me all around the world, back and forth in time, around the universe.

That time raised as many questions as it answered. It brought me in contact with heroes and villains, with hatred and with love. (By the way, since education was seen to be even more important than work, going to the library allowed me to escape some small amounts of work, and it allowed me to stay out until 9 p.m.)

The Revolt Against Learning

My grandparents' devotion to education would lead to their tremendous financial sacrifice for me to attend the seminary. Those most difficult days brought me in full contact with the white world for the first time and in contact with academic requirements that, initially, seemed crushing. Latin was a demon to be subdued and Latin class—well, that was a daily confirmation hearing. But, in spite of the angst, my love of learning grew. Both Native Son and Gone with The Wind, among other books, were read after lights out with the help of my trusty flashlight.

Education, with its dual role of preparation and personal growth had become a way of life by the time I went off to college in 1968 as a transfer student. I boarded the train in Savannah with my lifelong friend, Robert DeShay. Our train ride ended in New York, where we spent a few days with his uncle, then to Worcester on a Trailways bus. As we passed Holy Cross on our way to the bus depot, my heart pounded with apprehension, anticipation, and hope. Here was another challenge, another chance to escape the narrow confining world in which I grew up and the attendant lack of opportunity. Little did I know that the traditions of that institution as well as the traditions of the nation were on a collision course with challenges to authority. My years in the seminary had been orderly and, with the exception of the events that led me to leave, uninterrupted and uneventful. That would all change.

In the seminary, my life of educational and spiritual growth were only interrupted by sports, corporal works of mercy, and long, private discussions, accompanied by the heart-wrenching voice of Nina Simone, with an older black seminarian. We would later travel to Kansas City to participate in a march occasioned by the death of Dr. Martin Luther King. Though I remained in the seminary until the end of May, the assassination of Dr.

King effectively ended my attachment to the seminary. How could I stay there when the world seemed to be disintegrating around me? It all seemed so pointless. My dreams of becoming a priest had been dashed, my faith, shattered. I was consumed by almost uncontrolled anger and frustration. All that religion and education had seemed to promise no longer mattered to me. It seemed irrelevant.

Just as Richard Wright's Bigger Thomas had been consumed by the conflagration of prejudices, stereotypes, and circumstances beyond his control and understanding, I felt myself being similarly consumed. I stood at the brink of the great abyss of anger, frustration, and animosity. The summer before going to college served to reinforce this tremendous feeling of alienation. My grandfather asked that I leave his house; Robert Kennedy was assassinated; racial indignities seemed to continue unabated; and so much had changed for the worse in my hometown. I arrived at college with no hope in my religion, no faith in my country, and no desire to be in a predominantly white school again. But, in so many ways, I had no place else to go.

Someplace deep inside, however, there was some residual hope that there was hope. Perhaps, the lack of any alternatives forced this feeling on me. Perhaps it was nothing more than not knowing what to say to all those who had gone before me, who had remained hopeful when there was no reason to hope. Perhaps, it was just stubbornness. In any case, Holy Cross was my beacon on the hill.

My new roommate was also a transfer student, from Northeastern University. He had been an engineering student there, and would now major in biology. I decided to major in English, primarily because I entertained visions of becoming a journalist and because I had great difficulty with the spoken and written word, a prerequisite to communication and continued learning.

My new dormitory was a fabulous place to live. I would live there for a year. I made friends quickly, and they made every effort to make my roommate and me feel accepted. And my roommate was simply superb. He was a model student and an outstanding person. He would quietly have a tremendous impact on my academic performance.

In contrast to this rather normal transition were the events swirling around our country that would affect us all. There was, consistent with my own feeling, significant emphasis on admitting and accommodating black students. To make life better for us, some of the older black students decided that we should establish a Black Students' Union. Since I could type and edit, I was asked to type the Constitution and bylaws. This I did. I later became the correspondence secretary of BSU, a position I retained for most of my college years.

The challenges of a new school were as one could expect, but the times made this transition confusing to say the least. Unlike the safe harbor of the seminary, we, as black students, were right in the path of the upheavals taking place in our society. College campuses across New England and the country in general seemed to be fertile ground for protest and expressions of grievances against all the wrongs in our country. As blacks, we seemed to take the position that our grievance should always be at the top of the list, and we were to be the vanguard. We, after all, were the descendants of slaves, and our race had borne the brunt of discrimination.

All authority was questioned and challenged. So much that had been taken for granted in the past was now criticized and challenged—from dress codes to values and mores. Suddenly, little if anything was sacred, perhaps with the exception of our self-centered notion of autonomy—which we mistook for freedom. We were pulling away from the cultural mooring that had previously provided stability, structure, and civility—even as imperfections abounded. Major portions of our time and energy (intellectual and otherwise) were spent supporting and reinforcing the effort to rip away the cultural and moral structures that we felt were too confining. It seemed that we constantly engaged in an odd sort of narcissism and permanent temper tantrums. Distractions flourished. There were world problems about which to complain; governmental policies to protest; college rules to challenge; and so much capitalist greed and corruption to condemn. We were without sin, so we could righteously cast stones as we saw fit—with impunity.

At a time when we should have been quiet so that we could learn, it seemed that we already knew everything. And we were certainly superior to all those over thirty, who had ruined the country and the world. In a curious way, we had reversed the teacher/student relationship; those with knowledge were to listen to us, who, though without knowledge, had emotion, passion, grievances, and innocence. Our feelings gave legitimacy to the positions we took—even while our logic failed or didn't exist in the first instance. In fact, we were somehow authentic because we lacked the inhibitions of self-control, discipline, logic, and yes, civility.

Captive of the "Oppressive Society"

Because I was already predisposed to anger, confusion, and frustration, the environment which we as students created made it doubly difficult to take full advantage of the educational benefits of college. And I am certain that we made it impossible for some of the younger, more impressionable students, especially those who were black. For some reason that I can explain no more than I can explain having had any hope in the first place, I continued to plow on academically. Perhaps, initially, it was purely out of habit and a sense of obligation. But, even as I moved on, I became increasingly consumed by a seething anger.

During the first semester of my junior year, one of my closest friends was among the students disciplined for protesting the on-campus recruiting of a corporation that did business in South Africa. Because he was one of a number of black students in the protest, it was our view that he and the other black students were more easily identifiable for disciplinary purposes while many of the white students could not be quickly identified and thus escaped disciplinary actions. This injustice was proof positive for me that blacks could never be treated fairly on a predominantly white campus—or in a white society for that matter. I had finally had enough. Most of my fellow black students felt the same way; so we decided to leave.

As I packed all my belongings that night, I teetered precariously over the abyss. No one really cared. We were doomed. College didn't matter. Indeed, life itself didn't matter. I wanted to go home. But what would I tell my grandparents who had suffered far more indignities than I had? What would I tell my neighbors? What would I say to my friends who had always said that the "man" wasn't going to let me do anything? What, some day, would I say to my own son or daughter? What would I say to myself? I knew I could not stay; but I also knew I couldn't go home. After we had left campus, to my surprise and ultimately to my relief, wiser heads prevailed, and we returned.

My own personal anger continued to ferment well into the spring semester of my junior year. It was then, after a number of confrontational protests, that I finally began to question openly what had happened to me. It should have been obvious. I had become drunk with anger. I had become addicted to being a victim of oppression; and I was angry that whites controlled the fate of blacks. I was out of control with hostility. I was going to destroy either myself or someone else. Something had to change and change soon. I could not continue to let my passions rage out of control. I was consumed by animosity even though little had happened to me personally and even though I got along fine with all of the other students with whom I came in contact and even though I was doing just fine academically. I was angry for all oppression and injustice not mine personally.

Unfortunately, this anger was not helped by my living on a dormitory floor reserved for black students, which, though not totally segregated until my senior year, further isolated those black students who lived there from the rest of the student body. As a result, there were few if any forces to counter my own bitter feelings. Being up there was a mistake under any circumstances; it was disastrous at that time for me. The environment itself seemed to encourage me to continue in a direction that was dangerously negative. This seemed to be the abyss I had feared. I was addicted to the status of an oppressed person. I was a captive of the "oppressive society." All could be explained in terms of oppression. All facts and reasoning that disproved my feelings were rejected as lies and deception; all half-truths that supported my feelings were gospel. All individuals who agreed with me were good. All who disagreed were Uncle Toms or racists. All who partially agreed were half-steppers. I had become passionately obsessed with matters of race. Today, I sometimes hear of those who criticize me now, and I chuckle: If they only knew that I had thought that their reasonable efforts within the "system" suggested that they were "co-opted by the man" and that they were "sell-outs."

Some months ago I saw the movie Menace II Society. It is a discouraging movie. But the reality that it portrays is far more discouraging and tragic. In one scene, an adult is trying to convince a young man to discontinue a life of violence and drug dealing and leave south central Los Angeles for a better life. In doing so, he said something that caught my attention because I had repeated a similar observation to myself so many times. He said, and I am paraphrasing, "You can hold on to anger inside and let it eat you, or you can control it and make a difference." But this is easier said than done.

It has been unfortunate over the years to see anger such as mine accommodated. It is said that we are an emotional people; we are expressive; we feel deeply; we have rage. Often, it seems as though the cultural elite think that we are inherently unqualified to do much more than feel bad about what has happened to us in this country and, of course, follow their lead. Culturally, we are supposedly not attuned to precise or exacting analysis. I have found it curious how this could be complimentary. It always has seemed like a different way of reiterating the old stereotype that we made good singers and dancers. But, then, life is full of odd twists and turns.

Freedom from Our Own Passions

For reasons even they could not have fully understood, my grandparents were right that education was the door to freedom—freedom from the confining world of segregation and freedom from the destructive forces of our own passions.

Education is more than books, computers, and catalogues of facts. It should appeal to and enhance calm, sober judgment. It should encourage deep reflection about complicated, difficult problems. In the end, education, together with maturity and experience, should help us along the road to gaining wisdom. Education should also assist us in acquiring virtuous habits and ridding ourselves of nonvirtuous ones.

During those confusing times, as the events of the 1960s and my maelstrom of swirling emotions pulled me toward the abyss of permanent animus, any number of my professors pulled me back or at least kept me from going over the brink. They refused to accommodate my feelings; they demanded that I think rather than feel.

Though I could name a number of professors and courses, I will be content to use one course as an illustration: "Readings in Renaissance Prose." I can still remember being scared beyond comprehension when I first entered that class more than twenty-five years ago. I was clearly in over my head. But, for twenty-five years, I have been unable to shake Cavendish's "The Life and Death of Cardinal Wolsey" or Roper's "The Life of Sir Thomas More." From the former:

> Who list to read and consider with an indifferent eye this history may behold the wondrous mutability of vain honors, the brittle assurance of abundance, the uncertainty of dignities, the flattering of feigned friends, and the fickle trust to worldly princes. Whereof this Lord Cardinal hath felt both of the sweet and the sour in each degrees—as fleeting from honors, losing of riches, deposed from dignities, forsaken of friends, and the inconstantness of princes' favor. Of all which things he hath had in this world the full felicity as long as that Fortune smiled upon him; but when she began to frown, how soon was he deprived of all these dreaming joyous and vain pleasures! The which in twenty years with great travail, study, and pains obtained, were in one year and less, with heaviness, care, and sorrow, lost and consumed. O madness, O foolish desire, O fond hope, O greedy desire of vain honors, dignities, and riches, O what inconstant trust and assurance is in rolling Fortune!

And from Roper's biography of Thomas More: On his way to die,

> Sir Thomas More, as one that had been invited to some solemn feast, changed himself into his best apparel. Which Master Lieutenant spying, advised him to put it off, saying that he that should have it was but a javel [low fellow].
>
> "What, Master Lieutenant," quoth he, "shall I accompt him a javel that shall do me this day so singular a benefit? Nay, I assure you, were it cloth-of-gold, I would accompt it well bestowed upon him, as Saint Cyprian did, who gave his executioner thirty pieces of gold." And albeit at length, through Master Lieutenant's importunate persuasion, he altered his apparel, yet after the example of that holy martyr, Saint Cyprian, did he of that little money that was left him send one angel of gold to his executioner.

And so was he by Master Lieutenant brought out of the Tower and from thence led towards the place of execution. Where, going up the scaffold, which was so weak that it was ready to fall, he said merrily to Master Lieutenant: "I pray you, Master Lieutenant, see me safe up and, for my coming down, let me shift for myself."

Then desired he all the people thereabout to pray for him, and to bear witness with him that he should now there suffer death in and for the faith of the Holy Catholic Church. Which done, he kneeled down and after his prayers said, turned to the executioner and with a cheerful countenance spake thus to him:

"Pluck up thy spirits, man, and be not afraid to do thine office. My neck is very short. Take heed therefore thou strike not awry, for saving of thine honesty."

So passed Sir Thomas More out of this world to God upon the very same day in which himself had most desired.

My preference, of course, was and is to emulate Sir Thomas More. The wonderful rewards of that course, for which I received a modest grade of C+, were a hero and a model—a chance to compare fleeting success with principled dignity—even at the moment of death. In this era when dead white men have fallen into disrepute, I look back on the character and stature of Thomas More as a model. And in the twenty-five years that have drifted by since sitting submerged in that class, I have seen or learned about many more Cardinal Wolseys, rising as the wheel rises, but then being tragically crushed or splattered with mud as it descends.

Learning How to Live

Education occurs both in and outside the classroom. There are certain bumps and bruises that befall us all during life. The manner in which we deal with them will have a lot to say about how we deal with future difficulties and what kind of people we become. Education most certainly gives us the means by which to earn a living, but it also provides the means to learn how to live.

The penchant today for claiming victim status of one sort or another is a poor substitute for real education. Learning to grow beyond one's present condition has been replaced by simply shoveling the responsibility on others. This accomplishes no good and certainly leads to no growth. And it leads to the chain reaction of more anger on the part of the putative victims; resentment on the part of the alleged oppressor; suspicion on the part of both; and horror and incredulity on the part of those who watch this spectacle.

I know there are those who hear me with a smug arrogance that only untarnished youth or insulated cynicism can generate. But I am unimpressed with this uninformed and misguided arrogance; I have seen it and I have been there. My grandfather used to say, "Hard times make monkey eat Cayenne pepper." Hard times have a way of teaching us lessons that we refuse to learn in good times. That is the one university we all get to attend —tuition free. And learning the lessons that we must learn cannot forever be avoided by sweeping our difficulties under the rug of societal blame.

As the years have passed, I have thought deeply about the era in which I attended college. In that regard, I am probably not much different from so many others who reach mid-life and become more introspective and retrospective. We sort through the good times and the bad—we grow melancholy over the regrets. To my humble way of thinking, we threw the baby out with the bath water. Our attitude that the students are the intellectual equals of the professors makes no sense. And, to the extent that it is true, it certainly obviates the need to attend college at such great expense. And I believe we threw out civility. When I was young, my grandparents would insist that we conduct ourselves as gentlemen: mind our manners and watch our P's and Q's. Though I never understood what the "P" or the "Q" stood for, I knew what they meant. Good manners and civility allow us to move on to tackle the real problems, not fight constantly about the rules of engagement. Poor substitutes such as campus codes and political correctness are doomed to disrupting failure. They are artificial and arbitrary. Indeed, they are destined to promote conflict that is silly, dangerous, and distracting.

Everyone will be offended by something or someone; and an inordinate amount of time will be consumed arguing about who is offended and who has the more legitimate claim of victim status.

The study of the liberal arts, the education that pulled me back from the abyss of self-destruction, teaches us to confront and debate difficult ideas in a calm, civil way. It encourages analysis rather than fomenting passions, for the latter impedes the former, thus displacing the calm control that promotes further education.

Former Secretary of Education William Bennett has put it most eloquently:

> The case for the study of the liberal arts is not, then, a case for ideology: it is a case for philosophy and for thoughtfulness. Those who take such studies seriously live very different lives and come to very different conclusions about particulars. The tenets of Western civilization are not etched in stone; the West is the most self-critical of cultures. Reason is exalted, and reason leads to a look, a second look, and where necessary, readjustment, redefinition, and change.

I have often had occasion to think, with the benefit of hindsight and two decades of reality checks, how I would have pursued my college education were I given another chance.

I would steadfastly avoid activities that tend to inflame the passions rather than ignite the desire to learn, concentrating on a curriculum that closely approximated the old core requirements and traditional liberal arts education. I would surround myself with friends who were interested in and excited by ideas, not causes. (And I would play football—at least until I was hit hard enough to suggest conclusively that it was a bad idea to do so.) I deeply regret that I did not take advantage of all that college had to offer. And I am grateful that in spite of my obstinacy and resistance, so many wiser heads still found a way to expose me to a fine education. But I am convinced that I received far less than was made available to me. For this, I have no one to blame but myself.

A Common Culture

What I mean quite simply is that by focusing so passionately on the differences among us, I overlooked so much of what we have in common. Like it or not, we do have a common culture that informs our institutions and our conduct. We have a culture and a country that has borrowed much from other cultures, including those from which our respective ancestors came. I would celebrate and learn more about what we have in common as a starting point to understanding other cultures and to appreciating our differences. This approach, I believe, would encourage greater participation in all that higher education has to offer rather than reinforcing our differences to the point of intramural and cultural segregation.

I believe that education is, indeed, the second door to freedom. It can take us beyond the emotional confines of our passions, beyond the security of our preferences and to the boundless vistas of intellectual growth that only come from the calm, patient inquiry of our rational capacities—to think rather than just feel, to act methodically rather than react predictably.

Finally, it would be my hope that my education would provide me with the humility to know that there is much more to learn as life progresses and with the courage not to be intimidated by disagreements or vocal, faddish criticism. I would hope that I would not be afraid to ask myself at graduation: Have I taken full advantage of all that has been offered? Have I merely gone along with the crowd, or did I arrive at my own carefully reasoned conclusions? Am I prepared to think through problems and assume my responsibilities as a citizen, or am I content to agitate? Do I know more about the culture in which I live and its underlying principles and philosophy, or am I content to cast stones at its imperfections? Am I prepared to lead if called upon, or am I content to complain and brawl?

Each of us here will have that one moment in time when all that we have learned and all that we are will be called upon and required. None of us knows exactly what that challenge is or when it will occur. But taking advantage of all Hillsdale College has to offer will allow each student here to assert, with conviction, as Abraham Lincoln did: "I will prepare myself, and when the time comes, I will be ready."

❏ ❏ ❏

CLARENCE THOMAS is an Associate Justice of the United States Supreme Court. Prior to being nominated to this office by President George Bush in 1991, he served as a judge on the United States Court of Appeals for the District of Columbia Circuit, Chairman of the U.S. Equal Employment Opportunity Commission, and Assistant Secretary for Civil Rights in the U.S. Department of Education. Justice Thomas graduated cum laude from the College of the Holy Cross and earned a J.D. from Yale Law School before entering legal practice as Assistant Attorney General of Missouri and, later, as an attorney with the Monsanto Company.

Minority Schools and the Politics of Education

Thomas Sowell

January 1999

Dr. Sowell's delivered this speech at a Hillsdale College seminar, "Education in America: Schools and Strategies that Work," in Seattle, Washington.

❏ ❏ ❏

Will Rogers once said that it was not ignorance that was so bad, but as he put it, "all the things we know that ain't so." Nowhere is this more true than in American education today, where fashions prevail and evidence is seldom asked for or given. And nowhere does this do more harm than in the education of minority children.

The quest for esoteric methods of trying to educate these children proceeds as if such children had never been successfully educated before, when in fact there are concrete examples, both from history and from our own times, of schools that have been successful in educating children from low-income families and from minority families. Yet the educational dogma of the day is that you simply cannot expect children who are not middle class to do well on standardized tests, for all sorts of sociological and psychological reasons.

Those who think this way are undeterred by the fact that there are schools where low-income and minority students do score well on standardized tests. These students are like the bumblebees who supposedly should not be able to fly according to the theories of aerodynamics, but who fly anyway, in disregard of those theories.

The Dunbar School

While there are examples of schools where this happens in our own time— both public and private, secular and religious—we can also go back a hundred years and find the same phenomenon. In Washington, D.C., in the 1890s there were four academic public high schools—one black and three white. The black high school was called the M Street School and after 1916 it was renamed Dunbar High School. (I refer to it as Dunbar here.)

In standardized tests given in 1899, Dunbar averaged higher test scores than students in two of the three white high schools. This was not a fluke. It so happens that I have followed 85 years of the history of this black high school—from 1870 to 1955—and found it repeatedly equaling or exceeding national norms on standardized tests. Its academic performances on standardized tests remained good on into the mid-1950s.

When I first published this information more than twenty years ago, those few educators who responded at all dismissed the relevance of my findings by saying that these were "middle-class" children and therefore their experience was not "relevant" to the education of low-income minority children. Those who said this had no factual data on the incomes or occupations of the parents of these children—and I did.

The problem, however, was not that these dismissive educators did not have evidence. The more fundamental problem was that they saw no need for evidence. According to their doctrines, children who did well on standardized tests were middle class. These children did well on such tests, therefore, they were middle class.

Lack of evidence is not the problem. There was evidence on the occupations of the parents of the children at this school as far back as the early 1890s. As of academic year 1892–1893, there were 83 known occupations of the parents of the children attending Dunbar. Fifty-one parents were laborers and one was a doctor. That doesn't sound very middle class to me.

Over the years, a significant black middle class did develop in Washington and no doubt most of its members sent their children to Dunbar.

But that is wholly different from saying that most of the children at that school came from middle-class homes.

During the later period for which I collected data, there were far more children whose mothers were maids than there were whose fathers were doctors. For many years, there was only one academic high school for blacks in the District of Columbia and, as late as 1948, one-third of all black youngsters attending high school in Washington attended Dunbar High School. So this was not a "selective" school in the sense in which we normally use that term—there were no tests to take to get in, for example—even though there was undoubtedly self-selection in the sense that students who were serious went to Dunbar and those who were not had other places where they could while away their time without having to meet high academic standards.

A spot-check of attendance records and tardiness records showed that the M Street School at the turn of the century, and Dunbar High School at mid-century, had less absenteeism and less tardiness than the white high schools in the District of Columbia at those times. The school had a tradition of being serious, going back to its founders and early principals.

Among these early principals was the first black woman to receive a college degree in the United States—Mary Jane Patterson—from Oberlin College, Class of 1862. At that time, Oberlin had different academic curriculum requirements for men and women. Latin, Greek, and mathematics were required in the "gentlemen's course," as it was called, but not in the curriculum for ladies. Miss Patterson, however, insisted on taking Latin, Greek, and mathematics anyway. Not surprisingly, in her twelve years as principal of the black high school in Washington, she was noted for "a strong, forceful personality," for "thoroughness," and for being "an indefatigable worker." Having this kind of person shaping the standards and traditions of the school in its formative years undoubtedly had something to do with its later success.

Other early principals included the first black man to graduate from Harvard, Class of 1870. Four of the school's first eight principals graduated from Oberlin and two from Harvard. Because of restricted academic opportunities for blacks, Dunbar had three Ph.D.'s among its teachers in the 1920s.

Dunbar's Academic Success

One of the other educational dogmas of our times is the notion that standardized tests do not predict future performance for minority children, either in academic institutions or in life. Innumerable scholarly studies have devastated this claim intellectually, though it still survives and flourishes politically.

But the history of this black high school in Washington likewise shows a payoff for solid academic preparation and the test scores that result from it. Over the entire 85-year history of academic success of this school, from 1870 to 1955, most of its graduates went on to higher education. This was very unusual for either black or white high school graduates during this era. Because these were low-income students, most went to a local free teachers college, but significant numbers won scholarships to leading colleges and universities elsewhere.

Some Dunbar graduates began going to Harvard and other academically elite colleges in the early twentieth century. As of 1916, there were nine black students from the entire country attending Amherst College. Six were from Dunbar. During the period from 1918 to 1923, graduates of this school went on to earn 25 degrees from Ivy League colleges, Amherst, Williams, and Wesleyan. Over the period from 1892 to 1954, Amherst admitted 34 Dunbar graduates. Of these, 74 percent graduated, and more than one-fourth of these graduates were Phi Beta Kappa. No systematic study has been made of the later careers of the graduates of this school. However, when the late black educator Horace Mann Bond studied the backgrounds of blacks with Ph.D.'s, he discovered that more of them had graduated from Dunbar than from any other black high school in the country.

The first blacks to graduate from West Point and Annapolis also came from this school. So did the first black full professor at a major university (Allison Davis at the University of Chicago). So did the first federal judge, the first black general, the first black Cabinet member, the first black elected to the United States Senate since Reconstruction. During World War II, when black military officers were rare, there were more than two dozen Dunbar graduates holding ranks ranging from major to brigadier general.

All this contradicts another widely believed notion—that schools do not make much difference in children's academic or career success because income and family background are much larger influences. If the schools do not differ very much from one another, then of course it will not make much difference which one a child attends. But when they differ dramatically, the results can also differ dramatically.

How Politics Doomed Dunbar

Dunbar was not the only school to achieve success with minority children. But, before turning to some other examples, it may be useful to consider why and how this 85-year history of unusual success was abruptly turned into typical failure, almost overnight, by the politics of education.

As we all know, 1954 was the year of the famous racial desegregation case of *Brown v. Board of Education*. Those of us old enough to remember those days also know of the strong resistance to school desegregation in many white communities, including Washington, D.C. Ultimately, a political compromise was worked out. In order to comply with the law, without having a massive shift of students, the District's school officials decided to turn all public schools into neighborhood schools.

By this time, the neighborhood around Dunbar High School was run-down. This had not affected the school's academic standards. Black students from all over the city went to Dunbar, but very few of those who lived in its immediate vicinity did.

When Dunbar became a neighborhood school, the whole character of its student body changed radically—and the character of its teaching staff changed very soon afterward. In the past, many Dunbar teachers continued to teach for years after they were eligible for retirement because it was such a fulfilling experience. Now, as inadequately educated, inadequately motivated, and disruptive students flooded into the school, teachers began retiring, some as early as 55 years of age. Inside of a very few years, Dunbar became just another failing ghetto school, with all the problems that such schools have, all across the country. Eighty-five years of achievement simply vanished into thin air.

It is a very revealing fact about the politics of education that no one tried to stop this from happening. When I first began to study the history of Dunbar back in the 1970s, I thought that it was inconceivable that this could have been allowed to happen without a protest. I knew that the Washington school board in the 1950s included a very militant and distinguished black woman named Margaret Just Butcher who was also a graduate of Dunbar High School. Surely Dr. Butcher had not let all this happen without exercising her well-known gift of withering criticism.

Yet, I looked in vain through the minutes of the school board for even a single sentence by anybody expressing any concern whatever about the fate of Dunbar High School under the new reorganization plan. Finally, in complete frustration and bewilderment, I phoned Dr. Butcher herself. Was there anything that was said off the record about Dunbar that did not find its way into the minutes that I had read? "No," she said. Then she reminded me that racial "integration" was the battle cry of the hour in the 1950s. No one thought about what would happen to black schools, not even Dunbar.

Now, decades later, we still do not have racial integration in many of the urban schools around the country—and we also do not have Dunbar High School. Such are the ways of politics, where the crusade of the hour often blocks out everything else, at least until another crusade comes along and takes over the same monopoly of our minds.

Ironically, black high schools in Washington today have many of the so-called "prerequisites" for good education that never existed in the heyday of Dunbar High School, and yet the educational results are abysmal. "Adequate funding" is always included among these prerequisites, and today the per-pupil expenditure in the District of Columbia is among the highest in the nation. During its peak, Dunbar was starved for funds and its average class size was in the 40s. Its lunchroom was so small that many of its students had to eat out on the streets. Its blackboards were cracked, and it was 1950 before the school had a public address system. Yet, at that point, it had eighty years of achievement behind it—and only five more in front of it.

Other Successful Schools

Another black school that I studied—P.S. 91 in Brooklyn, New York—was housed in an even older building than the original Dunbar High School. It still had gas jets in the hallways, left over from the gaslight era. The surrounding neighborhood was so bad that a friend told me that I was "brave"—

he probably meant foolhardy—to park a car there. Yet the students in most of the grades in this predominantly black elementary school scored at or above the national norms on standardized tests.

This was not in any sense a middle-class school or a magnet school. It was just an ordinary ghetto school run by an extraordinary principal.

Educators usually like to give guided tours to selected (and often atypical) places, much like the Potemkin village tours in Czarist Russia. But, in P.S. 91, I was allowed to wander down the halls and arbitrarily pick out which classrooms I wanted to go into. I did this on every floor of the school. Inside those classrooms were black children much like children you can find in any ghetto across the country. Many came from broken homes and were on welfare. Yet, inside this school, they spoke in grammatical English, in complete sentences, and to the point. Many of the materials they were studying were a year or more ahead of their respective grade levels.

It so happened that I had to fly back to California right after visiting this school and did not get to talk to all the people I wanted to interview. I asked a mother who was head of the school's Parent–Teacher Association if I could call her at home after I got back to California and interview her over the phone. It turned out that she did not have a telephone. "I can't afford one," she said. That, too, hardly seemed middle class.

Others have found successful black schools operating in equally grim surroundings and under similar social conditions—for example, Catholic schools such as Holy Angel in Chicago, St. Gregory in New York, and East Catholic High in Detroit. Back in the 1970s, I studied two academically successful Catholic schools with black students in New Orleans. In both schools, a majority of the parental occupations were in the "unskilled and semi-skilled" category. Yet the dogma marches on that a middle-class background is necessary for academic success.

St. Augustine High School in New Orleans was a particularly striking example of achieving academic success while going against the grain of prevailing opinion in educational circles. It was established back in 1951, during the era of racial segregation in the South, as a school for black boys, presided over by an all-white staff from the Josephite order. None of these young priests had ever taken a course in a department or school of education. There was no unifying educational theory. To the horror of some outside members of the order, the school used corporal punishment. The school kept doing things that worked and discarded things that didn't.

The first black student from the South to win a National Merit Scholarship came from St. Augustine. So did the first Presidential Scholar of any race from the state of Louisiana. As of 1974, 20 percent of all Presidential Scholars in the history of the state had come from this school with about 600 black students.

Test scores were never used as a rigid cutoff for admission to St. Augustine. There were students with IQs in the 60s, as well as others with IQs more than twice that high. For individual students and for the school as a whole, the average IQ rose over the years—being in the 80s and 90s in the 1950s and reaching the national average of 100 in the 1960s. To put this in perspective, both blacks and whites in the South during this era tended to score below the national average on IQ and other standardized tests.

Most of these children did not come from middle-class families. Those whose parents were in professional or white-collar occupations were less than one-tenth as numerous as those whose parents worked in "unskilled and semi-skilled" occupations.

Secrets of Success

What are the "secrets" of such successful schools? The biggest secret is that there are no secrets, unless work is a secret. Work seems to be the only four-letter word that cannot be used in public today.

Aside from work and discipline, the various successful schools for minority children I studied had little in common with one another—and even less in common with the fashionable educational theories of our times. Some of these schools were public, some were private. Some were secular and some were religious. Dunbar High School had an all-black teaching staff, but St. Augustine in New Orleans began with an all-white teaching staff. Some of these schools were housed in old, run-down buildings and others in new, modern facilities. Some of their principals were finely attuned to the social and political nuances, while others were blunt individuals who could not have cared less about such things and would have failed "Public Relations 101."

None of these successful schools had a curriculum especially designed for blacks. Most had some passing recognition of the children's backgrounds. Dunbar High School, for example, was named for black poet Paul Laurence Dunbar, and it set aside one day a year to commemorate Frederick Douglass, but its curriculum could hardly be called Afrocentric. Throughout the 85 years of its academic success, it taught Latin. In some of the early years, it taught Greek as well. Its whole focus was on expanding the students' cultural horizons, not turning their minds inward. (For all I know, there may be some Afrocentric schools that are doing well. The point here is simply that this has not been an essential ingredient in the successful education of minority students.)

For those who are interested in schools that produce academic success for minority students, there is no lack of examples, past and present. Tragically, there is a lack of interest by the public school establishment in such examples. I think this goes back to the politics of education.

Put bluntly, failure attracts more money than success. Politically, failure becomes a reason to demand more money, smaller classes, and more trendy courses and programs, ranging from "black English" to bilingualism and "self-esteem." Politicians who want to look compassionate and concerned know that voting money for such projects accomplishes that purpose for them, and voting against such programs risks charges of mean-spiritedness, if not implications of racism.

We cannot recapture the past and there is much in the past that we should not want to recapture. But neither is it irrelevant. If nothing else, history shows what can be achieved, even in the face of adversity. We have no excuse for achieving less in an era of greater material abundance and greater social opportunities.

❏ ❏ ❏

THOMAS SOWELL is the Rose and Milton Friedman Senior Fellow in Public Policy at Stanford University's Hoover Institution on War, Revolution, and Peace. He earned his Ph.D. in economics from the University of Chicago and has taught at Amherst, Cornell, Brandeis, and UCLA. He has also been a scholar at the Urban Institute and at Stanford University's Center for

Advanced Study in the Behavioral Sciences. He writes a regular column for *Forbes*, as well as a nationally syndicated newspaper column. Among his nearly twenty books are *Knowledge and Decisions* (1980), *A Conflict of Visions* (1987), *Inside American Education* (1993), and a three-volume series—*Race and Culture* (1994), *Migrations and Cultures* (1996), and *Conquests and Cultures* (1998).

POLITICS

❑ ❑ ❑

The American Presidency
Statesmanship and Constitutionalism in the Balance

Walter Berns

January 1983

Dr. Berns delivered this speech at a Hillsdale College seminar, "Presidential Leadership: Past, Present, and Future," on the Hillsdale campus.

❏   ❏   ❏

America today is in need of leadership of the sort provided in the past by our greatest presidents, presidents whom we mean to honor and praise when we denominate them "statesmen." Our familiar habit of associating wisdom or propriety or goodness with constitutionality bespeaks our attachment to the Constitution and thereby to constitutionalism.

We are equally in favor, it seems, of statesmanship and of constitutionalism, and a strong argument can be made that we need them both.

The paradox that I want to explore here consists in, if not the incompatibility of the two—for, after all, the greatest of our presidents, Abraham Lincoln, displayed his statesmanship by saving the Constitution—then, at least, in the tension that exists between them.

It can be said truthfully that the Founding Fathers took such care in the writing of the Constitution because they—who were great statesmen—distrusted statesmen. They saw the necessity of constructing a system that did not depend on statesmanship. To leave room for statesmanship is to leave room for the exercise of discretion and, indeed, power, and power is dangerous.

"We shall never prevent the abuse of power if we are not prepared to limit power in a way which occasionally may also prevent its use for desirable purposes." That was written by a Nobel Laureate, a famous liberal (in the European sense of that term), and a friend of Hillsdale College, Friedrich Hayek.[1] As Werner Dannhauser has pointed out, however, Hayek, who advocates classical liberalism as a system where bad men can do the least harm, "never discusses whether liberalism is not, by the same token, the system in which good men, especially statesmen, can do the least good."[2]

If a statesman is someone who "takes his orders directly from God," and not from the laws of men, including the law of the constitutions men write, constitutionalism tends to believe that God doesn't speak audibly or unambiguously to men—even though some men claim otherwise, at least on behalf of their own aural powers. As Dannhauser went on to point out, "anyone who is inclined simply to dismiss the wisdom of the Founding Fathers in circumscribing the possibilities of statesmanship should first ponder the fact that this nation has been able to survive a large number of bad presidents."[3]

Statesmanship is the capacity to do what is good in the circumstances, as Professor Mansfield puts it,[4] and its possibility depends on the presence of persons who know what is good *and* enjoy the freedom to do it. Constitutionalism is acting according to fundamental laws designed to limit that freedom, laws of procedure and sometimes of substance.

The statesmen who wrote the Constitution of the United States were profound students of constitutionalism, of limited government. Indeed, the principles of constitutionalism cannot be separated from the principles of the American regime which are delineated in the Declaration of Independence. To understand the reasons for constitutionalism and the distrust of statesmanship, it is necessary to say something about the political philosophy that informs the Declaration of Independence .

The Declaration asserts the self-evident truth that all men are, by nature, endowed with certain unalienable rights and that they institute government "to secure these rights." By nature government does not exist; it is an artifact made by man. By nature rights do exist, but they are insecure; which is to say, men have rights but they cannot be enjoyed outside government or in the state of nature. To understand why this is so, we must turn to the founding father of liberalism, Thomas Hobbes.

Writing in the middle of the seventeenth century, more than a hundred years before the Declaration of Independence, Hobbes was the first political philosopher to take his bearings from the rights that men possess by nature. Because, as Hobbes argued, men are naturally selfish and vain, they seek power after power, which they can exercise only over other men. Since there is no government in the state of nature, the consequence is the state of war. The fundamental right of nature is self-preservation, but since everyone is himself the executor of that law, and there is no law to restrain him as he does whatever he thinks necessary to preserve his own life, the life of every man is "solitary, poor, nasty, brutish, and short." He needs government.

The trouble is, he brings into civil society all his passions, especially his vanity and the thirst for power. He is hard to govern. He insists on substituting his own judgment for that made by kings or the civil law. Especially if he is a priest—what we would call an intellectual—he teaches disobedience of the laws. The result, too frequently, is civil war.

Hobbes' solution to this was the contract by which all men agreed to give up their natural right, to do whatever is necessary to defend and preserve themselves, to a sovereign whom they create by this contract. Henceforth, the sovereign represents them all. Since in the state of nature each man was an absolute ruler, empowered to do anything to secure his rights, the sovereign who succeeds to these rights is an absolute ruler. His job is to preserve peace and thereby secure these rights.

But what is to prevent the sovereign from misruling? This problem was solved, in practice if not in principle, by the Englishman John Locke, sometimes referred to as "America's philosopher," who wrote a few years after Hobbes and accepted all of his principles. In Locke's teaching, however, when men enter into the contract with one another to institute government and secure their rights, they yield their natural rights not to a sovereign person but to the law. Every man yields his natural power to preserve himself and finds security in the laws.[5]

Now, these laws are, in principle, as absolute as Hobbes' sovereign. Whatever Hobbes' sovereign may do to secure rights, may in principle be done by Locke's civil society through law. But misrule by law is less likely than misrule by a sovereign. In the first place, everyone is subject to the laws, even those who make them. Then, secondly, the lawmaking or legislative power can be institutionalized, and institutions can themselves be subjected to laws or rules of procedure. For example, the legislative power can be divided—in a constitution made by the people who have yielded their natural rights—between two branches, and an executive can be given a share of it in the form of a veto. In short, protection against absolute power can be secured by means of carefully designed institutional devices. They make limited government possible, and this is constitutionalism.

Constitutionalism is an attempt to confine the rule of men over men to the rule of law. It is the attempt to convert the power that one man would exercise over others into a system whereby power takes the form of law that every man gives to himself. It should be clear that, stated in this essential form, constitutionalism and statesmanship are incompatible. They are incompatible because this constitutionalism recognizes or embodies the fundamental equality of all men, whereas statesmanship rests on inequality in an important respect: that some men, or some one man, knows better than all men (whose judgment is expressed in the law) what should be done.

Interestingly enough, modern statesmanship does not make this extreme claim. In what is probably the most instructive discussion of this subject, the late Herbert J. Storing asked whether the presidency is in the constitutional order or outside it. He meant by this whether the president's constitutional powers were confined to administering or enforcing the laws adopted by Congress, or, on the contrary, whether he was given some authority to act outside the law.

John Locke, the direct source of the principles of our political understanding, long ago formulated Storing's same question in this way: Can there be any room for prerogative in constitutional government, with prerogative defined as the power to act without the benefit of law and sometimes even against the letter of law? His answer was yes, and in the scope of that answer may be found the basis for the legitimacy of statesmanship under modern constitutionalism. This proves to be a constricted statesmanship. Here is Locke on prerogative:

> This power to act according to discretion for the public good, without the prescription of the law and sometimes even against it, is that which is called "prerogative"; for since in some gov-

ernments the lawmaking power is not always in being, and is usually too numerous and too slow for the dispatch requisite to execution, and because it is also impossible to foresee, and so by laws to provide for, all accidents and necessities that may concern the public, or to make such laws as will do no harm if they are executed with an inflexible rigor on all occasions and upon all persons that may come their way, therefore there is a latitude left to the executive power to do many things of choice which the laws do not prescribe.[6]

So prerogative, or the realm of statesmanship, is, in the first place (according to this authoritative account), the power to do what the laws would do if the lawmaking power were "in being." Its justification is not that a statesman knows better than the people but, rather, that the people are not assembled to make the law; they are home plowing the fields for the spring or fall planting. And prerogative is, in the second place, the power to do what the laws would do if the laws could foresee what should be done, as well as the power to make exceptions in the execution of the laws, exceptions governed by a judgment as to whether it would be good to apply them or not.

Let us apply these principles to one action taken by Lincoln shortly after he became president and was faced with armed insurrection. Armed bands of brigands were blowing up railroad tracks and bridges in Maryland, and otherwise doing whatever was in their power to prevent federal troops from reaching the capital at Washington in order to defend it against armies launched by the so-called Confederate States of America. The lawful government of Maryland did little to apprehend these brigands, and the national government could not depend on the judges to allow them to be convicted in a fair trial even if the Maryland executive brought them to trial.

Lincoln (to use the Constitution's language) suspended the privilege of the writ of habeas corpus. He authorized the army to apprehend, hold, and not to bring to trial anyone who interfered with the transportation of troops. A lawful use of prerogative? Yes, he insisted, because the Constitution authorized suspension of the privilege of habeas corpus, and, although its place in the Constitution suggests that this was a judgment to be made by Congress, Congress was not in session. Therefore, Lincoln did no more than the laws would have done had the lawmaking authority been able to act.

But what if it can be shown that Lincoln, who had the constitutional authority to call Congress into session, deliberately did not exercise it and, instead, did what, in his judgment, Congress ought to have done but which he was not sure Congress would do if given the opportunity? Does the Constitution, or fidelity to constitutionalism, permit this prerogative? To state the matter baldly, who is Abraham Lincoln to preempt the legislative authority—to take the law into his own hands?

Yet, are we not grateful to him for having done so? Are we really willing to abide rigidly by the rules of constitutionalism, laid down with the view to preventing bad men from doing harm, or do we see the Constitution as allowing, on exceptional occasions (and who defines such occasions), good men to do good? As I said at the beginning, we Americans are all in favor of constitutionalism *and* we are all in favor of statesmanship.

At least we are in favor of what might be called a democratic statesmanship, one that does not assert a claim of superiority on the part of the statesman—Lincoln, who was one of the most extraordinary men ever to live, made a practice of concealing himself behind a very democratic facade—and one that limits itself to actions designed to securing our rights. We would not brook, or tolerate, an Alexander, a Caesar, a Napoleon (the three "towering geniuses" the 29-year-old Lincoln referred to in his remarkable speech to the Young Men's Lyceum of Springfield)[7] or even a de Gaulle.

Such men impose a rule over others; they change the way of life of the people they rule; they change the constitution. They claim a superiority to the people, a right to govern. And from the very beginning, because of the Hobbes–Lockean principles embodied in our Declaration of Independence, we insist that the so-called government has no right to govern us.

This is why, whereas the British speak of the Churchill government, the Thatcher government, or the Disraeli or Gladstone governments, and even the Canadians speak of the Trudeau government, we Americans speak of the Washington, Lincoln, Carter, or Reagan *administrations*. The purpose of the Reagan Administration today, equally with that of the Washington Administration two centuries ago, is, as Storing has put it, to facilitate "the peaceful enjoyment of private life."[8] We may, on occasion, require extraordinary leadership, but, in principle, this is leadership required to so arrange our affairs that we can go about our private business. We want no one—as we would be inclined to put it—to mess around with our souls.

That there have been men of this order is suggested by this statement made by the greatest of German poets—indeed, one of the greatest poets simply—Goethe:

> A great dramatic poet if he is at the same time productive, and is actuated by a strong *noble* purpose, which pervades all his works, may succeed in making the soul of his pieces become the soul of the people. I should think that this was something well worth the trouble. From Corneille proceeded an influence capable of forming heroes. This was something for Napoleon, who had need of an heroic people. On which account, he said of Corneille, that if he were still living, he would make a prince of him.[9]

Lincoln was the American poet in this sense: He changed us with his words. But he did so always with reference to the Declaration of Independence and, as I said, he never pretended to be anything but a common man. As he said in response to a request for autobiographical details, "Why, it is great folly to attempt to make anything out of me or my early life. It can be condensed into a single sentence you will find in Gray's *Elegy*: 'The short and simple annals of the poor.' That's my life, and that's all you or anyone else can make of it."

It is sufficiently clear from the records of the period that the Founders, however attached they were to constitutionalism, and however distrustful they were of statesmanship, were as persuaded as was Locke that the president must be able to exercise prerogative, the power to act without the benefit of law and sometimes even against the law. The president was not to be elected by or responsible to the law-making body. He was to exercise a constitutionally established *executive* power, a power the best of our presidents have not hesitated to use: to seize private property, to emancipate slaves, to send troops against non-taxpaying whiskey distillers, or to Lebanon, Vietnam, Arkansas, and Mississippi, to spend money not appropriated and refuse to spend money appropriated, to send the fleet around the world, and so on; the list is a long one.

Nor was the president to be elected directly by the people, a procedure one of the Founders likened to submitting a choice of colors to a
blind man. Here, and in other of their constitutional provisions, they dis-
closed their principal apprehension concerning the future of government
in the United States, the fear that popular government (to which they were
firmly committed) would degenerate into populism, giving the people what
they want as soon as they want it.

From the Founders' point of view, nothing could be more inappropriate than such modern gimmicks as the constitutional amendment, proposed a few years ago by Senators Packwood and Abourezk, which would
have allowed a direct lawmaking by the people. As the Founders saw it, the
solution to the problems of democracy was *not* more democracy. On the
contrary, it was the provision of some distance between the people and
the political officials, distance to be used to refine the popular view, to do
what ought to be done rather than what the people want done, to provide
some scope for leadership or statesmanship.

The danger in our time is that political officials will do only what they
think is popular. Rather than government better than the people, the tendency—here in the words of Jimmy Carter—is to aim for government as
good as the people. It is as if our presidents, our legislators, and even our
judges, lack all confidence in their own judgment or know of no principled
way to act independently of the will of the people. Thus, the Supreme Court
ignores the Constitution, which it is sworn to uphold against even the
popular will, and renders judgments calculated to bring law and policy in
line with what it regards as popular.[10]

The danger we face today, in other words, is not statesmanship in the
sense in which the Founders used the term, but rather the opposite. The
danger is that the president, the judiciary, or the bureaucracy, will refuse to
abide by the rules of the law that come out of our constitutional system,
and will bend that law in what they regard as the direction indicated by the
popular will.

Here is merely one example of what I have in mind: Congress enacts the
Civil Rights Act of 1964, Title VII of which forbids an employer to discriminate
against any individual with respect to his "compensation, terms, conditions,
or privileges of employment, because of such individual's race, color, religion,

sex, or national origin." To make it absolutely clear that this did not require or permit what we now call affirmative action, Title VII went on to provide that this did not mean that any person, or group, should be given "preferential treatment." Yet, in case after case, the Supreme Court, with the acquiescence of Congress and the president, has upheld preferential treatment of one sort or another.

This ignoring of the law might be called statesmanship, but it is not statesmanship of the sort the Founders left room for in their constitutional system. It is the use of extraordinary power not, as in Lincoln's case, to preserve the constitutional order, but to undermine it. It is a false and dangerous statesmanship, exercised not to restrain the tendency of popular government to degenerate into populism, but rather to strengthen that tendency. And it is directly contrary to the Founders' intentions. As Storing said, "Any American statesman whose public face is populistic is not performing his highest duty, no matter how prudent and successful his specific policies may be."[11]

Notes

1. Friedrich Hayek, *The Road to Serfdom* (Chicago: The University of Chicago Press, 1944), p. 237.
2. Werner J. Dannhauser, "Reflections on Statesmanship and Bureaucracy," in Robert A. Goldwin (ed.), *Bureaucrats, Policy Analysts, Statesmen: Who Leads?* (Washington, D.C.: American Enterprise Institute, 1980), p. 120.
3. Ibid., p. 121.
4. Harvey C. Mansfield, Jr., *Statesmanship and Party Government: A Study of Burke and Bolingbroke* (Chicago & London: The University of Chicago Press, 1965), p. 17.
5. Locke, *Second Treatise of Civil Government*, seco. 87–89.
6. Ibid., sec. 160.
7. Roy P. Basler (ed.), *The Collected Works of Abraham Lincoln*, vol. I, p. 114.
8. Herbert J. Storing, "American Statesmanship: Old and New," in Goldwin, op. cit., p. 97.
9. Goethe, *Conversations with Eckermann*.
10. See, e.g., *Reynolds v. Sims*, 377 U.S. 533 (1964).
11. Storing, op. cit., p. 105.

❑ ❑ ❑

WALTER BERNS is the John M. Olin University Professor, Emeritus, at Georgetown University and a resident scholar at the American Enterprise Institute. He received his Ph.D. in political science from the University of Chicago and has taught at the University of Toronto, the University of Chicago, Cornell University, and Yale University. He is a member of the National Council on the Humanities and the Council of Scholars in the Library of Congress, and in 1983 he served as the alternate United States representative to the United Nations Commission on Human Rights. He has been a Guggenheim, Rockefeller, and Fulbright fellow and a Phi Beta Kappa lecturer. He has authored several books, including *Taking the Constitution Seriously* (1991) and *Making Patriots* (2001).

The Pyramid and the Eye: America in Modern History

George H. Nash

May 1983

Dr. Nash delivered this speech at a Hillsdale College seminar, "America Confronts Modernization: A Conservative View of the American Heritage," on the Hillsdale campus.

❏ ❏ ❏

From the days of the Puritans to the age of Ronald Reagan, a sense of uniqueness and of destiny has infused the American character. On board the ship *Arbella* as it sailed for New England in 1630, John Winthrop admonished his Puritan brethren: "...we must consider that we shall be a city upon a hill. The eyes of all people are upon us...." A century and a half later Hector St. John de Crèvecoeur, a Frenchman who had settled in New York, propounded in a classic little book a famous question: "What then is the American, this new man?" And he prophesied: "Here individuals of all nations are melted into a new race of men, whose labors and posterity will one day cause great changes in the world."

On the back of our one-dollar bill you find a replication of the Great Seal of the United States. One side of the seal features a majestic bald eagle holding arrows and an olive branch in its talons. The reverse side of the seal is less familiar—and more revealing. It shows an unfinished pyramid with the date 1776 engraved in Roman numerals on its base. Below the pyramid is a motto: *Novus Ordo Seclorum*—"A New Order of the Ages."

73

Adopted by the Continental Congress in 1782, the Great Seal of the United States symbolized America's self-image as it embarked upon nationhood. America, the seal suggested, was not simply another nation–state; it represented something novel in all history. Moreover, it portended the future —"a new order of the ages," a break with the past.

The Old World, with its kings, oligarchies, and regimes of oppression, was to be left behind forever. Now, in a vast and nearly empty land, there would be constructed a republic—"conceived in liberty," as Lincoln later put it, and dedicated to—to what? To a *proposition*, a creed, a set of truths held to be self-evident. America was to be a polity created by conscious design, an unprecedented experiment in self-government on a continental scale.

Land of Opportunity

In other ways than the political, America has long been perceived as an untraditional society. To millions upon million of immigrants through decade after decade of our history, America has been a land of opportunity, a refuse from the constricted, decadent, stratified, class-bound, traditional societies of Europe. Is it surprising that during our Civil War the British aristocracy was sympathetic to the "feudal" South, while the British working classes favored the more "modern" North? And America has beckoned precisely because it appeared to be *different* from the Old World.

What has it promised? It has promised freedom: free land, upward mobility, equality of opportunity, a chance to start over. It has been a land of stupendous social energy, a land wherein has flourished, as in no other society before or since, the social type known as the self-made man.

Benjamin Franklin is said to have remarked that America is a country where we ask of a person not "Who is he?" but "What can he do?" Think about that; it is a profound observation. In our commitment to a society based on individual merit and equality of opportunity we Americans have adopted two of the core values of modernity.

Still another way in which America has exhibited its modernity is in its dedication as a society to progress—or, to use a better word, to "improvement." Implanted deep in the American psyche is a conviction that social conditions around us *do not have to be that way*—that if evils exist we can eradicate them; that if, for example, corrupt politicians hold office we can throw the rascals out; that we are the masters of our fate and the captains of our souls. Passivity and fatalism are not a part of our national character.

This relentless American impulse for improvement—of society and of oneself—has taken the most various forms. Think of the extraordinary edifice of higher education that Americans in two centuries have established: from small liberal arts colleges like Hillsdale to behemoth universities. Think of the assumptions about human nature behind this commitment, and think also about its expansiveness: Americans increasingly seek education not just for a privileged elite but for ever broader segments of the population. A far higher percentage of Americans attends college, for example, than in any other country in the world.

"Born to Be a Reformer"

And consider this: Has there ever been a society as incessantly productive of reform movements as our own? I refer not only to such preeminent crusades as those for emancipation of the slaves, universal suffrage, and regulation of the trusts, but also to such causes as temperance, prison reform, aid to the Indians, the creation of orphanages, abolition of child labor, even the health food movement.

"What is man born for but to be a Reformer...?" wrote that enormously popular American philosopher Ralph Waldo Emerson. We are a restless people, and many of us believe that even our inner selves can be re-formed. It is a remarkably modern notion.

From Eli Whitney to Thomas Edison, from Henry Ford to Charles Lindbergh, from the Wright brothers to the astronauts, from the automobile to the home computer: No other society, to my knowledge, has honored science—above all, applied science—as lavishly as has ours.

This interest in technology, in gadgetry, in shaping and reshaping our environment, reflects another aspect of the modern temperament. We Americans like to think of ourselves as an optimistic, problem-solving people. During the election campaign of 1980, Ronald Reagan repeatedly denounced the drab, defeatist notion that American's challenges were insuperable, that our expectations must be lowered forever, that the "era of limits" had arrived. It was a theme that was persuasive with millions. In his inaugural address Mr. Reagan declared:

> The crisis we are facing today [requires] our willingness to believe in ourselves and to believe in our capacity to perform great deeds; to believe that together, with God's help, we can and will resolve the problems which now confront us. And after all, why shouldn't we believe that? We are Americans.

It is a significant datum that in our discourse we speak of something called the American Dream. No one ever talks about the British Dream, the Russian Dream, or the Japanese Dream. But the American Dream—that is something else. Instinctively we comprehend what it means: It means opportunity to achieve, to ascend the ladder, to transcend our origins, however humble. We sense that this is distinctively an *American* dream, that it is inextricably interwoven with our self-definition as a people. We sense further that ours is a land where dreams often enough find fulfillment, and that our society is unusual because of it.

America the Trailblazer

This belief in American uniqueness and destiny, in America as a trailblazing society, is not the sole property of the left. Consider this quotation:

> It was not because it was proposed to establish a nation, but because it was proposed to establish a nation on new principles, that July 4, 1776 has come to be regarded as one of the greatest days in history.

Who said this? Tom Paine? William O. Douglas? No; it was Calvin Coolidge in 1926. Now consider these words:

> By a classless America our forefathers meant far more than a sociological expression. There were to be no stratifications in

life that handicapped the rise of any boy from the bottom to the top. The human particles should move freely in the social solution. . . . This idea of a fluid classless society was unique in the world. It was the point at which our social structure departed from all others.

Who wrote this paean to classless America? Hubert Humphrey? Eugene Debs? Jane Fonda? No; it was Herbert Hoover in 1940.

America is different; it represents youth, freedom, energy, the future—a better future: this is a vision that has been central to our national identity.

The title of this CCA seminar is "America Confronts Modernization." Now if, as the social scientists tell us, the process of modernization entails social mobility, economic freedom, and the breakdown of class barriers; if it means equality of opportunity, increased popular participation in politics, and equal justice under law; if it means a social order that is not static and hierarchical but dynamic and future-oriented; it if means technological innovation and a spirit of improvement; then America for two hundred years—at least in its own self-understanding—has been a modernizing society.

"The most potent force in society," Herbert Hoover once reminded us, "is its ideals." From the late eighteenth century to the early twentieth, the dominant American ideal has been (to use a current term) "democratic capitalism." And in the long perspective of the Western history, democratic capitalism has been a virtual synonym for modernization.

New Order Now Old Hat?

Yet if America in many respects is a modern society (as I have used the term thus far), we must now examine an unsettling fact: that for more than half a century the identification of America with the future of mankind has been declining.

No longer, it seems, is America perceived as the harbinger of the new order of the ages. Instead today, over much of the earth, the inspiriting ideals of American experiment—the ideals of political equality and participation, of entrepreneurial freedom and economic growth, of social fluidity and equality of opportunity—are scorned, despised, and mocked.

Why has the American system lost its idealistic appeal as a model for other new nations? Some, I suppose, would claim that this was inevitable: that America, the nation of youth, has finally become middle-aged. Some would argue that America's sense of uniqueness was always a function of geographical isolation and that as America's isolation has disappeared, it has lost its immunity from the Old World and its ills. No longer, they would say, is America exempt from the disillusionment of history. Still other observers would point to America's racial problems, political corruption, unemployment, or environmental pollution and claim that the United States is no longer a success story, hence not a model for anybody.

These explanations have some plausibility, but they are not sufficient. For what has occurred in the past fifty or sixty years is not simply the discovery of an alleged gap between American ideals and American reality but a growing and massive rebellion against the ideals themselves.

To an influential number of American and European intellectuals in this century, other societies have supplanted America as the repositories of progress and modernity.

Political Pilgrims

Just after World War I, the eminent muckraking journalist Lincoln Steffens declared, "I have been over into the future—and it works." He was not referring to his own United States but to Russia. For him and so many others, communist Russia had come to portend the beneficent next phase in the evolution of mankind.

Lincoln Steffens was but an early example of one of the most extraordinary phenomena of the twentieth century: the rise of what Paul Hollander has called "political pilgrims"—deeply alienated Western intellectuals, many of them quite famous, who have repudiated their own societies, traveled to horribly repressive totalitarian regimes, and found therein the drawings of utopia.

Over the years, the particular earthly avatar of the new age has varied. In the 1920s and 1930s it was Soviet Russia; later it was Cuba and

Maoist China, Vietnam under Ho Chi Minh, and Chile under Salvador Allende. But always it was somewhere else—never America. And always it was totalitarian regime.

This profound inner defection of many of the West's most distinguished intellectuals from the American ethos of democratic capitalism is one of the most stunning and disturbing features of our time. It is a phenomenon, of course, that has many roots; but clearly it is linked to the rise, within the last century or so, of a new conception of modernity.

Unlike the modernizing principles to which I have referred earlier, this "new modernity" (as I shall call it) has not been primarily political or economic in its orientation. It has been, at bottom, literary, aesthetic, and, in a way, spiritual.

The pioneers of this new consciousness are familiar enough to us all: names like Nietzsche, Kierkegaard, and Sartre; Ibsen, Gide, and Baudelaire; Pound, Picasso, and the early Albert Camus.

Relativism, Negation, Despair

At the heart of this new modernity was a sense of relativism, negation, and despair. Where the old modernity asserted that certain truths were self-evident, the new modernity denied that universal truths exist.

Where the old modernity was bourgeois, the new modernity was bohemian, contemptuous of bourgeois culture.

Where the old modernity tended to be optimistic (after all, would not tomorrow be better than today?), the new modernity was not.

Where the old modernity tended to be rationalistic, the new modernity explored the irrational and the absurd.

Where the old modernity offered liberation from *external* constraints —from the barriers of class, race, national origin, and arbitrary government— the new modernity preached liberation from the *inner* constraints—from traditional morality, from artistic convention, from rationality itself.

Where the old modernity concentrated on getting ahead in the world and was relatively indifferent to questions of ultimate meaning, the new modernity was haunted by the conviction that life *has* no ultimate meaning; that God is dead.

This new modernity has penetrated very deeply into our civilization. It has become the *weltanschauung* of what Lionel Trilling has labeled the "adversary culture," a culture profoundly hostile to the old modernity and to the regime built in part upon it. How is it that this counterculture (to use another term for it) has become so pervasive? Writing more than a dozen years ago, Jeffrey Hart offered an answer. America in the past generation, he wrote, has witnessed a "cultural explosion":

> . . . paperbacks, Eliot reading his poems to fifty thousand students in a Midwestern football stadium, LP records, Mailer and Genet and de Sade appearing in mass circulation journals, the op-art and pop-art and porno phenomena. All of these things, along with affluence, the GI Bill and the assumption, implicit in democratic theory and increasingly the premise of government action, that absolutely everyone must go to college, have now given rise to a vast student proletariat. . . . Much of this proletariat absorbs the attitudes of the adversary culture.

Looking back on my own education I can attest to the acuity of Professor Hart's remark. Attending college in the Sixties, I was exposed to books like Paul Goodman's *Growing Up Absurd* and Norman O. Brown's *Life Against Death*, to plays like *Waiting for Godot* and the *Marat/Sade*. Teaching at Harvard in the early Seventies, I had a student tell me one day that all values are without rational foundation, that one can only choose arbitrarily among them. This was pure existentialism, of course, but where had he acquired such ideas?

A Sense of Our Goodness

As the new modernity has percolated down through our culture, the values of the old modernity have come increasingly to seem old-fashioned. Listen to the voices that dominate our public discourse (and I do not mean Mr. Reagan's). Listen carefully the next time someone uses the term "equality of opportunity" or "Protestant ethic" or "middle-class values" and see whether you do not detect a note of irony or disparagement.

It is significant that the political embodiment of "old-fashioned modernity" in the United Sates at present is the Republican party, the *conservative* party. It is in the Republican party and among people called conservatives and neoconservatives that one still hears the rhetoric of upward mobility and achievement, of liberty and democratic capitalism as the hope of all nations. These ideals of modernity—of the *old* modernity, that is—have become the property of conservatives.

But does this clash of modernities really matter? Does it matter that the new modernity has become a virtual orthodoxy among the secular intelligentsia? Does it matter that, as Midge Decter observed in a brilliant speech last year [1982], there is spreading throughout society a conviction that "nothing is worth dying for?"

Yes, it does matter, for two reasons. First, few men and women can live in a spiritual vacuum for long. If their society seems meaningless, they will in rage and frustration find or create meaning somewhere, even in violence, decadence, and revolution. Second, no society can survive without some sense of its own goodness. If many Americans no longer believe in our system, there are others in this world who believe in theirs—and are willing to enforce their beliefs at gunpoint.

Now is there a historical relationship between the two modernities? I have presented them as antagonists, but could there be some dialectical process by which the one inexorably gave birth to the other? Is there, in other words, an inevitable declension from democratic capitalism to socialist nihilism? There is a verse by Goldsmith that my New England ancestors used to recite:

> Ill fares the land
> To hastening ills a prey
> Where wealth accumulates
> And men decay.

More recently, Joseph Schumpeter, Daniel Bell, and others have suggested that capitalism creates the intellectual class that will ultimately destroy it—indeed, that capitalism generates its own fatal "cultural contradictions": That capitalism, with its ceaseless incitements to instant gratification of every taste, no matter how debased, eventually destroys the cultural matrix of decency, sobriety, and self-restraint upon which it—and republican self-government—depend.

Under God's Eye

Is this thesis true? Is the new modernity the necessary offspring of the old? In short, is the American way of life, in some ways a modern way of life, inherently and irremediably flawed?

I do not believe that it is. The Great Seal of the United States contains more than simply the motto *Novus Ordo Seclorum* and the image of an unfinished pyramid. Hovering above the pyramid is a symbolic unblinking eye: the eye of God. And placed above that is another Latin motto: *Annuit Coeptis*, meaning "He has favored [our] undertaking." Americans, I said earlier, are a restless people, but as Tocqueville long ago recognized, we have not been restless in everything, particularly in the realm of our formative philosophic and moral beliefs. And a powerful reason for this remarkable constancy amidst so much flux is that America, from the beginning, has evolved within a context of Christian religious faith.

I am not saying that the Founding Fathers sought to establish a Christian commonwealth or that America's public institutions have been explicitly religious in character. I am saying that the modernized impulses described earlier—the impulses of what I have called the old modernity—have operated, at least until recently, within a predominantly and persistently religious culture.

If the new modernity has not yet triumphed among us, it is because American culture has been molded and guided by the nonmodern and profoundly civilizing force of our Judeo-Christian religious heritage. While the American polity and economy are in some sense modern, American culture—at the level of ultimate beliefs about God and man—has been and perhaps remains primarily conservative.

Liberty, said Alexis de Tocqueville, "cannot be established without morality, nor morality without faith." If America is to survive, its indisputably modern elements, it seems to me, must be conjoined with what Russell Kirk has called the "permanent things," spiritual things, and the institutions that sustain them. Without this fusion, the American experiment may

GEORGE H. NASH

83

fail—not because it is a regime of liberty but because liberty alone cannot instruct us how to live. It is what we do with our liberty that will determine our own and our country's future, and for that guidance we must turn outside the market place and the polling booth.

Transcendent Sources

If the old modernity is not to succumb to the relativism and anti-religious nihilism of the new, it will have to draw on transcendent, premodern sources—on religious faith—to infuse our lives with meaning. Edmund Burke said it so well:

> Society cannot exist unless a controlling power upon will and appetite be placed somewhere, and the less of it there is within, the more there must be without. It is ordained in the eternal constitution of things, that men of intemperate minds cannot be free. Their passions forge their fetters.

It is the duty of conservatives—even while accepting and celebrating the ideals of the old modernity—to forge the internal checks and balances that will channel those ideals toward the permanent things.

I do not think that this will be easy. Still, if any of you are tempted to say that democratic capitalism itself is not worth purifying and preserving, or to conclude that the American experiment is too modern for your taste, I would ask you to indulge in a little act of imagination.

Imagine that when you leave this room you will be arrested and perhaps tortured for unlawful assembly; in large portions of the world at this very moment, this would be your fate.

Imagine that you could not obtain employment because of a government's whim; it happened to Lech Walesa recently.

Imagine that if you could not find a job you would be expelled from the city where you are now living; this is the case in the Soviet Union everyday.

Imagine that if you tried to practice your religious faith you were prohibited from going to college or pursing any but the most menial career. It happens all over the USSR in 1983.

The American heritage of which we are the heirs has bequeathed to us the "blessings of liberty." Freedom—to worship, to travel, to select and change careers. Freedom—to write, to publish, to attend meetings like this. Let us not lightly disparage these blessings. Free societies are a rarity in human history, and as the Vietnamese and Cuban boat people can tell you, they have their merits still.

American conservatives, then, unless they wish to live lives of reclusive despondency, must defend and civilize, not repudiate, the free society they have inherited. It will not, as I say, be easy: At times it will entail, in Whittaker Chambers's unforgettable metaphor, "a dance along a precipice." But in a world of spreading nihilism and tyranny, American conservatives must cherish their roots and perceive their true enemies with clarity. Conservatives must combat the new modernity, not the old.

George H. Nash graduated summa cum laude in 1967 from Amherst College and earned his Ph.D. in history from Harvard University in 1973. His dissertation was published in 1975 as *The Conservative Intellectual Movement in America Since 1945*. In subsequent years he has been writing a definitive, multi-volume biography of President Herbert Hoover. The latest volume to be published is *The Life of Herbert Hoover: Masters of Emergencies, 1917–1918* (1996).

The Moral Foundations of Republican Government

Edwin Meese III

September 1986

Mr. Meese delivered this speech at a Hillsdale College seminar, "The Authority of the Constitution: Procedural or Ethical?," on the Hillsdale campus.

❏   ❏   ❏

Taking the opportunity to pause and reflect on the roots of our freedom is always an important thing for us to do. But it is especially important now, as we prepare to celebrate the bicentennial of our Constitution. For our Constitution remains, as William Gladstone, the great British statesman, once described it, "the most wonderful work ever struck off at a given time by the brain and purpose of man."

Too frequently we view our Constitution primarily from the standpoint of litigation, as little more than a lawyer's brief or a judge's opinion. But it is, as you know, far more than that. Not only is the Constitution fundamental law, it is also the institutional expression of the philosophical foundation of our political order, the basis of our very way of life. George Roche has explained why this is so as clearly as anyone. "The Founding Fathers," he has written,

> derived their principles of limiting government and protecting individual rights from a belief in Natural Law; that is, a belief that God had ordained a framework of human dignity and responsi-

85

bility that was to serve as the basis for all human law and as the root assumption behind a written constitution.

During this bicentennial period especially it is crucial that we cast aside the notion that the Constitution is only a litigator's brief or a judge's opinion. Our task is to reawaken public opinion to the fact that our substantive constitutional values have a shape and content that transcend the crucible of litigation.

In order to successfully effect this reawakening, it is necessary to move beyond the current legal debate over jurisprudence. It is, in fact, necessary to move beyond current legal cases and controversies to the political and social milieu of the era in which our Constitution was written. We need to understand that generation of Founders not simply as a historical curiosity. Our obligation is to understand the Founders as they understood themselves.

Now this is no small task. And, obviously, my remarks are merely an introduction to what is, by any measure, an area of inquiry as intellectually complex as it is politically rich. I would like to offer a few general observations about the moral foundations of the government the Founders designed. In particular, I will argue that the ideas of natural rights and the consent of the governed are essential to understanding the moral character of our civil society. Further, I will discuss the institutional forms of the Founders' politics that facilitated the cultivation of virtue in our people— virtues upon which our form of government still depend.

In approaching this subject, we first need to remember that our Founders lived in a time of nearly unparalleled intellectual excitement. They were the true children of the Enlightenment. They sought to bring the new found faith in human reason to bear on practical politics. Hobbes and Locke, Harrington and Machiavelli, Smith and Montesquieu—these were the teachers of our Founders. These were the authors of celebrated works that had called into question long-prevailing views of human nature and thus of politics. Our nation was created in the light cast by these towering figures. That is what Alexander Hamilton meant in *The Federalist* when he argued that the "science of politic . . . like most other sciences, has received great improvement. The efficacy of various principles is now well understood, which were either not known at all, or imperfectly known to the ancients." Our Founders, in many ways, sought to give practical effect to David Hume's desire "that politics may be reduced to a science."

What, then, are the moral foundations of our republican form of government? Much of the answer, I believe, can be found in our charter of fundamental principles, the Declaration of Independence. I think it is worth recalling Thomas Jefferson's famous formulation of these first principles. "We hold these truths," he said, "to be self-evident,"

> That all men are created equal, that they are endowed by their Creator with certain inalienable rights, that among these are Life, Liberty, and the pursuit of Happiness. That to secure these rights, Governments are instituted among Men deriving their just powers from the consent of the governed.

Now these rights were neither the result of legal privilege nor the benevolence of some ruling class. They were rights that existed *in nature* before governments or laws were ever formed. As the physical world is governed by natural laws such as gravity so the political world is governed by other natural laws in the form of natural rights that belong to each individual. These rights, like the laws of gravity, antedate even mankind's recognition of them.

But because these rights were left unsecured by nature, as Jefferson said, governments are instituted among men. Thus there exists in the nature of things a natural standard for judging whether governments are legitimate or not. That standard is whether or not the government rests, in the phrase of the Declaration, upon the consent of the governed. Any political powers not derived from the consent of the governed are, by the laws of nature, illegitimate and hence unjust. Only by such a natural standard can arbitrary power be checked.

"Consent of the governed" is a political concept that is the reciprocal of the idea of equality. Because all men are created equal, nature does not single out who is to govern and who is to be governed. There is no divine right of kings, for example. Consent is the means whereby man's natural equality is made politically operable.

In this theory of government, this philosophy of natural rights and the consent of the governed, we find the most fundamental moral foundation of republican government. For it presupposes a universal moral equality that makes popular government not only politically possible but morally necessary.

However accustomed we have become to ideas of natural rights and the consent of the governed, we should never forget that these were, two centuries ago, morally revolutionary ideas. During this bicentennial period we should refresh ourselves as to the truth of these ideas.

Of course, it is one thing to argue that the only legitimate foundation of government is the consent of the governed, but it is quite another matter to put this theory into practice. The key here is the Declaration's maxim that in order to secure rights "governments are *instituted* among men." It is then, by the act of choosing, by the political act of constituting a government, that the moral standard of the consent of the governed is given definite shape and formidable weight. But such an act of creation is not easy.

That is what Alexander Hamilton had in mind when he introduced the first essay in *The Federalist* by asking "whether societies of men are really capable or not, of establishing good government from reflection and choice, or whether they are forever destined to depend, for their political constitutions, on accident and force." For after all was said and done, after the Revolution had been won, it remained to be seen whether the glowing rhetoric of the declaration could actually be made the standard of political practice.

One thing their recent experience with England had taught the Americans was the necessity of a constitution. And not just any sort of constitution would do. The celebrated English Constitution, after all, had allowed what they saw as a gross abuse of political power. That, we must remember, is what most of the Declaration of Independence is about: the long catalogue of abuses the Americans had suffered. This experience with the all-too-malleable English Constitution bolstered their own earlier inclinations—from the Mayflower Compact on—toward a *written* constitution. The one best way to hedge against arbitrary political power was to clearly stake out the lines and limits of the institutions that would wield power. Thus the purpose of our written Constitution was, as Walter Berns has said, to get it in writing.

This belief in a written constitution was the fulfillment of the more basic belief in the moral authority of the consent of the governed. A written constitution, when duly ratified, would stand as the concrete and tangible expression of that fundamental consent. This document would stand as testimony to the Founders' unfaltering faith in (to borrow the late scholar Alexander Bickel's term) the "morality of consent."

The question facing the Americans then became how to devise such a constitution that would, in the language of the Declaration, be "most likely to effect their Safety and Happiness." Indeed, as James Madison would bluntly put it later in *The Federalist*: "A good government implies two things; first, fidelity to the object of government, which is the happiness of the people; second, a knowledge of the means by which that object can be best attained."

After the War for Independence was won, the Americans set about to secure their revolution. The states began to draft their constitutions and the confederation of the states sought to draft a constitution for its purposes. By 1787, one thing had become clear. Popular government was not simply good government. The state governments, had in many instances, proved tyrannical. The national authority under the Articles of Confederation had proved inept. The period between 1776 and 1787 had shown many Americans that they did not yet possess that "knowledge of the means" by which the happiness of the people could best be secured.

By the time the Federal Convention came together in Philadelphia in May 1787, however, there was a collection of men who had thought through the causes of their present difficulties. They were convinced that the mechanics of republican government could be adjusted in order to defend against charges that it was "inconsistent with the order of society." What was at issue was the very question of the moral basis of the republican form: Could a republic be saved from its own excesses? A sufficient number of Americans believed it could. And they set about to do just that.

The new science of politics, Hamilton confidently argued, provided the "powerful means by which the excellencies of republican government may be retained and its imperfections lessened or avoided."

Now one of the basic problems of the old political order was what many began to see as an unhealthy reliance on the virtue of the people. In many ways, the earlier republicans in America, those historian Pauline Maier has dubbed the "Old Revolutionaries," had created their constitutions in light of their belief that somehow the Americans were a new breed of man, self-reliant, commonsensical, and, above all, civically virtuous. They had thought themselves uniquely capable of continuing self-denial and unfaltering devotion to the public good. As a result, the constitutional order they had created depended to a great degree on "Spartan habits" and Roman patriotism." By the mid-1780s it was clear to many that to love the public and to sacrifice personally for it was proving more easily said than done. Americans, too, it seemed, were corruptible. And this unhappy fact called into question the old assumption that Americans were some-how blessed with exceptional character.

Hamilton's perspicacious collaborator, Madison, was even more suc-cinct. "If the impulse and opportunity be suffered to coincide," he wrote in the famous tenth *Federalist Paper*, "we well know that neither moral nor reli-gious motives can be relied on as an adequate control." In what is arguably one of the most famous passages in American political writing, Madison laid the theoretical foundation for the Framers' "novel experiment" in popu-lar government. Reflecting on the institutional contrivances of the new Constitution, Madison, in *The Federalist*, No. 51 neatly captured his new theory of republican government. His theory, at its deepest level, relied on a cer-tain understanding of human nature. Thus, he wrote, "What is government itself but the greatest of all reflections on human nature? If men were an-gels, no government would be necessary. If angels were to govern men, neither external nor internal controuls would be necessary." However, he concluded, "In framing a government which is to be administered by men over men, the great difficulty lies in this; you must first enable the govern-ment to controul the governed; and in the next place, oblige it to controul itself." According to Madison the purpose of the Constitution's mechan-ics—separation of powers, bicameralism, representation, and so forth—was to hedge against an all too predictable human nature. The object was to offset "the defect of better motives." Good intentions were to be re-placed by good institutions.

To many, the most shocking feature of the Framers' new science of politics was its bold and nearly unqualified reliance on the power of com-merce to make civil society orderly. This was a truly radical step. Com-merce, you see, had long been thought to be the primary cause of corruption of the manners and the morals of free people. And private vice, the prevail-ing belief held, could never produce public virtue.

We take commerce so much for granted that this idea is puzzling to our generation. But to many of the founding generation, commerce produced greed and venality—it brought forth, as its critics said, the worst impulses of mankind. One Anti-Federalist critic of the proposed Constitution summed it up by arguing that such a reliance on commerce would encourage an "excessive fondness for riches and luxury" that would, if left untempered, and unchecked by a concern for public virtue, "totally subvert the government and erect a system of aristocratical or monarchaic tyranny," thereby losing "perhaps forever" the liberties of the people.

The new science of politics of the Constitution was as bold as those Founders who pushed the hardest for it. They were, as one historian has described them, young men of a continental vision. This was the time of Madison and Hamilton and Morris; the day of Adams and Franklin and Lee was quickly passing. They saw more in America than just America. They saw in the founding a great example for all the world. And they believed that commerce was an essential part of this vision.

So it was that these young nationalists rejected the cautious confederalism of the older generation of founders. Their object was not to secure a confederacy of small and virtuous republics of public-spirited citizens. Their object was—in the words of one of their guiding lights, Adam Smith—to establish a "great mercantile republic." Indeed, they sought to establish nothing less that a great republican empire of commerce.

Unleashed, these nationalists believed, the commercial power of self-interest that the Anti-Federalists feared could be turned to republican advantage. By drawing people together, by making them work together for their private gain, commerce could help to tame human nature. Brutish greed would become a prudent concern for profits. A nation of shopkeepers would not be characterized by crude self-interest but by what Alexis de Tocqueville would later celebrate as "enlightened self-interest." While commerce would surely depend upon human passions, it would also serve to moderate them. Commerce and constitutionalism together would make Americans free and prosperous at home and secure among the nations of the world. America would be, they believed, a new kind of republic in a world itself quite new.

But what of civic virtue? Would there be none? Surely there would have to be, because the new science of politics demanded it. As Madison pointed out in the Virginia ratifying convention, a certain degree of virtue was necessary if our form of civil society was to endure.

As we have seen, the political science of the Founding Fathers did not seek to inculcate virtue in its citizens by the terms of the Constitution. But that document, as I have said, is morally praiseworthy because it *does* protect natural rights and it *does* rest upon the consent of the governed. Still, the Founders understood the relevance of what I would call the "character question." They knew the oldest question of politics (the question Aristotle asked)—the question of what kind of people does a regime produce, what kind of character do they have—is always important.

Under the new political order of the Constitution, the cultivation of character was left to the states and the private sphere. Through the political principle of federalism, the Framers left to the people in their states sovereignty sufficient to legislate in these areas; state governments could attempt, under this scheme, directly to promote virtue among the people. In addition, family and church and private associations were expected to provide the support for the inculcation of virtue. And, in a curious way, even the thriving commercial republic the Founders envisioned would itself promote a new kind of public virtue. It would, of course, not be virtue in the classical or the Christian sense. Nor would it be the old small republican variety starkly Spartan in its demands. Rather, it would be what the late Martin Diamond accurately described as the "bourgeois virtues"—the virtues of honesty and decency that commerce itself, that business, presupposes.

But the question we must ultimately confront is how well has our Founders' constitutional handiwork in this regard fared? I suspect I will shock no one by suggesting that it fared very well for most of our history. For while not overtly concerned with morality, our Constitution, I submit, has produced the frame of government in which America has thrived as one of the most moral nations in the history of the world.

How is it that in America the moral concerns of republican government and the concomitant demand for individual liberty have been maintained in such a steady balance?

At its deepest level popular government—republican government—means a structure of government that not only rests upon the consent of the governed, but more importantly a structure of government wherein public opinion can be expressed and translated into public law and public policy. This is the deepest level precisely because public opinion over important public issues ultimately is a public debate over justice. It is naïve to think that people only base their opinions on their conceptions of their narrow self-interest. Very often public opinion and political debates do reflect deeper concerns—if you will, moral concerns.

It is this venting of the moral concerns of a people that is the very essence of political life. In a popular form of government it is not only legitimate but essential that the people have the opportunity to give full vent to their moral sentiments. Through deliberation, debate, and compromise a public consensus can be formed as to what constitutes the public good. It is this consensus over fundamental values that knits individuals into a community of citizens. And it is this liberty to debate and determine the morality of a community that is an important part of the liberty protected by our Constitution.

The toughest political problems deserve to have full and open public debate. Whether the issue is abortion, school prayer, pornography, or aid to parochial schools, the people within their communities within the several states must be allowed to deliberate over them and reach a consensual judgment.

This is not to say, of course, that the people must be allowed to choose any substantive end a majority at any given moment prefers. That is not good republican government; that is a simplistic notion of popular sovereignty. The political theory of our Constitution rejects such a simplistic theory. As one commentator has observed, "There are certain substantive things, such as slavery, that a democratic people may not choose because those substantive ends would be inconsistent with the fundamental premises that give majorities the right to decide."

But to deny the right—the liberty—of the people to choose certain other substantative ends reduces the American Constitution to moral relativism. In that direction lies the danger, to borrow Abraham Lincoln's phrase, of "blowing out the moral lights around us."

During the past several decades an aggressively secular liberalism often driven by an expansive egalitarian impulse has threatened many of the traditional political and social values the great majority of the American people still embrace. The strong gusts of ideology have indeed threatened to blow out the moral lights around us. This has been the result of our knocking down certain institutional barriers to national political power —in particular, the abandonment of an appreciation for the necessity of the separation of powers, and for the continuing political importance of federalism.

I would argue that the demise of these two institutional arrangements has had a disastrous impact on the moral foundations of republican government. I would further argue that these deleterious developments should be abandoned as the dangerous innovations that they are. For they violate our most fundamental political maxim: That in a system of popular government, the people have the liberty and the legitimate power within certain limits to define the moral, political, and legal content of their public lives. When we allow this principle to be transgressed, we risk severing the necessary link between the people and the polity. Indeed, we cut the moral chord that binds us together in our common belief that we have a vital role to play in deciding how we live our collective lives.

We have an obligation today—a moral obligation, if you will—to restore those institutional arrangements that the Founders knew to be essential to the nurturing of public virtue. We have an obligation to restrict the insensitive intrusiveness of the national government in order to allow the most important decisions to be made by the people, not by those Adam Ferguson once called the "clerks and accountants" of a large and distant bureaucracy. We have an obligation to allow the states and communities the maximum freedom possible to structure their politics and infuse them with the moral tone they find most conducive to their happiness. This is the moral obligation of our generation.

We may either reassert our right to govern ourselves or we can surrender to the stultifying leviathan of big government. We must restore those structures that will shore up our sagging moral foundations or we risk losing the liberties which rest upon those foundations.

A decade after the adoption of our Constitution, the Anti-Federalist Mercy Warren, with a good bit of melancholy, expressed her fear that in the end, her countrymen might be remembered as having been "too proud for monarchy, . . . too poor for nobility, and . . . too selfish and avaricious for a virtuous republic." While we may not ever be simply a virtuous people, we must surely endeavor to assuage Mercy Warren's fear by recognizing and perpetuating what Madison believed us to have: "sufficient virtue for self-government."

❏   ❏   ❏

Edwin Meese III is a Distinguished Visiting Fellow at the Hoover Institution and holds the Ronald Reagan Chair in Public Policy at the Heritage Institution. He served as counselor to President Reagan from 1981 to 1985 and as U.S. Attorney General from 1985 to 1988. He is the author of *With Reagan: The Inside Story* (1992).

Statesmanship and Its Betrayal

Mark Helprin

April 1998

Mr. Helprin delivered this speech at a Hillsdale College seminar, "Heroes for a New Generation and a New Century," in Scottsdale, Arizona.

❏ ❏ ❏

When Marco Polo entered Xanadu, the capital of the Great Khan, he crossed ring after ring of outer city, each more splendid and interesting than the one that had come before. He was used to greatness of scale, having traveled to the limits of the ordered world and then doubled that distance into the unknown, where no European had ever set foot, over the Hindu Kush and beyond the Pamir, and through the immense empty deserts of Central Asia. And yet after passing through the world's most ethereal regions he was impressed above all by Xanadu, a city of seemingly infinite expanse, the end of which he could not see, no matter in which direction he looked.

For almost a thousand years, this city floated at the peak of Western imagination. Unlike Jerusalem, it had vanished. Unlike Atlantis, someone had actually seen it. Even during the glory of the British Empire, Coleridge held it out for envy. But no more. Now it has been eclipsed, with ease, by this, our country, founded not as a Xanadu but with the greatest humility, and on the scale of yeomen and their small farms, and as the cradle of simple gifts.

This country was not expected to be what it became. It was expected to be infinite seeming in its rivers, prairies, and stars, not in cities with hundreds of millions of rooms, passages, and halls, and buildings a quarter-mile high. It was expected to be rich in natural silence and the quality of light rather than in uncountable dollars. It was expected to be a place of unfathomable numbers, but of blades of grass and grains of wheat and the crags of mountains rather than millions upon millions of motors spinning and humming at any one time, and wheels turning, fires burning, voices talking, and lights shining.

But this great inventory of machines, buildings, bridges, vehicles, and an incomprehensible number of smaller things, is what we have. A nation founded according to a vision of simplicity has become complex. A nation founded with disdain for power has become the most powerful nation.

When letters took a month by sea and the records of the United States government could be moved in a single wagon pulled by two horses, we had great statesmanship. We had men of integrity and genius: Washington, Hamilton, Franklin, Jefferson, Adams, Madison, and Monroe. These were men who were in love with principle as if it were an art, which, in their practice, they made it. They studied empires that had fallen, for the sake of doing what was right in a small country that had barely risen, and were able to see things so clearly that they surpassed in greatness each and every one of the classical models that they had approached in awe.

Now, lost in the sins and complexity of a Xanadu, when we desperately need their high qualities of thought, their patience for deliberation, and their unerring sense of balance, we have only what we have. Which is a political class that in the main has abandoned the essential qualities of statesmanship, with the excuse that these are inappropriate to our age. They are wrong. Not only do they fail to honor the principles of statesmanship, they fail to recognize them, having failed to learn them, having failed to want to learn them.

In the main, they are in it for themselves. Were they not, they would have a higher rate of attrition, falling with the colors of what they believe rather than landing always on their feet—adroitly, but in dishonor. In light of their vows and responsibilities, this constitutes not merely a failure but a betrayal. And it is a betrayal not only of statesmanship and principle but of country and kin.

Why is that? It is because things matter. Even though it be played like a game, by men who excel at making it a game, our life in this country, our history in this country, the sacrifices that have been made for this country, the lives that have been given to this country, are not a game. My life is not a game. My children's lives are not a game. My parents' lives were not a game. Your life is not a game.

Yes, it is true, we do have great accumulated stores—of power, and wealth, and decency—against which those who pretend to lead us can draw when, as a result of their vanities and ineptitudes, they waste and expend the gifts of previous generations. The margin of error bequeathed to them allows them to present their failures as successes.

They say, as we are still standing, and a chicken is in the pot, what does it matter if I break the links between action and consequence, work and reward, crime and punishment, merit and advancement? I myself cannot imagine a military threat (and never could), so what does it matter if I weld shut the silo hatches on our ballistic missile submarines? What does it matter if I weld shut my eyes to weapons of mass destruction in the hands of lunatics who are building long-range missiles? Our jurisprudence is the envy of the world, so what does it matter if, now and then, I perjure myself, a little? What is an oath? What is a pledge? What is a sacred trust? Are not these things the province of the kinds of people who were foolish enough to do without all their lives, to wear the ruts into the Oregon Trail, to brave the seas, to die on the beaches of Normandy and Iwo Jima and on the battlefields of Shiloh and Antietam, for me, so that I can draw from America's great accounts, and look good, and be presidential, and have fun, in all kinds of ways?

That is what they say, if not in words then, indelibly, in actions. They who, in robbing Peter to pay Paul, present themselves as payers and forget that they are also robbers. They who, with studied compassion, minister to some of us at the expense of others. They who make goodness and charity a public profession, depending for their election upon a well-manured embrace of these things and the power to move them not from within themselves or by their own sacrifices but, by compulsion, from others. They who, knowing very little or next to nothing, take pride in eagerly telling everyone else what to do. They who believe absolutely in their recitation of pieties not because they believe in the pieties but because they believe in themselves.

Nearly four hundred years of America's hard-earned accounts—the principles we established, the battles we fought, the morals we upheld for century after century, our very humility before God—now flow promiscuously through our hands, like blood onto sand, squandered and laid waste by a generation that imagines history to have been but a prelude for what it would accomplish. More than a pity, more than a shame, it is despicable. And yet, this parlous condition, this agony of weak men, this betrayal and this disgusting show, are not the end of things.

Principles are eternal. They stem not from our resolution or lack of it but from elsewhere where, in patient and infinite ranks, they simply wait to be called. They can be read in history. They arise as if of their own accord when in the face of danger natural courage comes into play and honor and defiance are born. Things such as courage and honor are the mortal equivalent of certain laws written throughout the universe. The rules of symmetry and proportion, the laws of physics, the perfection of mathematics, even the principle of uncertainty, are encouragement, entirely independent of the vagaries of human will, that not only natural law but our own best aspirations have a life of their own. They have lasted through far greater abuse than abuses them now. They can be neglected, but they cannot be lost. They can be thrown down, but they cannot be broken.

Each of them is a different expression of a single quality, from which each arises in its hour of need. Some come to the fore as others stay back, and then, with changing circumstance, those that have gone unnoticed rise to the occasion.

Rise to the occasion. The principle suggests itself from a phrase, and such principles suggest easily and flow generously. You can grab them out of the air, from phrases, from memories, from images.

A statesman must rise to the occasion. Even Democrats can do this. Harry Truman had the discipline of plowing a straight row ten, twelve, and fourteen hours a day, of rising and retiring with the sun, of struggling with temperamental machinery, of suffering heat and cold and one injury after another. After a short time on a farm, presumptions about ruling others tend to vanish. It is as if you are pulled to earth and held there.

The man who works the land is hard put to think that he would direct armies and nations. Truman understood the grave responsibility of being the president of the United States, and that it was a task too great for him or for anyone else to accomplish without doing a great deal of injury—if not to some, then to others. He understood that, therefore, he had to transcend himself. There would be little enjoyment of the job, because he had to be always aware of the enormous consequences of everything he did. Contrast this with the unspeakably vulgar pleasure in the office of President Clinton.

Truman, absolutely certain that the mantle he assumed was far greater than he could ever be, was continually and deliberately aware of the weight of history, the accomplishments of his predecessors, and, by humble and imaginative projection, his own inadequacy. The sobriety and care that derived from this allowed him a rare privilege for modern presidents, to give to the presidency more than he took from it. It is not possible to occupy the Oval Office without arrogantly looting its assets or nobly adding to them. May God bless the president who adds to them, and may God damn the president who loots them.

America would not have come out of the Civil War as it did had it not been led by Lincoln and Lee. The battles raged for five years, but for a hundred years the country, both North and South, modeled itself on their character. They exemplified almost perfectly Churchill's statement, "Public men charged with the conduct of the war should live in a continual stress of soul."

This continual stress of soul is necessary as well in peacetime, because for every good deed in public life there is a counterbalance. Benefits are given only after taxes are taken. That is part of governance. The statesman, who represents the whole nation, sees in the equilibrium for which he strives a continual tension between victory and defeat. If he did not understand this, he would have no stress of soul, he would be merely happy—about money showered upon the orphan, taken from the widow. About children sent to day care, so that they may be long absent from their parents. About merciful parole of criminals, who kill again. Whereas a statesman knows continual stress of soul, a politician is happy, for he knows not what he does.

It is difficult for individuals or nations to recognize that war and peace alternate. But they do. No matter how long peace may last, it will end in war. Though most people cannot believe at this moment that the United States of America will ever again fight for its survival, history guarantees that it will. And, when it does, most people will not know what to do. They will believe of war, as they did of peace, that it is everlasting.

The statesman, who is different from everyone else, will, in the midst of common despair, see the end of war, just as during the peace he was alive to the inevitability of war, and saw it coming in the far distance, as if it were a gray wave moving quietly across a dark sea.

The politician will revel with his people and enjoy their enjoyments. The statesman, in continual stress of soul, will think of destruction. As others move in the light, he will move in darkness, so that as others move in darkness he may move in the light. This tenacity, that is given to those of long and insistent vision, is what saves nations.

A statesman must have a temperament that is suited for the Medal of Honor, in a soul that is unafraid to die. Electorates rightly favor those who have endured combat, not as a matter of reward for service, as is commonly believed, but because the willingness of a soldier to give his life is a strong sign of his correct priorities, and that in future he will truly understand that statesmen are not rulers but servants. It seems clear even in these years of squalid degradation that having risked death for the sake of honor is better than having risked dishonor for the sake of life.

No matter what you are told by the sophisticated classes that see virtue in every form of corruption and corruption in every form of virtue, I think you know, as I do, that the American people hunger for acts of integrity and courage. The American people hunger for a statesman magnetized by the truth, unwilling to give up his good name, uninterested in calculation only for the sake of victory, unable to put his interests before those of the nation. What this means in practical terms is no focus groups, no polls, no triangulation, no evasion, no broken promises, and no lies. These are the tools of the chameleon. They are employed to cheat the American people of honest answers to direct questions. If the average politician, for fear that he may lose something, is incapable of even a genuine yes or no, how is he supposed to rise to the great occasions of state? How is he supposed to face a destructive and implacable enemy? How is he supposed to understand the rightful destiny of his country, and lead it there?

At the coronation of an English monarch, he is given a sword. Elizabeth II took it last, and as she held it before the altar, she heard these words:

> Receive this kingly Sword, brought now from the altar of God and delivered to you by us, the Bishops and servants of God, though unworthy. With this Sword do justice, stop the growth of iniquity, protect the holy Church of God, help and defend widows and orphans, restore the things that are gone to decay, maintain the things that are restored, punish and reform what is amiss, and confirm what is in good order; that doing these things you may be glorious in all virtue; and so faithfully serve our Lord.

Would that we in America come once again to understand that statesmanship is not the appetite for power but—because things matter—a holy calling of self-abnegation and self-sacrifice. We have made it something else. Nonetheless, after and despite its betrayal, statesmanship remains the manifestation, in political terms, of beauty, and balance, and truth. It is the courage to tell the truth, and thus discern what is ahead. It is a mastery of the symmetry of forces, illuminated by the genius of speaking to the heart of things.

Statesmanship is a quality that, though it may be betrayed, is always ready to be taken up again merely by honest subscription to its great themes. Have confidence that even in idleness its strengths are growing, for it is a providential gift given to us in times of need. Evidently we do not need it now, but as the world is forever interesting the time will surely come when we do. And then, so help me God, I believe that, solely by the grace of God, the corrupt will be thrown down and the virtuous will rise up.

❏   ❏   ❏

MARK HELPRIN was raised on the Hudson and in the British West Indies. After receiving degrees from Harvard College and Harvard's Graduate School of Arts and Sciences, he did postgraduate work at the University of Oxford and served in the British merchant navy, the Israeli infantry, and the Israeli air force. He was published in the *New Yorker* for almost a quarter of a century, and his stories and essays have appeared in the *Atlantic Monthly*, *New Criterion*, *Commentary*, the *New York Times*, *The Wall Street Journal*, and many other publications in the United States and abroad. Translated into more than a dozen languages, his books include *A Dove of the East and Other Stories* (1975); *Refiner's Fire* (1977); *Ellis Island and Other Stories* (1981); *Winter's Tale* (1983); *Memoir from Antproof Case* (1995); and (with illustrations by Chris Van Allsburg) *Swan Lake* (1989); *A City in Winter* (1996), and *The Veil of Snows* (1997). He is best known for *A Soldier of the Great War* (1991).

Civility and Citizenship in Washington's America and Ours

Charles R. Kesler

December 2000

Dr. Kesler delivered this speech at a Hillsdale College seminar, "The Morality of Civility," on the Hillsdale campus.

❏ ❏ ❏

As we meet here to consider the connection between civility and citizenship, that connection seems to have become weakened, at least in certain select Florida counties. As shocking as some of the shenanigans in those counties might seem, perhaps they should not come as a complete surprise. After all, the same people who now seem to love Election Day, to the point of wanting it to go on forever, have for years been markedly *unenthusiastic* about Constitution Day. Perhaps this is because they understand the Constitution to "evolve" or change from year to year—or at least from election to election, depending on who wins. This changeability is what today's liberals mean when they say we have a "living Constitution." It does not represent constitutionalism in the older sense of the word. Nor, I would argue, is it a formula for good government, because it undermines the constitutional morality that is essential to the connection between citizenship and civility in democratic or popular governments.

105

The Constitution as Teacher

Consider the moral problem faced by our Founding Fathers in the late eighteenth century. Looking back over the history of previous popular governments—which James Madison, for one, did extensively—they discovered a generic problem. This problem arises from the basic idea of democracy—the idea that the people ought to be the source of all law. The problem is this: If the people are the source of the law, why should they respect it? Why should they not simply look on the law as a tool or a convenience with which to achieve their private ends? Most republics had failed precisely because they had not solved this moral conundrum. The people, being the source of the law, had failed to distinguish their rights from their desires, and had come to believe that whatever they wanted passionately enough was their right. This is the path down which democracies descend—the path of tyranny of the majority, which Madison presents in *The Federalist Papers* as the characteristic fault of republican regimes.

The genius of the American Constitution is shown in nothing more than in its ability to tutor the American people in a way to overcome this fault and make them law-abiding. Don't we all today look up to the Constitution as an authority for us, even though, technically speaking, its only legal and moral authority comes from the fact that it was ratified over 200 years ago by a generation that is dead and gone? Of course, as each state enters the Union, it must agree to abide by the Constitution. And whenever we amend the Constitution, we in a sense endorse it. But in fact, the American people have legislated themselves a Constitution only once, in 1787 and 1788, and since then we have looked on it as authoritative. Thus for Americans, the *oldest* law is the *highest* law. This is not a normal or an automatic outcome of popular government. Most of the time, republics and the people who move their politics tend to think that if they make a law "A" one day, and a law "B" that contradicts "A" the next day, the newer law supersedes the old. What is unusual about the Constitution is that this rule is completely reversed in respect of it. The oldest law is the most authoritative, and is indeed the only law that "the people" as such have ever passed. Other law is statute law, law made by representatives of the people. Thus every other law needs to be adjudged in light of the only law that is genuinely ours, the Constitution.

Creating this new category of law, the Constitution, which is created by "we the people" and yet ascends above us, was a great breakthrough in political science and a great achievement of the American Founders.

The Importance of Washington

The theory of the Constitution is contained in *The Federalist Papers*, but the moral authority which backs up this theory is George Washington—our first president, and the only president elected unanimously by the Electoral College. There is a real sense in which the prestige of the Constitution depends on the fact that Washington stands behind it. Certainly he had an enormous amount to do with its original success. We can see how and why this is by considering the connection of civility and citizenship. The problem of this connection can be stated succinctly. Many countries have citizenship without the restraints of civility; nor is it unusual for nonfellow citizens to be civil. But how is it possible to combine civility and citizenship in healthy and mutually reinforcing ways?

To be "civil," in ordinary usage, means to be polite, respectful, decent. It is a quality implying, in particular, the restraint of anger directed toward others. In this sense, civility is not the same thing as warmth and indeed implies a certain coolness: Civility helps to cool the too-hot passions of citizenship. When citizens are civil to one another despite their political disagreements, they reveal that these disagreements are less important than their resolution to remain fellow citizens. They agree on the fundamental political questions, even if they differ on secondary issues. Without this fundamental agreement, citizenship would be self-contradictory and finally self-destructive. The French Revolution remains the unforgettable modern example of citizenship's self-destruction in the absence of civility. Citizen Brissot, Citizen Danton, Citizen Robespierre—one by one they fell victim to ever more radical and exclusive definitions of the good citizen. Tyranny itself is this process of exclusion carried to its logical extreme.

Still, it would be a great mistake to believe that the opposite of tyranny is simply a concord of opinion. Political friendship can be based on better or worse opinions. The criteria for evaluating them must therefore be extrinsic to the opinions themselves. In other words, even as citizenship requires civility, so civility points beyond itself to permanent and objective moral standards—to the nature of "civil government" and, higher still, to the moral and theoretical concerns of what is rightly called civilization. Here the example of Washington is invaluable.

Civility in the first place is a matter of shaping young people's character. The tools of this art include precepts, examples, exhortation, and shame. It is not surprising, then, to find that one of the earliest writings of the young Washington, laboriously entered into his copybook, is a set of 110 "Rules of Civility and Decent Behavior in Company and Conversation." For the most part these are useful lessons for reducing any adolescent to a civilized state: for example, "Shake not the head, feet, or legs; roll not the eyes; lift not one eyebrow higher than the other, wry not the mouth, and bedew no man's face with your spittle by [approaching too near] him [when] you speak." These rules are a playful (though serious) reminder that civility consists first of all in good manners. "Every action done in company," reads the first rule, "ought to be with some sign of respect to those that are present."

Civility in this sense stands athwart the contemporary ethic of self-expression. Nevertheless, good manners aim not to crush but to form individual character. Washington's list begins with what might be dismissed today as mere social conformity; but it ends, "Labor to keep alive in your breast that little spark of celestial fire called conscience." Conformity to social custom is a part of good manners, but it is justified because it frees us to cultivate the distinctions that matter. Civility allows for, and at its best is, the fanning of that "spark of celestial fire" in man to produce a steady blaze of moral seriousness.

Washington's civility is thus a species of honor or of concern with honor. Explaining to his wife why he had had to accept the command of the Continental army, he wrote:

> It was utterly out of my power to refuse this appointment, without exposing my character to such censures, as would have reflected dishonor upon myself, and given pain to my friends. This, I am sure, could not, and ought not, to be pleasing to you, and must have lessened me considerably in my own esteem.

Washington's consciousness of his own honor, reflected in and re-flecting the honorableness of his friends, provided the touchstone of his conduct. At the highest level, his civility was thus a form of magnanimity. As Aristotle explains, the magnanimous man accepts external honors as the highest tribute that can be paid him, but regards all such popular offer-ings as vastly inferior to his own sense of dignity and propriety.

One of the most instructive displays of Washington's magnanimity was his response to Colonel Lewis Nicola's letter, on May 22, 1782, pro-posing that Washington be made king. At this time the Continental Army was still assembled, and its soldiers were deeply aggrieved due to the fact that they had not been paid what they had been promised by Congress for their service. Washington might well have led this justly disgruntled army to Philadelphia to assume the role of king or dictator. Instead he replied to Nicola's proposal as follows:

> With a mixture of great surprise and astonishment I have read with attention the Sentiments you have submitted to my perusal. ... I am much at a loss to conceive what part of my conduct could have given encouragement to an address which to me seems big with the greatest mischiefs that can befall my Coun-try. If I am not deceived in the knowledge of myself, you could not have found a person to whom your schemes are more disagreeable. ... Let me conjure you then, if you have any regard for your Country, concern for yourself or posterity, or respect for me, to banish these thoughts from your Mind, and never com-municate, as from yourself, or any one else, a sentiment of the like nature.

What is remarkable here is the letter's tone: not outraged or accusa-tory, it was calculated to shame. And indeed, Nicola was so ashamed that he wrote three apologies in as many days.

In this short letter, Washington refused the honor of being king on the remarkable grounds that it was beneath him! Honor without principle would be infamy; true honor lay in performing just and noble deeds for their own sake, not for the sake of extrinsic rewards. And in the most fundamental sense, the letter's tone was "civil"; it was not the voice of a commander upbraiding his inferior officer, but of one civilian to another. The foundation of civilian control of the military was the civility of the commanding general—his reasonable control of his militant passions.

Thus did Washington's civility lay the basis and set the standard for republican citizenship in America. His virtues may be considered the final cause of the new regime, even as they played an indispensable role in its efficient causation—the victories won by the Continental Army. Be that as it may, the formal cause of the new order was something different. This was the great principle, proclaimed in the Declaration of Independence, "that all men are created equal." It is a matter of some academic and political dispute today how this was understood at the time. Certainly, however, there should not be any dispute over how Washington understood it.

In his General Orders to the Army on March 1, 1778, Washington wrote that the fortitude of

> the virtuous officers and soldiery of this Army . . . not only under the common hardships incident to a military life, but also under the additional sufferings to which the peculiar situation of these States have exposed them, clearly proves them worthy of the enviable privilege of contending for the rights of human nature, the Freedom and Independence of their Country.

In addition to Washington's own honor, then, there is an honor due to human nature, which honor may be called the rights of man. It is an "enviable privilege" to contend for them because they are something special: They are based on what is special to man—his rank in Creation. Man's possession of reason distinguishes him from the beasts, but his imperfect possession of reason—above all the fact that his passions may cloud his reason—distinguishes him from the divine being, the kind of being whose rationality is perfect and unaffected by desire. As the in-between being, man's dignity derives from his place in this ordered universe.

Civility and Citizenship in the Founding

Washington expressed the whole purpose of the Revolution—in words that would be echoed, I might note, in the Hillsdale College Articles of

Incorporation—as follows: "The establishment of Civil and Religious Liberty was the Motive which induced me to the Field. . . ." In the Christian West prior to the American founding, citizenship and civility were both endangered. Christianity, when established by temporal authorities, had the distressing if somewhat paradoxical tendency both to sap obedience to civil laws and to invite civil coercion in matters of faith. By virtue of the first tendency, citizenship became peculiarly problematic. By virtue of the second, civility became swamped by fanaticism and hypocrisy. Restoring the foundations of civility and citizenship under these conditions was the great accomplishment of the American Founding. It did this in the name of civil and religious liberty, not explicitly of virtue, for the deepest cause of the civil war within the Christian West had really been the dispute over the meaning of virtue—not only between competing religions, but between the rational and revealed accounts of virtue, skeptical reason, and faithful obedience. But this was a debate that had to be carried on at the highest intellectual and spiritual levels. It could not be conducted politically, and any attempt to do so was bound to be tyrannical. This had been the cause of the holocausts of the Old World. In America, people would have the liberty to carry on this transpolitical debate while cultivating the civic and religious friendship that was its precondition and product.

Two principles were required: a ground of citizenship and a ground for separating citizenship from church membership. Both were found in the doctrine of the rights of man. In the first place, the basis of political obligation was found in the consent of each individual, premised on the grounds of their natural freedom and equality. At the same time, religious liberty is secured by virtue of the limited nature of the social contract. "Civil government" and "civil liberties" are made possible by excluding questions of revealed truth from determination by political majorities. Majority rule and minority rights can be made consistent only on this basis. Limited government is thus essential to the rule of law. But the justice of limited or moderate government for all times and places depends upon the limits of human knowledge, whether viewed in terms of Socratic ignorance or man's inferiority to God. In light of these limits, the separation of church and state means that revelation is not forced to overrule the protests of human reason, nor reason compelled to pass judgment on the claims of revelation. The limits of human wisdom from every point of view thus affirm the justice of limited government and of citizenship governed by civility. Both are embodied in the Constitution of 1787.

Civility and Citizenship Today

The principle that binds our political parties together—as it binds American citizens together—is allegiance to the Constitution and constitutional morality. And as I recently observed in *The Claremont Review of Books*, the disturbing thing about the election of 2000 was how thin that allegiance sometimes seemed. In the days after November 7, it was widely and repeatedly suggested that because the Vice President appeared to have won a plurality of the nationwide popular vote, he somehow must have won Florida's popular vote, whether or not the election tally confirmed it. Furthermore, it was suggested that his national plurality meant that he somehow deserved Florida's electoral votes and thus the presidency. Those proposing these arguments seemed to be saying that it was not how Americans actually voted but how they meant to—or should have—voted that counts. This is a theory that hitherto has been at home only in banana republics and the phony "people's republics" of the Communist world. In any event, they never backed away from the notion that the moral high ground was held by the popular vote, not by the Electoral College. So it was not surprising to hear that Senator-elect Hillary Rodham Clinton promises as her first official act to support an amendment to abolish the Electoral College.

The Electoral College is a crucial part of the Framers' machinery for combining democracy with constitutionalism and the rule of law. It ensures that the president will be chosen not by a plebiscitary majority but by a constitutional one, distributed by states and moderated by the need to accommodate a variety of interests and viewpoints. Without the Electoral College, our political party system would fragment, smaller and more extremist parties would proliferate, and election fraud would multiply enormously. To abolish the Electoral College would be to strike at the heart of the Constitution.

The constitutional majority is, in fact, the only majority that has ever governed the United States as a free country. We don't determine which party controls the Senate or the House of Representatives by pointing to the raw national vote totals rung up by each party. We count the votes by state or by congressional district, and control of the House or Senate goes to whichever party has won more of the individual races. The same principle applies to the presidency. Whoever wins the majority of the electoral votes cast by the states is thereby elected president. This is not really a question of democracy. The principles of one man, one vote, majority-rule democracy apply scrupulously in every state. Rather the issue is democracy with federalism (the Electoral College) versus democracy without federalism (a national popular vote).

In any case, one prays that current events in Florida do not herald other such attempts to break the customary, unwritten rules of our constitutional democracy. These habitual rules are fostered by the Constitution, and nourish it in turn. We undermine and weaken them at the peril of our country.

To conclude: The Founding Fathers were hopeful but not sanguine about the prospects of the American experiment in free government. In his famous Circular Letter of June 14, 1783, Washington wrote:

> The foundation of our empire was not laid in the gloomy age of Ignorance and Superstition, but at an Epocha when the rights of mankind were better understood and more clearly defined, than at any former period; the researches of the human mind, after social happiness, have been carried to a great extent; the Treasures of knowledge, acquired through a long succession of years, by the labours of Philosophers, Sages and Legislatures, are laid open for our use, and their collected wisdom may be happily applied in the Establishment of our forms of Government; the free cultivation of Letters, the unbounded extension of Commerce, the progressive refinement of manners, the growing liberality of sentiment, and above all, the pure and benign light of Revelation, have had a meliorating influence on mankind and increased the blessings of Society. At this auspicious period, the United States came into being as a Nation, and if their Citizens should not be completely free and happy, the fault will be entirely their own.

The auspices could not have been more favorable, but the political lesson was that the freedom and happiness of the American people, and the destiny of the civilization they represent, depend on their conduct. As shown in their list of grievances against the British king in the Declaration of Independence, the Founders were well aware that "cruelty and perfidy scarcely paralleled in the most barbarous ages" could be committed by "the Head of a civilized nation"—were aware more generally that ages of science and commerce could be just as barbarous, in some respects more barbarous, than ages of "Ignorance and Superstition."

It was precisely such a threat from within that faced the United States less than seventy-five years later in the Civil War, when civility and citizenship were rent in two by the controversy over slavery. It was in the midst of this crisis that Abraham Lincoln, leaving Springfield for the nation's capital, declared somberly that he went "with a task before me greater than that which rested upon Washington." In contemplating the future of American citizenship and civility, we ought to remember how he bore that task— and what he may have learned to help him bear it, as an avid student of the life of Washington, and of the constitutional morality it embodied and upheld.

❏   ❏   ❏

CHARLES R. KESLER is a professor of government and the director of the Henry Salvatori Center at Claremont McKenna College. He received his A.B. in social studies and his A.M. and Ph.D. in government at Harvard University. He is editor of and contributor to *Saving the Revolution: The Federalist Papers and the American Founding* (1987) and co-editor, with William F. Buckley, Jr., of *Keeping the Tablets: Modern American Conservative Thought* (1988). He has published widely in newspapers and periodicals such as *The Wall Street Journal*, the *Los Angeles Times*, the *Washington Times*, *National Review*, and the *Weekly Standard*, and is editor-in-chief of *The Claremont Review of Books*.

ECONOMICS

❑ ❑ ❑

Whatever Happened to Free Enterprise?

Ronald Reagan

January 1978

Then Governor Reagan delivered this speech on the Hillsdale College campus as part of the Ludwig von Mises Lecture Series.

❑ ❑ ❑

During the presidential campaign last year [1976], there was a great deal of talk about the seeming inability of our economic system to solve the problems of unemployment and inflation. Issues such as taxes and government power and costs were discussed, but always these things were discussed in the context of what *government* intended to do about it. May I suggest for your consideration that government has already done too much about it? That indeed, government, by going outside its proper province, has caused many if not most of the problems that vex us.

How much are we to blame for what has happened? Beginning with the traumatic experience of the Great Depression, we the people have turned more and more to government for answers that government has neither the right nor the capacity to provide. Unfortunately, government as an institution always tends to increase in size and power, and so government attempted to provide the answers.

The result is a fourth branch of government added to the traditional three of executive, legislative, and judicial: a vast federal bureaucracy that is

117

now being imitated in too many states and too many cities, a bureaucracy of enormous power which determines policy to a greater extent than any of us realize, very possibly to a greater extent than our own elected representatives. And it can't be removed from office by our votes.

To give you an illustration of how bureaucracy works in another country, England in 1803 created a new civil service position. It called for a man to stand on the cliffs of Dover with a spy glass and ring a bell if he saw Napoleon coming. They didn't eliminate that job until 1945. In our own country, there are only two government programs that have been abolished. The government stopped making rum on the Virgin Islands, and we have stopped breeding horses for the cavalry.

We bear a greater tax burden to support that permanent bureaucratic structure than any of us would have believed possible just a few decades ago. When I was in college, governments—federal, state, and local—were taking a dime out of every dollar earned and less than a third of that paid for the federal establishment. Today, governments—federal, state, and local—are taking 44 cents out of every dollar earned, and two-thirds of that supports Washington. It is the fastest growing item in the average family budget, and yet it is not one of the factors used in computing the cost of living index. It is the biggest single cost item in the family budget, bigger than food, shelter, and clothing all put together.

When government tells us that in the last year the people in America have increased their earning 9 percent, and since the inflation is 6 percent, we are still percentage points better off, or richer than we were the year before, government is being deceitful. That was *before* taxes. After taxes, the people of America are 3 percentage points worse off, poorer than they were before they got the 9 percent raise. Government profits by inflation.

At the economic conference in London several months ago, one of our American representatives there was talking to the press. He said you have to recognize that inflation doesn't have any single cause and therefore has no single answer. Well, if he believed that, he had no business being at an economic conference. Inflation is caused by one thing, and it has one answer. It is caused by government spending more than government takes in, and it will go away when government stops doing that, and not before.

Government has been trying to make all of us believe that somehow inflation is like a plague, or the drought, or the locusts coming, trying to make us believe that no one has any control over it and we just have to bear it when it comes along and hope it will go away. No, it is simpler than that. From 1933 until the present, our country has doubled the amount of goods and services that are available for purchase. In that same period we have multiplied the money supply by 23 times. So $11.50 is chasing what one dollar used to chase. And that's all that inflation is: a depreciation of the value of money.

Ludwig von Mises once said, "Government is the only agency that can take a perfectly useful commodity like paper, smear it with some ink, and render it absolutely useless."

There are 73 million of us working and earning by means of private enterprise to support ourselves and our dependents. We support, in addition, 81 million other Americans totally dependent on tax dollars for their year-round living. Now it's true that 15 million of those are public employees and they also pay taxes, but their taxes are simply a return to government of dollars that first had to be taken from the 73 million. I say this to emphasize that the people working and earning in private business and industry are the only resource that the government has.

In Defense of Free Enterprise

More than anything else, a new political economic mythology, widely believed by too many people, has increased government's ability to interfere as it does in the marketplace. Profit is a dirty word, blamed for most of our social ills. In the interest of something called consumerism, free enterprise is becoming far less free. Property rights are being reduced, and even eliminated, in the name of environmental protection. It is time that a voice be raised on behalf of the 73 million independent wage earners in this country, pointing out that profit, property rights, and freedom are inseparable, and you cannot have the third unless you continue to be entitled to the first two.

Even many of us who believe in free enterprise have fallen into the habit of saying when something goes wrong: "There ought to be a law."

Sometimes I think there ought to be a law against saying: "There ought to be a law." The German statesman Bismarck said, "If you like sausages and laws you should never watch either of them being made." It is difficult to understand the ever-increasing number of intellectuals in the groves of academe, present company excepted, who contend that our system could be improved by the adoption of some of the features of socialism.

In any comparison between the free market system and socialism, nowhere is the miracle of capitalism more evident than in the production and distribution of food. We eat better, for a lower percentage of earnings, than any other people on earth. We spend about 17 percent of the average family's after-tax income for food. The American farmer is producing two and one-half times as much as he did sixty years ago with one-third of the man-hours on one-half the land. If his counterparts worldwide could reach his level of skill, we could feed the entire world population on one-tenth of the land that is now being farmed .

The biggest example comes, I think, when you compare the two superpowers. I am sure that most of you are aware that some years ago the Soviet Union had such a morale problem with the workers on the collective farms that they finally gave each worker a little plot of ground and told him he could farm it for himself and sell in the open market what he raised. Today, less than 4 percent of Russia's agricultural land is privately farmed in that way, and on that 4 percent is raised 40 percent of all of Russia's vegetables, and 60 percent of all its meat.

Some of our scholars did some research on comparative food prices. They had to take the prices in the Russian stores and our own stores and translate them into minutes and hours of labor at the average income of each country. With one exception they found that the Russians have to work two to ten times as long to buy the various food items than do their counterparts here in America. The one exception was potatoes. There the price on their potato bins equaled less work time for them than it did for us. There was one hitch though—they didn't have any potatoes.

In spite of all the evidence that points to the free market as the most efficient system, we continue down a road that is bearing out the prophecy of Tocqueville, a Frenchman who came here 130 years ago. He was attracted by the miracle that was America. Think of it: Our country was only 70 years old and already we had achieved such a miraculous living standard, such productivity and prosperity, that the rest of the world was amazed. So he came here and he looked at everything he could see in our country trying to find the secret of our success, and then went back and wrote a book about it. Even then, 130 years ago, he saw signs prompting him to warn us that if we weren't constantly on the guard, we would find ourselves covered by a network of regulations controlling every activity. He said if that came to pass we would one day find ourselves a nation of timid animals with government the shepherd.

Was Tocqueville right? Well, today we are covered by tens of thousands of regulations to which we add about 25,000 new ones each year.

The Cost of Government Regulation

A study of 700 of the largest corporations has found that if we could eliminate unnecessary regulation of business and industry, we would instantly reduce the inflation rate by half. Other economists have found that overregulation of business and industry amounts to a hidden five-cent sales tax for every consumer. The misdirection of capital investment costs us a quarter of a million jobs. That is half as many as the president wants to create by spending $32 billion over the next two years. And with all of this comes the burden of government-required paperwork.

If affects education—all of you here are aware of the problems of financing education, particularly at the private educational institutions. I had the president of a university tell me the other day that government-required paperwork on his campus alone has raised the administrative costs from $65,000 to $600,000. That would underwrite a pretty good faculty chair. Now the president of the Eli Lilly drug company says his firm spends more man-hours on government-required paperwork than they do on heart and cancer research combined. He told of submitting one ton of paper, 120,000 pages of scientific data—most of which he said were absolutely worthless for FDA's purposes—in triplicate in order to get a license to market an arthritis medicine. So, the United States is no longer first in the development of new health-giving drugs and medicines. We're producing 60 percent fewer than we were fifteen years ago.

And it is not just the drug industry which is over-regulated. How about the independent men and women of this country who spend $50 billion a year sending 10 billion pieces of paper to Washington where it costs $20 billion each year in tax money to shuffle and store that paper away? We are so used to talking billions—does anyone realize how much a single billion is? A billion minutes ago Christ was walking on this earth. A billion hours ago our ancestors lived in caves, and it is questionable as to whether they had discovered the use of fire. A billion dollars ago was 19 hours in Washington, D.C. And it will be another billion in the next 19 hours, and every 19 hours until they adopt a new budget at which time it will be almost a billion and a half.

It all comes down to this basic premise: If you lose your economic freedom, you lose your political freedom and, in fact, all freedom. Freedom is something that cannot be passed on genetically. It is never more than one generation away from extinction. Every generation has to learn how to protect and defend it. Once freedom is gone, it is gone for a long, long time. Already, too many of us, particularly those in business and industry, have chosen to switch rather than fight.

We should take inventory and see how many things we can do ourselves that we have come to believe only a government can do. Let me take one that I am sure everyone thinks is a government monopoly and properly so. Do you know that in Scottsdale, Arizona, there is no city fire department? There, the per capita cost for fire protection and the per capita fire loss are both one-third of what they are in cities of similar size. And the insurance rates reflect this. Scottsdale employs a private, profit-making, fire fighting company, which now has about a dozen clients out in the Western states.

Sometimes I worry if the great corporations have abdicated their responsibility to preserve the freedom of the market place out of fear of retaliation or a reluctance to rock the boat. If they have, they are feeding the crocodile hoping he'll eat them last. You can fight city hall, and you don't have to be a giant to do it. In New Mexico there is a little company owned by a husband and wife. The other day two OSHA inspectors arrived at the door. They demanded to come in order to go on a hunting expedition to see if there were any violations of their safety rules. The wife, who happens to be company president, said "Where's your warrant?" They said, "We don't need one." She said, "You do to come in here, " and shut the door. Well, they went out and got a warrant, and they came back, but this time she had her lawyer with her. He looked at the warrant and said it does not show probable cause. A federal court has since upheld her right to refuse OSHA entrance.

Why don't more of us challenge what Cicero called the arrogance of officialdom? Why don't we set up the communications between organizations and trade associations to rally others to come to the aid of an individual like that, or to an industry or profession when they are threatened by the barons of bureaucracy, who have forgotten that we are their employers? Government by the people works when the people work at it. We can begin by turning the spotlight of truth on the widespread political and economic mythology that I mentioned.

A recent poll of college and university students (they must have skipped this campus) found that the students estimated that business profits in America average 45 percent. That is nine times the average of business profts in this country. It was understandable that the kids made that mistake, because the professors in the same poll guessed that the profits were even higher.

Then there is the fairy tale born of political demagoguery that the tax structure imposes unfairly on the low earner with loopholes designed for the more affluent. The truth is that at $23,000 of earnings you become one of that exclusive band of 10 percent of the wage-earners in America paying 50 percent of the income tax but only taking 5 percent of all the deductions. The other 95 percent of the deductions are taken by the 90 percent of the wage-earners below $23,000 who pay the other half of the tax.

The most dangerous myth is that business can be made to pay a larger share of taxes, thus relieving the individual. Politicians preaching this are either deliberately dishonest, or economically illiterate, and either one should scare us. Business doesn't pay taxes, and who better than business could make this message known? Only people pay taxes, and people pay as consumers every tax that is assessed against a business. Passing along their tax costs is the only way businesses can make a profit and stay in operation.

The federal government has used its taxing power to redistribute earnings to achieve a variety of social reforms. Politicians love those indirect business taxes, because it hides the cost of government. During the New Deal days, an undersecretary of the treasury wrote a book in which he said that taxes can serve a higher purpose than just raising revenue. He said they could be an instrument of social and economic control to redistribute the wealth and income and to penalize industries and economic groups.

We need to put an end to that kind of thinking. We need a simplification of the tax structure. We need an indexing of the surtax brackets, a halt to government's illicit profiteering through inflation. It is as simple as this: Every time the cost-of-living index goes up one percent, the government's revenue goes up one and one-half percent. Above all we need an overall cut in the cost of government. Government spending isn't a stimulant to the economy; it is a drag on the economy. Only a decade ago, about 15 percent of corporate gross income was required to pay the interest on corporate debt; now it is 40 percent. Individuals and families once spent about 8 percent of their disposable income on interest on consumer debt, installment buying, mortgages, and so forth. Today, it is almost one-fourth of their total earnings. State and government in the last fifteen years has gone from $70 billion to $220 billion. The total private and public debt is growing four times as fast as the output of goods and services.

Again, there is something we can do. Congressman Jack Kemp (R-NY) has a bill before Congress designed to increase productivity and to create jobs for people. Over a three-year period, it calls for reducing the income tax for all of us by a full one-third. And also it would reduce the corporate tax from 48 to 45 percent. The base income tax would no longer be 20 percent but 14 percent, and the ceiling would be 50 percent instead of 70 percent. Finally, it would double the exemption for smaller businesses before they get into the surtax bracket. It would do all of the things that we need to provide investment capital, increase productivity, and create jobs.

We can say this with assurance, because it has been done twice before: in the 1920s under Harding and Coolidge and again in the 1960s under John F. Kennedy. In the 1960s, the stimulant to the economy was so immediate that even government's revenues increased because of the broadening base of the economy. Kemp's bill is gaining support but unfortunately the majority in Congress is concerned with further restrictions on our freedom.

To win this battle against Big Government, we must communicate with each other. We must support the doctor in his fight against socialized medicine, the oil industry in its fight against crippling controls and repressive taxes, and the farmer, who hurts more than most because of government harassment and rule-changing in the middle of the game. All of these issues concern each one of us, regardless of what our trade or profession may be. Corporate America must begin to realize that it has allies in the independent businessmen and -women, the shopkeepers, the craftsmen, the farmers, and the professions. All these men and women are organized in a great variety of ways, but right now we only talk in our own organizations about our own problems. What we need is a liaison between these organizations to realize how much strength we as a people still have if we will use that strength.

In regard to the oil industry, is there anyone who isn't concerned with the energy problem? Government caused that problem while we all stood by unaware that we were involved. Unnecessary regulations and prices and imposed price limits back in the 1950s are the direct cause of today's crisis. Our crisis isn't because of a shortage of fuel; it is a surplus of government. Now we have a new agency of enormous power, with 20,000 employees and a $10.5 billion budget. That is more than the gross earnings of the top seven oil companies in the United States. The creation of the Department of Energy is nothing more than a first step toward nationalization of the oil industry.

While I believe no one should waste a natural resource, the conservationists act as if we have found all the oil and gas there is to be found in this continent, if not the world. Do you know that 57 years ago our government told us we only had enough for 15 years? Nineteen years went by and they told us we only had enough left for 13 more years, and we've done a lot of driving since then and we'll do a lot more if government will do one simple thing: get out of the way and let the incentives of the marketplace urge the industry out to find the sources of energy this country needs.

We have had enough of sideline kibitzers telling us the system they themselves have disrupted with their social tinkering can be improved or saved if we will only have more of that tinkering or even government planning and management. They play fast and loose with a system that for 200 years made us the light of the world. The refuge for people all over the world who just yearn to breathe free. It is time we recognized that the system, no matter what our problems are, has never failed us once. Every time *we* have failed the system, usually by lacking faith in it, usually by saying that we have to change and do something else. A Supreme Court Justice has said the time has come, is indeed long overdue, for the wisdom, ingenuity, and resources of American business to be marshaled against those who would destroy it.

What specifically should be done? The first essential for the businessman is to confront the problem as a primary responsibility of corporate management. It has been said that history is the patter of silken slippers descending the stairs and the thunder of hobnail boots coming up. Back through the years we have seen people fleeing the thunder of those boots to seek refuge in this land. Now too many of them have seen the signs, signs that were ignored in their homeland before the end came, appearing here. They wonder if they will have to flee again, but they know there is no place to run to. Will we, before it is too late, use the vitality and the magic of the marketplace to save this way of life, or will we one day face our children, and our children's children, when they ask us where we were and what we were doing on the day that freedom was lost?

❏ ❏ ❏

RONALD WILSON REAGAN was born in Tampico, Illinois, on February 6, 1911. He graduated from Eureka College, worked as a radio sports announcer, and made more than fifty movies as a Hollywood film actor. From 1942 to 1945 he served in the U.S. Army, making training films. He was discharged with the rank of captain, and in 1947 was elected president of the Screen Actors Guild. A New Deal Democrat as a young man, Mr. Reagan joined the Republican party in 1962. A staunch anti-communist, he launched his political career in 1964 with a live national television address on behalf of presidential candidate Barry Goldwater. In 1966, he was elected Governor of California and served eight years. He nearly won the Republic presidential nomination in 1976, falling only sixty delegates short of defeating the incumbent president, Gerald R. Ford, Jr. In 1980, Mr. Reagan was elected the 40th President of the United States, and in 1984 he was re-elected to a second term, winning every state except Minnesota.

The Moral Sources
of Capitalism

George Gilder

December 1980

Mr. Gilder delivered this speech at Hillsdale College as part
of the Ludwig von Mises Lecture Series.

❑ ❑ ❑

"Businessmen are bastards": This crude view of men of commerce, once
famously pronounced by President John F. Kennedy, sums up the sentiments of socialist thinkers in America and around the world, from Jane
Fonda to the remaining followers of the late Chairman Mao. In fact, the
idea that businessmen are bastards is such a cliché among the progressive and enlightened men of the left that most of them would be hurt and
startled if a businessman responded by calling them the bigots that they
objectively are.

Early in 1980, however, these same words were vehemently uttered
by a conservative professor of economics at a major American college. Yet
conservatives are considered to be the friends of business. In fact, this
economist in particular was wearing a handsome Adam Smith necktie and
imagined himself to be staunchly defending private enterprise at the very
time he made his rude remark about businessmen.

What is most extraordinary about this economist's view is not its
extremity, vehemence, or apparent incongruity, but the fact that it was a
perfectly ordinary statement for such a man to make. It sums up what has

been the prevailing attitude of the leading defenders of free enterprise ever since the time of Adam Smith. Although Smith himself did not use such bawdy language, he insisted that businessmen were in general an unattractive lot who "seldom gather together except to conspire against the public interest." According to Smith the motive force of a capitalist economy is self-concern, which is a more polite way of depicting what a leftist would call avarice or greed. "Not from benevolence," said Smith, "do we expect our bread from the baker" but from self-interest. "As by an invisible hand," Smith immortally maintained, these individual acts of avarice flow together to promote the general welfare, even though few of the businessmen are concerned with any aim beyond their own enrichment.

These arguments of Adam Smith, espoused in *The Wealth of Nations*, the masterwork of capitalist economics, recur in various forms throughout the literature of free enterprise and lend to many of these writings a strangely anti-business cast. The general idea is that businessmen are useful sorts but you wouldn't want your daughter to marry one. Just as English aristocrats still sometimes express disdain for people "in trade," so American intellectuals, even on the right, often depict capitalists as crude, boorish, and predatory figures.

Although one might suppose that such men should be kept on a short rein by the government, the conservatives argue on the contrary that governments should keep out of the fray and allow the disciplines of the free market to keep the predators in line. In essence, these economists answer President Kennedy by saying, "Yes, businessmen are bastards, but the best thing to do is let them loose, to fight it out among themselves, and may the best bastard win."

Needless to say, conservative economists offer many other, more sophisticated arguments against the growth of the state. Most of what they say about the virtues of free markets is luminously true. Nonetheless, their essential view of the nature and motivation of capitalists, inherited from Adam Smith, is insidiously false and fails to explain in any convincing way the sources of economic growth and progress. It just won't do any longer to suggest that businessmen are bad guys, or ambitious dolts, or self-serving money grubbers, and then conclude that if they are given maximum freedom, they will build the new Jerusalem: a good and bountiful society. Capitalism needs no such labored and paradoxical defense. The fact is that capitalism is good and successful not because it miraculously transmutes personal avarice and ambition into collective prosperity but because it calls forth, propagates, and relies upon the best and most generous of human qualities.

Capitalism begins with giving. This is a growing theme of "economic anthropology," from Melville Herskovits's pioneering book by that name to Marvin Harris's *Cannibals and Kings*. The capitalists of primitive society were tribal leaders who vied with one another in giving great feasts. Similarly, trade began with offerings from one family to another or from one tribe to its neighbor. The gifts, often made in the course of a religious rite, were presented in hopes of an eventual gift in return. The compensation was not defined beforehand. But in the feasting process it was expected to be a return with interest, as another "big man" or *mumi* as he was called among the Siuai in the Solomon Islands, would attempt to excel the offerings of the first.

Harris describes the process:

> A young man proves himself capable of becoming a *mumi* by working harder than everyone else and by carefully restricting his own consumption of meat and coconuts. Eventually, he impresses his wife, children, and near relations with the seriousness of his intentions, and they vow to help him prepare for his first feast. If the feast is a success, his circle of supporters widens and he sets to work readying an even greater display of generosity. He aims next at the construction of a men's clubhouse, and if this is also a success his circle of supporters—people willing to work for the feast to come—grows still larger and he will begin to be spoken of as a *mumi*. . . . Even though larger and larger feasts mean that the *mumi*'s demands on his supporters become more irksome, the overall volume of production goes up. . . .

Helen Codere describes potlatching, a similar sequence of work and saving, capital accumulation and feasting, performed among the Kwakiutl of the northwestern United States: "The public distribution of property by an individual is a recurrent climax to an endless series of cycles of accumulating property—distributing it in a potlatch—being given property—again accumulating and preparing." The piles of food and other gifts and ceremonial exchanges could mount to dumbfounding quantities. One South Sea offering mentioned by Herskovits consisted of 10,000 coconuts and ten baskets of fish.

These competitions in giving are contests of altruism. A gift will only elicit a greater response if it is based on an understanding of the needs of others. In the most successful and catalytic gifts, the giver fulfills an unknown need or desire in a surprising way. The recipient is startled and gratified by the inspired and unexpected sympathy of the giver and is eager to repay him. In order to repay him, however, the receiver must come to understand the giver. Thus the contest of gifts leads to an expansion of human sympathies. The circle of giving (the profits of the economy) will grow as long as the gifts are consistently valued more by the receivers than by the givers.

What the tribal givers were doing, by transcending barter, was to invent a kind of money: a mode of exchange that by excluding exact contractual planning allowed for freedom and uncertainty. Money consists of liabilities, debts, or promises. By giving someone a dollar, you both acknowledge a debt to him of a certain value, and you pass on to him an acknowledgment of debt given to you by someone else. But the process has to start somewhere, with a giver and a gift, a feast and a *mumi*, an investment and an investor.

By giving a feast, a *mumi* imposed implicit debts on all his guests. By attending it, they accepted a liability to him. Through the gifts or investments of primitive capitalism, man created and extended obligations. These obligations led to reciprocal gifts and further obligations in a growing fabric of economic creation and exchange, with each giver hoping for greater returns but not assured of them, and with each recipient pushed to produce a further favor. This spreading out of debts could be termed expanding the money supply. The crucial point is that for every liability (or feeling of obligation on the part of the guest), there was a previous asset (meal) given to him. The *mumi*, as a capitalist, could not issue demands or impose liabilities or expand money without providing commensurate supplies. The demand was inherent in the supply—in the meal.

The next step above potlatching was the use of real money. The invention of money enabled a pattern of giving to be extended as far as the reach of faith and trust—from the *mumi's* tribe to the world economy. Among the most important transitional devices was the Chinese *Hui*. This became the key mode of capital formation for the overseas Chinese in their phenomenal successes as tradesmen and retailers everywhere they went, from San Francisco to Singapore. A more sophisticated and purposeful development of the potlatching principle, the *Hui* began when the organizer needed money for an investment. He would raise it from a group of kin and friends and commit himself to give a series of ten feasts for them. At each feast a similar amount of money would be convivially raised and given by lot or by secret bidding to one of the other members. The rotating distribution would continue until every member had won a collection. Similar systems, called the *Ko* or *Tanamoshi*, created savings for Japanese; and the West African *Susu* device of the *Yoruba*, when transplanted to the West Indies, provided the capital base for Caribbean retailing. This mode of capital formation also emerged prosperously among West Indians when they migrated to American cities. All these arrangements required entrusting money or property to others and awaiting returns in the uncertain future.

That supply creates its own demand is a principle of classical economics called Say's Law. It has come to be expressed, and refuted, in many interesting technical forms. But its essential point is potlatching. Capitalism consists of providing first and getting later. The demand is implicit in the supply. Without a monetary economy, such gifts were arrayed in expectation of an immediate profit in prestige and a later feast of interest, and they could be seen as a necessary way to escape the constraints of barter, to obviate the exact coincidence of wants and values required by simple trading. In most cases, the feasts and offerings were essentially entrepreneurial. They entailed the acquisition of goods at a known cost with the intention of acquiring in exchange—in this case, over an extended period—goods of unknown value. As devices of savings and investment, they depended for success on the continued honesty and economic returns of all members. The entrepreneurs succeed only to the extent they are sensitive to the needs of others, and to the extent that others succeed. Altruism is the essence of capitalism.

Capitalist production entails faith—in one's neighbors, in one's society, and in the compensatory logic of the cosmos. Search and you shall find, give and you will be given unto, supply creates its demand. It is this cosmology, this sequential logic, that essentially distinguishes the free from the socialist economy. The socialist economy proceeds from a rational definition of needs or demands to a prescription of planned supplies. In a socialist economy, one does not supply until the demands have already been determined and specified. Rationality rules, and it rules out the awesome uncertainties and commensurate acts of faith that are indispensable to an expanding and innovative system.

The gifts of advanced capitalism in a monetary economy are called investments. One does not make gifts without some sense, possibly unconscious, that one will be rewarded, whether in this world or the next. Even the Biblical injunction affirms that the giver will be given unto. The essence of giving is not the absence of all expectation of return, but the lack of a predetermined return. Like gifts, capitalist investments are made without a predetermined return.

These gifts or investments are experimental in that the returns to the giver are unknown; and whether gains or losses, they are absorbed by him. Because the vast majority of investments fail, the moment of decision is pregnant with doubt and promise and suffused to some degree with faith. Because the ventures are experiments, however, even the failures in a sense succeed, even the waste is often redeemed. In the course of time, perhaps even with the passage of generations, the failures accumulate as new knowledge, the most crucial kind of capital, held by both the entrepreneurs themselves and the society at large.

This new knowledge is a deeper kind than is taught in schools or acquired in the controlled experiments of social or physical science, or gained in the experience of socialist economies. For entrepreneurial experiments are also adventures, with the future livelihood of the investor at stake. He participates with a heightened consciousness and passion and an alertness and diligence that greatly enhance his experience of learning. The experiment may reach its highest possibilities, and its crises and surprises may be exploited to the utmost.

This motivational advantage will often decide the success or failure of enterprises or nations otherwise equally endowed. Harvey Leibenstein of Harvard has presented a large body of evidence which shows that the key factor in productivity differences among firms and between countries is neither the kind of allocational efficiency stressed in economic texts nor any other measurable input in the productive process. The differences derive from management, motivation, and spirit; from a factor he cannot exactly identify but which he calls *X-efficiency*. He quotes Tolstoy in *War and Peace*:

> Military science assumes the strength of an army to be identical to its numbers. . . . [In fact it] is the product of its mass and some unknown x . . . the spirit of the army. . . . To define and express the significance of this unknown factor . . . is a problem for science . . . only solvable if we cease arbitrarily to substitute for the unknown x itself the conditions under which that force becomes apparent—such as the commands of the general, the equipment employed and so on . . . and if we recognize this unknown quantity in its entirety as being the greater or lesser desire to fight and to face danger.

In other words, measurable inputs, such as those that can be calculated in a planned economy, do not determine output. Leibenstein shows that productivity differences between workers doing the same job in a particular plant are likely to vary as much as four to one, that differences as high as 50 percent can arise between plants commanding identical equipment and the same size labor force that is paid identically. Matters of management, motivation, and spirit—and their effects on willingness to innovate and seek new knowledge—dwarf all measurable inputs in accounting for productive efficiency, both for individuals and groups and for management and labor. A key difference is always in the willingness to transform vague information or hypotheses into working knowledge: Willingness, in Tolstoy's terms, transferred from the martial to the productive arts, "to fight and face danger," to exert efforts and take risks.

Socialism presumes that we already know most of what we need to know to accomplish our national goals. Capitalism is based on the idea that we live in a world of unfathomable complexity, ignorance, and peril, and that we cannot possibly prevail over our difficulties without constant efforts of initiative, sympathy, discovery, and love. One system maintains that we can reliably predict and elicit the outcomes we demand. The other asserts that we must give long before we can know what the universe will return. One is based on empirically calculable human power; the other on optimism and faith. These are the essential visions that compete in the world and determine our fate.

When faith dies, so does enterprise. It is impossible to create through the mechanisms of rational self-interest a system of collective regulation and safety that does not finally deaden the moral sources of the willingness to face danger and fight, that does not dampen the spontaneous flow of gifts and experiments which extend the dimensions of the world and the circles of human sympathy.

Walter Lippmann was much closer to the truth of the system than many of its more conservative apologists when in 1936, the midst of the Great Depression, he wrote that capitalism is based on "an ideal that for the first time in human history" gave men "a way of producing wealth in which the good fortune of others multiplied their own." At long last "the Golden Rule was economically sound . . . and for the first time men could conceive a social order in which the ancient moral aspiration of liberty, fraternity, and equality was consistent with the abolition of poverty and the increase of wealth." Once "the worldly policy was to be predatory. The claims of the spirit were otherworldly." But with the rise of capitalism "the vista was opened at the end of which men could see the possibility of the good society on this earth. At long last the ancient schism between the world and the spirit . . . was potentially closed."

To defend capitalism—even to understand it—you have to comprehend that businessmen are not bastards, but the heroes of the modern age—crucial vessels of those generous and creative impulses that give hope to an evermore populous humanity in overcoming its continuing scarcities and conflicts. In a world always divided in part between the givers and the takers, businessmen are among the most persistent and ingenious of donors and all of us who benefit should be thankful.

How is it then that the contrary view is so prevalent in the world—that most observers of capitalism see businessmen not as givers but as takers? There are many reasons, including envy, ignorance, and the corruption of many businessmen by the snares of the state. But the key source of confusion is what can be called the materialist fallacy: the belief that wealth consists chiefly not of human knowledge and creativity, generosity and love, but of a limited fund of "natural resources," always in danger of running out, and the accumulated inheritance of physical capital embodied in farms, factories, and machines.

This belief is one of the oldest of human delusions, from the period of empire when men imagined that wealth was land, to the era of mercantilism when they fantasized that it was gold, won through a favorable balance of trade, and continuing on to today when the world believes that wealth is oil, and grasps at real estate and gold as well. Contemporary economists, liberal and conservative, make a similar error when they define wealth as physical property and capital assets and measure it in quantitative terms.

As long experience should show us, however, resources and machines are nearly useless without entrepreneurs and willing workers. Iran before the revolution was replete with oil and factories, but all their resources availed them little, because they lacked in the generosity and discipline of entrepreneurs. Hong Kong and Taiwan have little material endowment, but their businessmen provide wealth for the world. Japan and Germany possess few natural resources and saw much of their material capital destroyed during World War II, but they have thrived by liberating enterprise. Throughout history, most of mankind has lived cramped and impoverished lives in materially affluent countries because of an absence of the metaphysical capital that is most crucial to progress: the trust in others, the hope for the future, the faith in a providential God that allows freedom and prompts the catalytic gifts of capitalism.

Without these essentially spiritual dimensions, the success of capitalism is inexplicable except where it is already occurring. The great flaw of the bastard capitalism theory is that it cannot explain economic growth under the conditions where it is most needed: a depressed and impoverished economy in which there is little to take, and as John Kenneth Galbraith has written, the most "rational" course is to accept one's poverty rather than fight hopelessly against it. This perception has prompted Galbraith and many other leftist thinkers to give up on further world development and predict "lean years" of scarcity, entropy, and decay. A blindness to the spiritual sources of wealth thus is leading many "progressive" writers into a strange revival of the dismal science of the 19th century economics. No Ricardian law of rents, no Malthusian cycle of population was ever more coldly remorseless in its rejection of the dreams of the poor than Richard Barnet's "entropy theory" or Barry Commoner's "closing circle" of ecological limits to growth.

Adam Smith's self-interest, however, is little more persuasive than Marxist ideas of exploitation and taking as an explanation of capitalist prosperity. The pursuit of self-interest would lead not to the always risky and unpromising ventures of capitalism in an uncertain and perilous world but to the quest for safety and security in an ever-growing welfare state. The only way to escape the vicious cycles of poverty is through the expanding circles of creative giving, the investments of brave men with hope for the future, trust in their fellow men, and faith in providence. This impulse of philanthropy is the prime gift of business success.

Capitalism can be summed up in the language of scripture: *Give and you will be given unto, search and you shall find. . . . Cast your bread upon the waters and it will return to you manyfold.* Or even in the language of economics: *Supply creates its own demand.* Capitalism is not impugned but affirmed in the Biblical parables: the parable of the talents, in which Jesus praises the man who invests and multiplies his money, or even in the parable of the rich man, who is told to give away rather than hoard his wealth.

"Where your treasure is, so your heart is also." It is Marxism and statism that are based on the materialist fallacy, that believe in the treasure of things. It is capitalism that is based on the treasure of ideas and spirit. To the extent that capitalists are bastards—predatory and materialistic, hoarding and miserly, hedonistic and prodigal—they betray the essence of capitalism and balk its growth. The fable of Midas is the story not of perils and contradictions of capitalist wealth but of the pitfalls of materialism itself. The real capitalists have the anti-Midas touch, turning the hoards of gold and liquidity, through an alchemy of creative spirit, into the productive capital of real wealth. And the foundation of wealth is always giving, not taking. The deepest truth of capitalism is faith, hope, and love.

❏ ❏ ❏

GEORGE GILDER is Chairman of Gilder Publishing LLC, a Senior Fellow at the Discovery Institute, a contributing editor of *Forbes*, and a frequent writer for *The Economist*, the *Harvard Business Review*, *The Wall Street Journal*, and other publications. A graduate of Exeter Academy and Harvard University, his books include *Visible Man* (1978), the best-selling *Wealth and Poverty* (1981), *The Spirit of Enterprise* (1984), *Microcosm* (1989), *Men and Marriage* (1992), and *Telecosm* (2000). In 1986, President Reagan presented him the White House Award for Entrepreneurial Excellence.

"I, Pencil"

Leonard E. Read

June 1992

The following is a reprint of a classic 1958 essay.

❏ ❏ ❏

I am a lead pencil—the ordinary wooden pencil familiar to all boys and girls and adults who can read and write. (My official name is "Mongol 482." My many ingredients are assembled, fabricated, and finished by Eberhard Faber Pencil Company, Wilkes-Barre, Pennsylvania.)

Writing is both my vocation and my avocation; that's all I do.

You may wonder why I should write a genealogy. Well, to begin with, my story is interesting. And, next, I am a mystery—more so than a tree or a sunset or even a flash of lightning. But, sadly, I am taken for granted by those who use me, as if I were a mere incident and without background. This super-cilious attitude relegates me to the level of the commonplace. This is a species of the grievous error in which mankind cannot too long persist without peril. For, as a wise man, G. K. Chesterton, observed, "We are perishing for want of wonder, not for want of wonders."

I, Pencil, simple though I appear to be, merit your wonder and awe, a claim I shall attempt to prove. In fact, if you can understand me—no, that's too much to ask of anyone—if you can become aware of the miraculous-ness that I symbolize, you can help save the freedom mankind is so unhap-pily losing. I have a profound lesson to teach. And I can teach this lesson

141

better than can an automobile or an airplane or a mechanical dishwasher because—well, because I am seemingly so simple.

Simple? Yet, not a single person on the face of this earth knows how to make me. This sounds fantastic, doesn't it? Especially when you realize that there are about one and one-half billion of my kind produced in the U.S. each year.

Pick me up and look me over. What do you see? Not much meets the eye—here's some wood, lacquer, the printed labeling, graphite lead, a bit of metal, and an eraser.

Innumerable Antecedents

Just as you cannot trace your family tree back very far, so is it impossible for me to name and explain all my antecedents. But I would like to suggest enough of them to impress upon you the richness and complexity of my background.

My family tree begins with what in fact is a tree, a cedar of straight grain that grows in Northern California and Oregon. Now contemplate all the saws and trucks and rope and the countless other gear used in harvesting and carting the cedar logs to the railroad siding. Think of all the persons and the numberless skills that went into their fabrication: the mining of ore, the making of steel and its refinement into saws, axes, motors; the growing of hemp and bringing it through all the stages to heavy and strong rope; the logging camps with their beds and mess halls, the cookery and the raising of all the foods. Why, untold thousands of persons had a hand in every cup of coffee the loggers drink!

The logs are shipped to a mill in San Leandro, California. Can you imagine the individuals who make flat cars and rails and railroad engines and who construct and install the communication systems incidental thereto? These legions are among my antecedents.

Consider the millwork in San Leandro. The cedar logs are cut into small, pencil-length slats less than one-fourth of an inch in thickness. These are kiln-dried and then tinted for the same reason women put rouge on their faces. People prefer that I look pretty, not a pallid white. The slats are waxed and kiln-dried again. How many skills went into the making of the tint and kilns, into supplying the heat, the light and power, the belts, motors, and all the other things a mill requires? Are sweepers in the mill among my ancestors? Yes, and also included are the men who poured the concrete for the dam of a Pacific Gas & Electric Company hydroplant which supplies the mill's power. And don't overlook the ancestors present and distant who have a hand in transporting sixty carloads of slats across the nation from California to Wilkes-Barre.

Complicated Machinery

Once in the pencil factory—$4,000,000 in machinery and building, all capital accumulated by thrifty and saving parents of mine—each slat is given eight grooves by a complex machine, after which another machine lays leads in every other slat, applies glue, and places another slat atop—a lead sandwich, so to speak. Seven brothers and I are mechanically carved from this "wood-clinched" sandwich.

My "lead" itself—it contains no lead at all—is complex. The graphite is mined in Ceylon. Consider the miners and those who make their many tools and the makers of the paper sacks in which the graphite is shipped and those who make the string that ties the sacks and those who put them aboard ships and those who make the ships. Even the lighthouse keepers along the way assisted in my birth—and the harbor pilots.

The graphite is mixed with clay from Mississippi in which ammonium hydroxide is used in the refining process. Then wetting agents are added such as sulfonated tallow—animal fats chemically reacted with sulfuric acid. After passing through numerous machines, the mixture finally appears as endless extrusions—as from a sausage grinder—cut to size, dried, and baked for several hours at 1,850 degrees Fahrenheit. To increase their strength and smoothness the leads are then treated with a hot mixture which includes candililla wax from Mexico, paraffin wax, and hydrogenated natural fats.

My cedar receives six coats of lacquer. Do you know all of the ingredients of lacquer? Who would think that the growers of castor beans and the refiners of castor oil are a part of it? They are. Why, even the processes by which the lacquer is made a beautiful yellow involves the skills of more persons than one can enumerate!

Observe the labeling. That's a film formed by applying heat to carbon black mixed with resins. How do you make resins and what, pray, is carbon black?

My bit of metal—the ferrule—is brass. Think of all the persons who mine zinc and copper and those who have the skills to make shiny sheet brass from these products of nature. Those black rings on my ferrule are black nickel. What is black nickel and how is it applied? The complete story of why the center of my ferrule has no black nickel on it would take pages to explain.

Then there's my crowning glory, inelegantly referred to in the trade as "the plug," the part man uses to erase the errors he makes with me. An ingredient called "factice" is what does the erasing. It is a rubber-like product made by reacting rape seed oil from the Dutch East Indies with sulfur chloride. Rubber, contrary to the common notion, is only for binding purposes. Then, too, there are numerous vulcanizing and accelerating agents. The pumice comes from Italy; and the pigment which gives "the plug" its color is cadmium sulfide.

Vast Web of Know-How

Does anyone wish to challenge my earlier assertion that no single person on the face of this earth knows how to make me?

Actually, millions of human beings have had a hand in my creation, no one of whom even knows more than a very few of the others. Now, you may say that I go too far in relating the picker of a coffee berry in far-off Brazil and food growers elsewhere to my creation; that this is an extreme position. I shall stand by my claim. There isn't a single person in all these millions, including the president of the pencil company, who contributes more than a tiny, infinitesimal bit of know-how. From the standpoint of know-how the only difference between the miner of graphite in Ceylon and the logger in Oregon is in the type of know-how. Neither the miner nor the logger can be dispensed with, any more than the chemist at the factory or the worker in the oil field—paraffin being a byproduct of petroleum.

Here is an astounding fact: Neither the worker in the oil field nor the chemist nor the digger of graphite or clay nor anyone who mans or makes the ships or trains or trucks nor the one who runs the machine that does the knurling on my bit of metal nor the president of the company performs his singular task because he wants *me*. Each one wants me less, perhaps, than does a child in the first grade. Indeed, there are some among this vast multitude who never saw a pencil nor would they know how to use one. Their motivation is other than me. Perhaps it is something like this: Each of these millions sees that he can thus exchange his tiny know-how for the goods and services he needs or wants. I may or may not be among these items.

No Human Mastermind

There is a fact still more astounding: The absence of a mastermind, of anyone dictating or forcibly directing these countless actions that bring me into being. No trace of such a person can be found. Instead, we find the Scottish economist and moral philosopher Adam Smith's famous "Invisible Hand" at work in the marketplace. This is the mystery to which I earlier referred.

It has been said that "only God can make a tree." Why do we agree with this? Isn't it because we realize that we ourselves could not make one? Indeed, can we even describe a tree? We cannot, except in superficial terms. We can say, for instance, that a certain molecular configuration manifests itself as a tree. But what mind is there among men that could even record, let alone direct, the constant changes in molecules that transpire in the life span of a tree? Such a feat is utterly unthinkable!

I, Pencil, am a complex combination of miracles; a tree, zinc, copper, graphite, and so on. But to these miracles which manifest themselves in Nature an even more extraordinary miracle has been added: the configuration of creative human energies—millions of tiny bits of know-how configurating naturally and spontaneously in response to human necessity and desire and in the absence of any human necessity and desire and in the absence of any human masterminding! Since only God can make a tree, I insist that only God could make me. Man can no more direct millions of bits of know-how so as to bring a pencil into being than he can put molecules together to create a tree.

That's what I meant when I wrote earlier, "If you can become aware of the miraculousness which I symbolize, you can help save the freedom mankind is so unhappily losing." For, if one is aware that these bits of know-how will naturally, yes, automatically, arrange themselves into creative and productive patterns in response to human necessity and demand—that is, in the absence of governmental or any other coercive masterminding—then one will possess an absolutely essential ingredient for freedom: a faith in free men. Freedom is impossible without this faith.

Once government has had a monopoly on a creative activity—the delivery of the mail, for instance—most individuals will believe that the mail could not be efficiently delivered by men acting freely. And here is the reason: Each one acknowledges that he himself doesn't know how to do all the things involved in mail delivery. He also recognizes that no other individual could. These assumptions are correct. No individual possesses enough know-how to perform a nation's mail delivery any more than any individual possesses enough know-how to make a pencil. In the absence of a faith in free men—unaware that millions of tiny kinds of know-how would naturally and miraculously form and cooperate to satisfy this necessity—the individual cannot help but reach the erroneous conclusion that the mail can be delivered only by governmental masterminding.

Testimony Galore

If I, Pencil, were the only item that could offer testimony on what men can accomplish when free to try, then those with little faith would have a fair case. However, there is testimony galore; it's all about us on every hand. Mail delivery is exceedingly simple when compared, for instance, to the making of an automobile or a calculating machine or a grain combine or a milling machine, or to tens of thousands of other things.

Delivery? Why, in this age where men have been left free to try, they deliver the human voice around the world in less than one second; they deliver an event visually and in motion to any person's home when it is happening; they deliver 150 passengers from Seattle to Baltimore in less than four hours; they deliver gas from Texas to one's range or furnace in New York at unbelievably low rates and without subsidy; they deliver each four pounds of oil from the Persian Gulf to our Eastern Seaboard—halfway around the world—for less money than the government charges for delivering a one-ounce letter across the street! [*Ed.: Some things have changed since this essay ran in 1958!*]

Leave Men Free

The lesson I have to teach is this: Leave all creative energies uninhibited. Merely organize society to act in harmony with this lesson. Let society's legal apparatus remove all obstacles the best it can. Permit creative know-how to freely flow. Have faith that free men will respond to the "Invisible Hand." This faith will be confirmed. I, Pencil, seemingly simple though I am, offer the miracle of my creation as testimony that this is a practical faith, as practical as the sun, the rain, a cedar tree, and the good earth.

❏ ❏ ❏

Born in 1898, LEONARD READ founded the Foundation for Economic Education in 1946. In addition to numerous articles that appeared in FEE's monthly journal, *The Freeman*, and elsewhere, he wrote seventeen books and lectured extensively throughout the U.S. and abroad. For ten years, he was the manager of the National Chamber of Commerce's Western Division, and in 1939 he became the general manager of the Los Angeles Chamber. He was one of the founders of the Mont Pèlerin Society. Mr. Read passed away in 1983.

Economic Liberties
and the Law

Richard W. Duesenberg

April 1994

Mr. Duesenberg delivered this speech at a Hillsdale College
seminar, "Politicization of the Law: Landmark Decisions and
Trends in U.S. Legal History," on the Hillsdale campus.

❏ ❏ ❏

The Cost of Regulation

The cost of government regulation is truly staggering—it is also a barometer
of how free we Americans are to pursue our own interests and to determine
the course of our own lives.

In the late 1970s, Washington University's Center for the Study of
American Business estimated that the total annual cost of implementing
government regulations was about $64 billion. By the late 1980s, its esti-
mate more than doubled to reach $137 billion. Other studies reveal even
starker figures. The Rochester Institute of Technology estimated in 1990
that federal regulations were costing Americans $395–$510 *billion*, or $4,100–
$5,400 per household, each year.

Financial costs are not the only burden. Regulations also result in a
tremendous loss of one of our most valuable and limited resources—time.
In the 1980s, the U.S. Office of Management and Budget reported that the
private sector was spending over 5 *billion hours* a year just to meet government paperwork demands. It is spending even more time on compliance in

the 1990s. It is no wonder that regulation discourages the creation of new businesses, new jobs, new products, and new services.

Today, every single aspect of business activity requires seeking the approval of one or more government agencies. A businessman may not even interview a job applicant without first knowing all the federal and state regulations that govern the interview process. These determine whom he may interview, what questions he may ask, and how he may determine an applicant's qualifications. Regulations also dictate to the person seeking a job, from stipulating the number of hours he may work to limiting the kind of the work he may perform.

Looking to invest in a business? You need a lawyer to help sort through all the complex regulations related to raising and investing capital. Erecting or remodeling a building? If you are very lucky, you will get a permit, but then be prepared for even more costly restrictions. Setting salaries or other compensation? Call your lawyer again to find out all the regulations on minimum benefit levels, nondiscrimination, selective disclosures, etc. Developing a product? Send tons of reports to the government and cross your fingers in the hope that you will get permission to sell it—within a decade, that is. Setting a price? Not without checking with the state once again to see if it considers that price "fair" and "equitable." And that's just getting started in your new business—it is even tougher to *stay* in business.

Each of us is affected—intimately—every day by regulation. Without approval from the government, we cannot drive an automobile. We cannot establish a school to educate our children. We cannot make the smallest improvement to our home or other property. We cannot practice any profession. We cannot even contract an illness without being reported to some bureaucratic authority. And, of course, up to half of what we earn is confiscated by local, state, and federal tax collectors.

Economic Liberties and the Constitution

Government control over our lives has increased as protections of our economic liberties have decreased. But this is a fairly recent phenomenon. Throughout most of our history, we have been free from the heavy yoke of regulation. We have viewed government with suspicion, and we have been protected *from* government, not *by* government. We have also recognized that there is no meaningful freedom without freedom of enterprise—our political and economic liberties are interdependent.

Over 200 years ago, our economic liberties were foremost in the minds of the framers of the Constitution. In *The Federalist*, No. 10, James Madison argued that men have different "faculties," that is, different talents and abilities, and that this is why property rights are essential: "From the protection of different and unequal faculties of acquiring property, the possession of different degrees and kinds of property immediately results." And he emphasized, "The protection of these faculties is the first object of government."

Madison furthermore criticized the "rage" for "an equal distribution of property," and condemned it as an "improper or wicked project." On laws impairing the obligation of contracts, he wrote that they were "contrary to the first principles of the social compact and to every principle of sound legislation."

In his *Defense of the Constitutions of Government*, John Adams also raised the issue of property rights as "natural rights":

> property is surely a right of mankind as really as liberty. . . . The moment the idea is admitted into society that property is not as sacred as the laws of God, and that there is not a force of law and public justice to protect it, anarchy and tyranny commence.

Does this resound with self-interest from the landed and propertied classes? Of course it does. But, more important, this natural rights view explains why America has not only been "the land of the free" but "the land of opportunity" for millions of men and women of every race, every social class, and every economic condition.

It may seem surprising that the framers referred only briefly to property rights in the Constitution. This was mainly because the document was so short, consisting merely of a preamble and seven articles. But it was also because the framers believed that a lengthy defense of any form of rights was unnecessary. Rights originated with the people, not with the state: delegation *to* government, not *from* it—that was the idea. As Alexander Hamilton expressed it, "[T]he people surrender nothing; and as they retain everything, they have no need of particular reservations."

So the document that emerged from conference on September 17, 1787, and that was effectively ratified on June 21, 1788, made only two references of any significance to property. In Section 9 of Article I, there was a proscription against bills of attainder (depriving the accused of rights without judicial trial) and *ex post facto* legislation (retroactive punishment for activities that were once legal). In Section 10, the same prohibitions were applied to state legislatures, and there was an added restriction against laws impairing the obligation of contracts.

But there were even more important references to property rights in the Bill of Rights attached to the Constitution. The famous language of the Fifth Amendment was: "No person shall . . . be deprived of life, liberty, or property, without due process of law; nor shall private property be taken for public use without just compensation."

Keep in mind that the framers had a very broad definition of "property" that not only included land, merchandise, and contracts but much more. Madison explained that it meant "that dominion which one man claims and exercises over the external things of the world, in exclusion of every other individual." He added, "In its larger and juster meaning, it embraces everything to which a man may attach a value and have a right; and which leaves to everyone else the like advantage."

Property, then, extends to our opinions and the free communication of them, our religious beliefs, our safety, and our liberty of person. "In a word," Madison concluded, "as a man is said to have a right to his property, he may be equally said to have a property in his rights."

Economic Liberties and the Early Supreme Court

It was with this broad definition of property rights, springing from natural rights philosophy, that the early Supreme Court began its work. From the start, the justices interpreted the Constitution to mean that the government could not abridge the rights of its citizens except in rare circumstances, and that even then it would have to provide compelling proof that intervention was necessary. In one of the earliest cases involving property rights, Justice William Paterson wrote:

The right of acquiring and possessing property, and having it protected, is one of the natural, inherent, and inalienable rights of man. . . . No man would become a member of a community in which he could not enjoy the fruits of his honest labor and industry.

He judged that the legislature had no authority to make an act divesting one citizen of his freehold and vesting it in another without just compensation, and in ringing terms he concluded with the declaration that such conduct

> is inconsistent with the principles of reason, justice, and moral rectitude; it is incompatible with the comfort, peace, and happiness of mankind; it is contrary to the principles of social alliance in every free government. . . .

In an 1810 case, *Fletcher v. Peck*, Chief Justice John Marshall relied on both natural rights language and the contracts clause to declare unconstitutional a Georgia statute canceling title to a 35-million-acre tract of land that had been purchased in good faith. But it was a dissenting opinion written near the end of his tenure on the Court that best describes Marshall's view. "Individuals," he wrote,

> do not derive from government their right to contract, but bring that right with them into society; that obligation is not conferred on contract by positive law, but is intrinsic, and is conferred by the act of the parties. This results from the right which every man retains to acquire property, to dispose of that property according to his own judgment, and to pledge himself for a future act. These rights are not given by society but are brought into it.

Justice Joseph Story expressed the same view in an 1829 opinion:

> The fundamental maxims of a free government seem to require, that the rights of personal liberty and private property should be held sacred. At least no court of justice in this country would be warranted in assuming that the power to violate and disregard

them, a power so repugnant to the common principles of justice and civil liberty, lurked under any general grant of legislative authority, or ought to be implied from any general expressions of the will of the people. The people ought not to be presumed to part with rights so vital to their security and well being. . . .

Unfortunately, the early Court failed to take advantage of some important opportunities to protect property rights. For example, in 1798 the Court ruled that the *ex post facto* clause only applied to criminal cases. (It was not unanimous on the point, and many subsequent justices and legal scholars have argued that the position was in error.) Since much of today's legislation has a retroactive effect, the Court's failure to use the *ex post facto* clause broadly has had a huge negative impact on the protection of lawful private action recently, especially in the area of environmental law. As for the contract clause, an 1827 decision upholding a state bankruptcy law gave government a power over individuals and businesses that might not otherwise have emerged.

But even with its weak interpretations of these provisions, the early Supreme Court was a strong defender of economic liberties in general. In a case applying the Fourteenth Amendment against a piece of state legislation that made it illegal to purchase insurance from an unlicensed out-of-state carrier, the Court found that the amendment

means not only the right of the citizen to be free from the mere physical restraint of his person, as by incarceration, but the term is deemed to embrace the right of the citizen to be free in the enjoyment of all his faculties; to be free to use them in all lawful ways; to live and work where he will; to earn his livelihood by any lawful calling; to enter into all contracts which may be proper, necessary, and essential to his carrying out to a successful conclusion the purposes above mentioned.

The Court also reiterated the principle that if the government chose to restrict an individual's "inalienable right" to pursue any of the commonplace occupations of life, then it bore the burden of justifying its action.

Probably the most famous case declaring a statute unconstitutional because it infringed upon freedom of contract was *Lochner* v. *New York*. The state of New York had passed a law limiting the number of hours that could be worked in one week in a bakery. It was justified on health grounds, but if one looked behind the statute, its political *raison d'être* was not hard to find. An employer had been indicted for violations, so it was a criminal case. His defense was that the state law violated his liberty of contract, that is, his liberty to engage a worker for whatever number of hours per week he was willing to pay and the worker was willing to labor.

The Court declared the New York law unconstitutional, not because a state could not pass health-related legislation, but because if it used its police power to restrict economic liberties, it had to show that the exercise of those powers was fair, reasonable, and appropriate. Whether the act in question met those standards could be answered "in a few words," the Court declared. "There is no reasonable ground for interfering with the liberty of person or the right of free contract, by determining the hours of labor, in the occupation of a baker." Bakers could decide that for themselves. After all, the Court reasoned, they were citizens of average intelligence, not wards of the state, and they did not need its help to determine how many hours they were willing to work. The mere assertion of health considerations was not enough for the state to save its legislation.

Lochner was an early 20th-century decision—1905 to be exact. The Court had reached the zenith of its protection of economic liberties, primarily through the due process clause of the Fifth and Fourteenth Amendments.

Economic Liberties and the Modern Supreme Court

Oliver Wendell Holmes, who was just beginning a thirty-year career as a Supreme Court justice, filed a dissenting opinion. He criticized the Court's decision for being based, he alleged, "upon an economic theory which a large part of the country does not entertain." But whether he agreed or disagreed with that theory, he insisted, had nothing to do with "the right of the majority to embody their opinion in the law." Consistent with this, in 1915 Justice Holmes wrote another dissenting opinion:

> Regulation means the prohibition of something, and [in interstate commerce] I cannot doubt that the regulation may prohibit any part of such commerce that Congress sees fit to forbid.

Such language signaled that a truly monumental shift in constitutional interpretation was about to take place. The principle that government derives its authority only from the individual was being supplanted by the principle that legislation becomes legitimate through the action of the majority.

The framers of the U.S. Constitution feared the rule of the majority. In *The Federalist*, No. 51, Madison wrote that it was critically important that a republic guard the rights of the minority. He was aware that democracy can justify its own expansion of power better than any other political system. A government that is derived from the authority of the people is, after all, seemingly authorized to do everything.

But the fear of the majority faded in the first several decades of the 20th century; constitutional protections of economic liberties—which we may call "substantive due process"—were gradually abandoned. In case after case, price support laws, price discrimination laws, minimum wage laws, laws setting fees in various industries, laws limiting work hours in various trades, laws on union organization and membership, laws on child labor, and laws on product contents kept coming back to the Court. And Holmes was joined on the bench by other pro-interventionist justices like Louis Brandeis, William Douglas, and Hugo Black. Finally, in the mid-20th century, the constitutional edifice the framers built collapsed.

Keep in mind the historical setting for this drama: The Great Depression had ravaged society, and socialist factions had risen to power in Europe. Intellectuals everywhere had been seduced by the temptations of the Left. A leading theologian, Reinhold Niebuhr, idealized socialist Germany as the place "where all the social and political forces of modern civilization have reached their most advanced form."

The abandonment of constitutional protections of economic liberties meant that the state no longer had to prove the necessity of intervention. In *Nebbia v. New York*, a 1933 decision upholding milk price controls, the Supreme Court pronounced that the guarantee of due process "demands only that the law shall not be unreasonable, arbitrary, or capricious." Many years later, Justice Black would add with satisfaction that the "modern" Court refused

to sit as a "superlegislature to weigh the wisdom of legislation," and we emphatically refuse to go back to the time when courts

used the Due Process Clause to "strike down state laws regulat-
ing business and industrial conditions because they may be
unwise, improvident, or out of harmony with a particular school
of thought."

Unbounded legislative discretion, coupled with the principle that "the
majority rules," became the new standard for constitutional interpretation.
Justices could, at their own discretion, grant or deny economic liberties. So-
called "personal liberties" (like the "right of privacy," which is nowhere mentioned in the Constitution) outweighed economic liberties.

The Pursuit of Happiness

But to most Americans, the pursuit of happiness *is* the pursuit of economic liberties. Being able to hang from a tree and utter vulgar epithets at
the emperor is not nearly so dear to us as being able to own and dispose of
property, to engage freely in our own chosen trade or profession, to pass
our possessions on to our heirs.

While there are indications that the Court might be resuming some
sensitivity to property (e.g., under the takings clause), the deference it gives
to legislative action is still near-absolute. If a law or regulation simply
stresses "urgent need" or "the public interest," the Court is sure to let it
stand. The judicial review process is so biased that only the most absurd
edicts are found unconstitutional.

Legal scholar Bernard Siegan has noted that this bias has led to the
impeding of the democratic process. If the Court refuses to review the legitimacy of economic regulation, then the government is essentially free to
dominate the entire American business community and, indeed, the life of
every American citizen. This is socialism—and socialism does not work any
better in this country than it has anywhere else. We just seem to be the only
country that still doesn't want to admit it. Our most pressing social and
economic problems have only been made worse by government intervention. Even more alarming is the loss of freedom that has accompanied growing government involvement in our affairs. But freedom is valueless to the
government planner. He requires coercive force in order to have his way, and

he regards centralized planning as far superior to the untidy, unpredictable actions and decisions of free men and women.

Recently, Hillary Clinton was quoted as saying that one of the federal government's tasks is "redefining who we are as human beings in the post-modern age." Heaven help us! We've had enough politicians in this century who have made redefining humanity their goal. Millions of lives have been destroyed as a result. We should recall that the framers of the Constitution did not try to "redefine" or "remake" human beings. They sought to understand them and to protect their natural rights. They also stood firm with John Locke, who warned in his *Second Treatise on Civil Government*:

> He who attempts to get another man into his absolute power does thereby put himself into a state of war with him. . . . For I have reason to conclude that he who would get me into his power without my consent would use me as he pleased when he had got me there, and destroy me too when he had a fancy to it; for nobody can desire to have me in his absolute power unless it be to compel me by force to that which is against freedom, that is make me a slave.

❑   ❑   ❑

RICHARD W. DUESENBERG is a retired senior vice president, general counsel, and secretary of Monsanto Company. He has also served as chairman of the American Society of Corporate Secretaries, chairman of the American Bar Association's Section of Corporation Banking, a member of the New York Stock Exchange's Legal Advisory Committee, and a board director of the National Judicial College. He is an elected member of the American Law Institute and a member of the boards of directors of Valparaiso University, the Opera Theatre of St. Louis, the St. Louis Symphony Orchestra, and the Lutheran Brotherhood. He is co-author of one volume and author of two volumes on commercial codes and has written numerous articles for law journals and other publications.

The Moral Case
for the Flat Tax

Steve Forbes

October 1996

Steve Forbes delivered the following speech at a Hillsdale College seminar, "The Future of American Business," in Chicago, Illinois.

❏ ❏ ❏

Capitalism works better than any of us can conceive. It is also the only truly *moral* system of exchange. It encourages individuals to devote their energies and impulses freely to peaceful pursuits, to the satisfaction of others' wants and needs, and to constructive action for the welfare of all. The basis of capitalism is not greed. You don't see misers creating Wal-Marts and Microsofts.

Think about it for a moment. Capitalism is truly miraculous. What other system enables us to cooperate with millions of other ordinary people—whom we will never meet but to whom we will gladly provide goods and services—in an incredible, complex web of commercial transactions? And what other system perpetuates itself, working every day, year in, year out, with no single hand guiding it?

Capitalism is a moral system if only because it is based on *trust*. When we turn on a light, we assume there will be electricity. When we drive into a service station, we assume there will be fuel. When we walk into a restaurant, we assume there will be food. If we were to make a list of all the basic things that capitalism provides—things that we take for granted—it would fill an encyclopedia.

Three years have passed since I wrote those words in a September 1993 issue of Hillsdale College's speech digest, *Imprimis*, called "Three Cheers for Capitalism." I still firmly believe in them, but the vast majority of liberals—and, sadly, many conservatives—persist in viewing capitalism as merely an economic system, forgetting, as Warren Brookes wrote in *The Economy in Mind* (1982), that economics is a metaphysical rather than a mathematical science, "in which intangible spiritual values and attitudes are at least as important as physical assets and morals more fundamental than the money supply." He concluded that "a national economy, like an individual business or a specific product, is the sum of the spiritual and mental qualities of its people, and its output of value will be only as strong as the values of society."

Flat tax advocates like myself are often criticized for focusing too much on "dollars and cents" issues instead of on moral issues. But as the philosopher and essayist Ralph Waldo Emerson said 150 years ago: "A dollar is not value, but representative of value, and, at last, of moral value." More recently, scholars like former education secretary Bill Bennett and Nobel Prize-winning economist Milton Friedman have pointed out that every time you take a dollar out of one person's pocket and put it into another's, you are making a moral decision.

The High Price of Taxes

Taxes are not simply a means of raising revenue; they are also a price. The taxes on our income, capital gains, and corporate profits are the price we pay for the privilege of working, the price we pay for being productive, and the price we pay for being innovative and successful. If the price we pay becomes too high, we get less of these things. If the price we pay is lowered, we get more of them. So taxes are a barrier to progress, and they punish rather than reward success.

The Kemp–Roth bill of 1981 and the tax reform bill of 1986 reduced individual income tax rates to levels we hadn't seen in more than half a century, and they helped create an unrivaled period of prosperity. Yet today, many of our policymakers ignore or deny the positive benefits of those tax cuts. They also fail to realize that it is people, not policies, who make an economy run.

Remember, says investor and philanthropist Theodore J. Forstmann, "No government has ever borne the cost of anything. Taxes cost *people*. Tax cuts do not cost *government*." Families with children are hardest hit by high taxes. According to the Family Research Council, a family of four at the median income in 1948 paid 2 percent of its income in taxes; in 1994 the figure was 25 percent. That is why families feel they are on a treadmill and the treadmill is winning.

If we want to do something to help families in this country, I can't think of a better option than the flat tax. True, the across-the-board tax cuts proposed by Republican and even some Democratic leaders are an important step in the right direction and will do enormous good, but we should not stop there. We should scrap the existing tax code. Just think about what a monstrosity this code is. The Gettysburg Address runs about 200 words. The Declaration of Independence runs about 1,300 words. The Holy Bible runs about 773,000 words. But our federal income tax code runs about seven million words and is growing longer every year.

How Taxes Corrupt

Political Corruption

Today's tax code is incomprehensible, even to tax collectors, and it is the principal source of corruption in our nation's capital. Politicians have been trading favors and loopholes for political contributions and support for so long that they have come to think that this is acceptable, even virtuous, behavior. And there are now almost 13,000 registered lobbyists and special interest groups who together represent the largest private sector industry in Washington, D.C. Over half of them are there for the precise purpose of manipulating the tax code to their own advantage. As House Majority Leader

Dick Armey warns, this not only costs our economy billions of dollars but turns the political process into a free-for-all for special interests.

Washington attorney Leonard Garment says, "Whatever corruption may exist here is what happens wherever government is given large amounts of money to dispense, great power over people's lives, and great discretion in using that power, whether it is in a poverty program, or the Small Business Administration, or the Department of Defense. . . . It is a corruption that occurs almost universally when government has too much discretionary power and individuals too little."

Civic Corruption

Taxes also have a corrosive impact on our civic life. Our individual sense of responsibility and trust is destroyed—eaten by the acid of big government spending sprees and confiscatory taxes. Today, many of us view taxes as a form of legalized plunder, and we have little faith that the earnings we are forced to surrender to Uncle Sam will be used wisely or properly. So we do not scruple to look for ways to avoid compliance with the tax code whenever possible. We don't think of ourselves as "tax cheats" but as "tax rebels." But no matter what we call ourselves, we have the uneasy sense that high taxes, like welfare, can steal our sense of self-reliance and integrity.

Cultural Corruption

When we look around our nation, we see more illegitimacy, more illiteracy, more crime, more drug abuse, more broken families, and more members of a permanent underclass than ever before. In the name of "compassion," we have spent trillions of tax dollars on all these crises, and all we have done is to make them worse.

If we truly wish to be compassionate, we should adopt a flat tax that exempts the poorest citizens and offers all Americans real and practical ways to climb the ladder of successful living. Moreover, the flat tax allows us, not the federal government, to decide how best to solve our own problems. It puts responsibility back into the equation and sends a powerful moral message.

What Is the Flat Tax?

The flat tax is a simple, fair, and uniform system. It is a sound system, with widespread support from Nobel Prize-winning economists as well as former cabinet members and other political leaders. And it is a moral system because it means more take-home pay for wage earners, more savings and investment, more businesses, more jobs, more efficiency, more products and services, more price cuts, and more personal decisions as opposed to state planning. When people can keep more of what they earn, they tend to spend it on their children's education, on preparing for careers, on solving social problems, on going to church, and on volunteering instead of working overtime. The flat tax can actually provide a moral imperative to rebuild our lives and our communities.

Under my flat tax proposal, every individual would have a tax exemption of $13,000; every child, $5,000. For a family of four, the first $36,000 of income would be free. (There would be generous exemptions for smaller and larger families and for single individuals, too.) Currently, a family of four typically owes over $3,000 in taxes for the first $36,000 in income. With the flat tax, they would owe nothing, and their income over $36,000 would be taxed at 17 percent rate. There would be no tax on personal savings, pensions, Social Security benefits, capital gains, or inheritances. For businesses, the 17 percent rate on net profits would also apply, and investments would be written off in the first year. Constantly changing and complicated depreciation schedules would be eliminated. The IRS would no longer be able to define arbitrarily the life of an asset.

The flat tax would get America's economy moving again. But it has been attacked through a nationwide campaign of misinformation based mainly on six myths:

> Myth 1: *The flat tax would raise taxes on the middle class.* How many families of four do you know that have $36,000 of exemptions under the current tax code? The flat tax will actually lower taxes on the middle class. Yet one New Hampshire state official ran ads during the last presidential primary saying the flat tax would hike taxes on families of four in his state by $2,000–$3,000. How

did he come up with these numbers? He ignored the $36,000 tax exemption and applied the 17 percent to their entire income.

Myth 2: *The flat tax would hurt the housing industry and property owners.* But even President Clinton's Treasury Department acknowledges that the flat tax would lower interest rates by one-fourth to one-third. Lower interest rates mean lower down payments and monthly mortgage payments. More people can become homeowners for the first time, and current homeowners can save more of their earnings for other expenses. The need for mortgage deductions (which would be phased out gradually rather than all at once) would end because the flat tax would bring far greater savings and superior benefits.

Myth 3: *The flat tax would destroy municipal bonds.* The lower interest rates introduced by the flat tax would not hurt existing municipal bonds or future ones. New purchasers would be more concerned with where their money was going than how their taxes were affected. This would lead to greater accountability in public finance, and bond prices would even be likely to rise a little as general interest rates came down.

Myth 4: *The flat tax would hurt charitable giving.* The American people don't need to be bribed by the tax code to give when they live under a fair and equitable system. We were a generous and giving nation long before the federal income tax was instituted. And the tax cuts in the 1980s actually resulted in a huge, historic increase in charitable giving. In short, when the American people have more, they give more.

Myth 5: *The flat tax is a giveaway because investment income, or what liberal economists love to call "unearned income," would not be taxed.* Wrong: Under the flat tax, all income would be taxed. But investment income would be taxed only once instead of two or three times as the current code mandates. When a company makes a profit, it would pay a 17 percent rate tax.

Myth 6: *The flat tax would increase the budge deficit.* The only way we are going to cure the budget deficit is by cutting government spending and cutting taxes. This will lead to an economic boom. In the 1960s and 1980s, tax cuts increased rather than decreased government revenues. Why? Because, as I mentioned earlier, taxes are a price. When the American people can keep more of the resources they create, they create more resources. And whenever tax rates are reduced, compliance goes up because people find it easier to work productively than to figure out how to get around the shoals of the tax code.

The flat tax would mean more than just a financial savings—it would save time, too. Right now, individuals and businesses spend more than five billion hours a year filling out tax forms. The flat tax form would be the size of a postcard and would take almost no time to fill out. Imagine what we could achieve with all the time we would save. Imagine the benefits for our families, our schools, our churches, our charities, our communities, and our businesses.

Let Individuals Choose

There is a moral case for the flat tax because the flat tax is fundamentally about freedom. I am not talking about the freedom that the great free market economist Ludwig von Mises condemned as the freedom to "let soulless forces operate." That is not freedom at all; that is just tyranny in another guise. Rather, I am talking about the freedom to "let individuals choose."

Time and time again, the evidence has shown that the federal government cannot preserve our families, reawaken our faith, restore our values, solve our social problems, or create prosperity. Only free individuals can.

❏ ❏ ❏

STEVE FORBES is the president and chief executive officer of Forbes Inc. and editor-in-chief of *Forbes*. He graduated cum laude in 1966 from Brooks School in North Andover, Massachusetts, and received a B.A. in history from Princeton in 1970. At Princeton, he was the founding editor of *Business Today*, the country's largest magazine published by students for students. From 1993 to 1996 he served as Chairman of the Board of Directors of Empower America and from 1996 to 1999 he was the honorary chairman of Americans for Hope, Growth and Opportunity. He serves on several boards, including those of Princeton University, the Ronald Reagan Presidential Foundation, and the National Taxpayers Union. In 1996 and 2000, he was a candidate for the Republican presidential nomination, campaigning on the pro-growth agenda.

The Real Cost of Regulation

John Stossel

May 2001

Mr. Stossel delivered the following speech at a Hillsdale College seminar, "Taxes, Freedom, and America's Future," in Fort Myers, Florida.

❏ ❏ ❏

When I started thirty years ago as a consumer reporter, I took the approach that most young reporters take today. My attitude was that capitalism is essentially cruel and unfair, and that the job of government, with the help of lawyers and the press, is to protect people from it. For years I did stories along those lines—stories about Coffee Association ads claiming that coffee "picks you up while it calms you down," or Libby-Owens-Ford Glass Company ads touting the clarity of its product by showing cars with their windows rolled down. I and other consumer activists said, "We've got to have regulation. We've got to police these ads. We've got to have a Federal Trade Commission." And I am embarrassed at how long it took me to realize that these regulations make things worse, not better, for ordinary people.

The damage done by regulation is so vast, it is often hard to see. The money wasted consists not only of the taxes taken directly from us to pay for bureaucrats, but also of the indirect cost of all the lost energy that goes into filling out the forms. Then there is the distraction of creative power. Listen to Jack Faris, president of the National Federation of Independent Business: "If you're a small businessman, you have to get involved in gov-

167

ernment or government will wreck your business." And that's what happens. You have all this energy going into lobbying the politicians, forming the trade associations and PACs, and trying to manipulate the leviathan that has grown up in Washington, D.C. and the state capitals. You have many of the smartest people in the country today going into law, rather than into engineering or science. This doesn't create a richer, freer society. Nor do regulations only depress the economy. They depress the spirit. Visitors to Moscow before the fall of communism noticed a dead-eyed look in the people. What was that about? I don't think it was about fear of the KGB. Most Muscovites didn't have intervention by the secret police in their daily lives. I think it was the look that people get when they live in an all-bureaucratic state. If you go to Washington, to the Environmental Protection Agency, I think you'll see the same thing.

One thing I noticed that started me toward seeing the folly of regulation was that it didn't even punish the obvious crooks. The people selling the breast-enlargers and the burn-fat-while-you-sleep pills got away with it. The Attorney General would come at them after five years, they would hire lawyers to gain another five, and then they would change the name of their product or move to a different state. But regulation *did* punish *legitimate* businesses.

When I started reporting, all the aspirin companies were saying they were the best, when in fact aspirin is simply aspirin. So the FTC sued and demanded corrective advertising. Corrective ads would have been something like, "Contrary to our prior ads, Excedrin does not relieve twice as much pain." Of course these ads never ran. Instead, nine years of costly litigation finally led to a consent order. The aspirin companies said, "We don't admit doing anything wrong, but we won't do it again." So who won? Unquestionably the lawyers did. But did the public? Aspirin ads are more honest now. They say things like, "Nothing works better than Bayer"—which, if you think about it, simply means, "We're all the same." But I came to see that the same thing would have happened without nearly a decade of litigation, because markets police themselves. I can't say for certain *how* it would have happened. I think it is a fatal conceit to predict how markets will work. Maybe Better Business Bureaus would have gotten involved. Maybe the aspirin companies would have sued each other. Maybe the press would have embarrassed them. But the truth would have gotten out. The more I watched the market, the more impressed I was by how flexible and reasonable it is compared to government-imposed solutions.

Market forces protect us even where we tend most to think we need government. Consider the greedy, profit-driven companies that have employed me. CBS, NBC, and ABC make their money from advertisers, and they have paid me for twenty years to bite the hand that feeds them. Bristol-Myers sued CBS and me for $23 million when I did the story on aspirin. You would think CBS would have said, "Stossel ain't worth that." But they didn't. Sometimes advertisers would pull their accounts, but still I wasn't fired. Ralph Nader once said that this would never happen except on public television. In fact the opposite is true: Unlike PBS, almost every local TV station has a consumer reporter. The reason is capitalism: More people watch stations that give honest information about their sponsors' products. So although a station might lose some advertisers, it can charge the others more. Markets protect us in unexpected ways.

Alternatives to the Nanny State

People often say to me, "That's okay for advertising. But when it comes to health and safety, we've got to have OSHA, the FDA, the CPSC" and the whole alphabet soup of regulatory agencies that have been created over the past several decades. At first glance this might seem to make sense. But by interfering with free markets, regulations almost invariably have nasty side effects. Take the FDA, which saved us from thalidomide—the drug to prevent morning sickness in pregnant women that was discovered to cause birth defects. To be accurate, it wasn't so much that the FDA saved us, as that it was so slow in studying thalidomide that by the end of the approval process, the drug's awful effects were being seen in Europe. I am glad for this. But since the thalidomide scare, the FDA has grown tenfold in size, and I believe it now does more harm than good. If you want to get a new drug approved today, it costs about $500 million and takes about ten years. This means that there are drugs currently in existence that would improve or even save lives, but that are being withheld from us because of a tiny chance they contain carcinogens. Some years ago, the FDA held a press conference to announce its long-awaited approval of a new beta-blocker, and predicted it would save 14,000 American lives per year. Why didn't anybody stand up at the time and say, "Excuse me, doesn't that mean you killed 14,000 people last year by not approving it?" The answer is, reporters don't think that way.

Why, in a free society, do we allow government to perform this kind of nanny-state function? A reasonable alternative would be for government to serve as an information agency. Drug companies wanting to submit their products to a ten-year process could do so. Those of us who choose to be cautious could take only FDA-approved drugs. But others, including people with terminal illnesses, could try nonapproved drugs without sneaking off to Mexico or breaking the law. As an added benefit, all of us would learn something valuable by their doing so. I would argue further that we don't need the FDA to perform this research. As a rule, government agencies are inefficient. If we abolished the FDA, private groups like the publisher of *Consumer Reports* would step in and do the job better, cheaper, and faster. In any case, wouldn't that be more compatible with what America is about? Patrick Henry never said, "Give me absolute safety or give me death!"

Lawyers and Liability

If we embrace the idea of free markets, we have to accept the fact that trial lawyers have a place. Private lawsuits could be seen as a supplement to Adam Smith's invisible hand: the invisible fist. In theory they should deter bad behavior. But because of how our laws have evolved, this process has gone horribly wrong. It takes years for victims to get their money, and most of the money goes to lawyers. Additionally, the wrong people get sued. A Harvard study of medical malpractice suits found that most of those getting money don't deserve it, and that most people injured by negligence don't sue. The system is a mess. Even the cases the trial lawyers are most proud of don't really make us safer. They brag about their lawsuit over football helmets, which were thin enough that some kids were getting head injuries. But now the helmets are so thick that kids are butting each other and getting other kinds of injuries. Worst of all, they cost over $100 each. School districts on the margin can't afford them, and as a result some are dropping their football programs. Are the kids from these schools safer playing on the streets? No.

An even clearer example concerns vaccines. Trial lawyers sued over the diphtheria–pertussis–tetanus vaccine, claiming that it wasn't as safe as it might have been. Although I suspect this case rested on junk science, I don't know what the truth is. But assuming these lawyers were right, and that they've made the DPT vaccine a little safer, are we safer? When they sued, there were twenty companies in America researching and making vaccines. Now there are four. Many got out of the business because they said, "We don't make that much on vaccines. Who needs this huge liability?" Is America better off with four vaccine makers instead of twenty? No way.

These lawsuits also disrupt the flow of information that helps free people protect themselves. For example, we ought to read labels. We should read the label on tetracycline, which says that it won't work if taken with milk. But who reads labels anymore? I sure don't. There are twenty-one warning labels on stepladders—"Don't dance on stepladders wearing wet shoes," etc.—because of the threat of liability. Drug labels are even crazier. If anyone were actually to read the two pages of fine print that come with birth control pills, they wouldn't need to take the drug. My point is that government and lawyers don't make us safer. Freedom makes us safer. It allows us to protect *ourselves*. Some say, "That's fine for us. We're educated. But the poor and the ignorant need government regulations to protect them." Not so. I sure don't know what makes one car run better or safer than another. Few of us are automotive engineers. But it's hard to get totally ripped off buying a car in America. The worst car you can find here is safer than the best cars produced in planned economies. In a free society, not everyone has to be an expert in order for markets to protect us. In the case of cars, we just need a few car buffs who read car magazines. Information gets around through word-of-mouth. Good companies thrive and bad ones atrophy. Freedom protects the ignorant, too.

Admittedly there are exceptions to this argument. I think we need some environmental regulation, because now and then we lack a market incentive to behave well in that area. Where is the incentive for me to keep my waste-treatment plant from contaminating your drinking water? So we need some rules, and some have done a lot of good. Our air and water are cleaner thanks to catalytic converters. But how much regulation is enough? President Clinton set a record as he left office, adding 500,000 new pages to the *Federal Register*—a whole new spiderweb of little rules for us to obey. How big should government be? For most of America's history, when we grew the fastest, government accounted for 5 percent or less of GDP. The figure is now 40 percent. This is still less than Europe. But shouldn't we at least have an intelligent debate about how much government should do? The problem is that to have such a debate, we need an informed public. And here I am embarrassed, because people in my business are not helping that cause.

Fear-Mongering: A Risky Business

A turning point came in my career when a producer came into my office excited because he had been given a story by a trial lawyer—the lazy reporter's best friend—about Bic lighters spontaneously catching fire in people's pockets. These lighters, he told me, had killed four Americans in four years. By this time I had done some homework, so I said, "Fine. I'll do the exploding lighter story after I do stories on plastic bags, which kill 40 Americans every four years, and five-gallon buckets, which kill 200 Americans (mostly children) every four years." This is a big country, with 280 million people. Bad things happen to some of them. But if we frighten all the rest about ant-sized dangers, they won't be prepared when an elephant comes along. The producer stalked off angrily and got Bob Brown to do the story. But several years later, when ABC gave me three hour-long specials a year in order to keep me, I insisted the first one be called, "Are We Scaring Ourselves to Death?" In it, I ranked some of these risks and made fun of the press for its silliness in reporting them.

Risk specialists compare risks not according to how many people they kill, but according to how many days they reduce the average life. The press goes nuts over airplane crashes, but airplane crashes have caused fewer than 200 deaths per year over the past twenty years. That is less than one day off the average life. There is no proof that toxic-waste sites like Love Canal or Times Beach have hurt anybody at all, despite widely reported claims that they cause 1,000 cases of cancer a year. (Even assuming they do, and assuming further that all these cancer victims die, that would still be less than four days off the average life.) House fires account for about 4,500 American deaths per year—eighteen days off the average life. And murder, which leads the news in most towns, takes about 100 days off the average life. But to bring these risks into proper perspective, we need to compare them to far greater risks like driving, which knocks 182 days off the average life. I am often asked to do scare stories about flying—"The Ten Most Dangerous Airports" or "The Three Most Dangerous Airlines"—and I refuse because it is morally irresponsible. When we scare people about flying, more people drive to Grandma's house, and more are killed as a result. This is statistical murder, perpetuated by regulators and the media.

Even more dramatic is the fact that Americans below the poverty line live seven to ten fewer years than the rest of us. Some of this difference is self-induced: Poor people smoke and drink more. But most of it results from the fact that they can't afford some of the good things that keep the rest of us alive. They drive older cars with older tires; they can't afford the same medical care; and so on. This means that when bureaucrats get obsessed about flying or toxic-waste sites, and create new regulations and drive up the cost of living in order to reduce these risks, they shorten people's lives by making them poorer. Bangladesh has floods that kill 100,000 people. America has comparable floods and no one dies. The difference is wealth. Here we have TVs and radios to hear about floods, and cars to drive off in. Wealthier is healthier, and regulations make the country poorer. Maybe the motto of OSHA should be: "To save four, kill ten."

Largely due to the prevalence of misleading scare stories in the press, we see in society an increasing fear of innovation. Natural gas in the home kills 200 Americans a year, but we accept it because it is old. It happened before we got crazy. We accept coal, which is awful stuff, but we are terrified of nuclear power, which is probably cleaner and safer. Swimming pools kill over 1,000 Americans every year, and I think it is safe to say that the government wouldn't allow them today if they didn't already exist. What about vehicles that weigh a ton and are driven within inches of pedestrians by 16-year-olds, all while spewing noxious exhaust? Cars, I fear, would never make it off the drawing board in 2001.

What has happened to America? Why do we allow government to make decisions for us as if we were children? In a free society we should be allowed to take risks, and to learn from them. The press carps and whines about our exposure to dangerous new things—invisible chemicals, food additives, radiation, etc. But what is the result? We are living longer than ever. A century ago, most people my age were already dead. If we were better informed, we would realize that what is behind this longevity is the spirit of enterprise, and that what gives us this spirit—what makes America thrive—isn't regulation. It is freedom.

❏   ❏   ❏

JOHN STOSSEL joined the ABC newsmagazine 20/20 in 1981, and began his critically acclaimed series of one-hour primetime specials in 1994. He has received nineteen Emmy Awards and has been honored five times for excellence in consumer reporting by the National Press Club. Among his other awards are the George Polk Award for Outstanding Local Reporting and the George Foster Peabody Award. Mr. Stossel is a 1969 graduate of Princeton University with a B.A. in psychology.

RELIGION

❏   ❏   ❏

The Great Liberal Death Wish

Malcolm Muggeridge

May 1979

Mr. Muggeridge delivered the following speech at a Hillsdale
College seminar, "The Humane Holocaust: The Auschwitz
Formula," on the Hillsdale campus.

❑ ❑ ❑

"The Great Liberal Death Wish" is a subject that I have given a lot of thought
to and have written about, and it would be easy for me to read to you a long
piece that I have written on the subject. But somehow in the atmosphere of
this delightful college, I want to have a shot at just talking about this notion
of the great liberal death wish as it has arisen in my life, as I have seen it, and
the deductions I have made from it. I should also plead guilty to being responsible for the general heading of these lectures, namely, "The Humane
Holocaust: The Auschwitz Formula."

Later on I want to say something about all this, showing how this
humane holocaust, this dreadful slaughter that began with fifty million
babies last year, will undoubtedly be extended to the senile old and the
mentally afflicted and mongoloid children, and so on, because of the large
amount of money that maintaining them costs. It is all the more ironical
when one thinks about the holocaust western audiences, and the German
population in particular, have been shuddering over, as it has been presented on their TV and cinema screens. Note this compassionate or humane
holocaust, if, as I fear, it gains momentum, will quite put that other in the

shade. And, as I shall try to explain, what is even more ironical, the actual considerations that led to the German holocaust were not, as is commonly suggested, due to Nazi terrorism, but were based upon the sort of legislation that advocates of euthanasia, or "mercy killing," in this country and in Western Europe, are trying to get enacted. It is not true that the German holocaust was simply a war crime, as it was judged to be at Nuremberg. In point of fact, it was based upon a perfectly coherent, legally enacted decree approved and operated by the German medical profession before the Nazis took over power. In other words, from the point of view of the Guinness *Book of Records* you can say that in our mad world it takes about thirty years to transform a war crime into compassionate act.

But I am going to deal with that later. I want first of all to look at this question of the great liberal death wish. And I was very delighted that you should have got here for this CCA program the film on Dostoevsky for which I did the commentary, because his novel *The Devils*[1] is the most extraordinary piece of prophecy about this great liberal death wish. All the characters in it, the circumstances of it, irresistibly recall what we mean by the great liberal death wish. You cannot imagine what a strange experience it was doing that filming in the USSR. I quoted extensively from the speech that Dostoevsky delivered when the Pushkin Memorial was unveiled in Moscow, and his words were considered to be, in terms of then current ideologies, about the most reactionary words ever spoken. They amounted to a tremendous onslaught on this very thing that we are talking about, this great liberal death wish, as it existed in Russia in the latter part of the last century. The characters in the book match very well the cast of the liberal death wish in our society and in our time. You even have the interesting fact that the old liberal, Stephen Trofimovich Verkovensky, who is a sort of male impersonator of Mrs. Eleanor Roosevelt, with all the sentimental notions that go therewith, is the father of Peter Verkovensky, a Baader Meinhof character, based on a Russian nihilist of Dostoevsky's time, Sergey Nechayef. To me, it is one of the most extraordinary pieces of modern prophecy that has ever been. Especially when Peter Verkovensky says, as he does, that what we need are a few generations of debauchery—debauchery at its most vicious and most horrible—followed by a little sweet bloodletting, and then the turmoil will begin. I put it to you that this bears a rather uneasy resemblance to the sort of thing that is happening at this moment in the Western world.

Now I want to throw my mind back to my childhood, to the sitting room in the little suburban house in south London where I grew up. On Saturday evenings my father and his cronies would assemble there, and they would plan together the downfall of the capitalist system and the replacement of it by one which was just and humane and egalitarian and peaceable, etc. These were my first memories of a serious conversation about our circumstances in the world. I used to hide in a big chair and hope not to be noticed, because I was so interested. And I accepted completely the views of these good men, that once they were able to shape the world as they wanted it to be, they would create a perfect state of affairs in which peace would reign, prosperity would expand, men would be brotherly, and considerate, and there would be no exploitation of man by man, nor any ruthless oppression of individuals. And I firmly believed that, once their plans were fulfilled, we would realize an idyllic state of affairs of such a nature. They were good men, they were honest men, they were sincere men. Unlike their prototypes on the continent of Europe, they were men from the chapels. It was a sort of spillover from the practice of nonconformist Christianity, not a brutal ideology, and I was entirely convinced that such a brotherly, contented, loving society would come to pass once they were able to establish themselves in power.

My father used to speak a lot at open air meetings, and when I was very small I used to follow him around because I adored him, as I still do. He was a very wonderful and good man. He'd had a very harsh upbringing himself, and this was his dream of how you could transform human society so that human beings, instead of maltreating one another and exploiting one another, would be like brothers. I remember he used to make quite good jokes at these outdoor meetings when we had to set up our little platform, and a few small children and one or two passersby had gathered briefly to listen. One joke I particularly appreciated and used to wait for even though I had heard a hundred times ran like this: "Well, ladies and gentlemen," my father would begin, "you tell me one thing. What is it that it is his majesty's navy and his majesty's stationery office and his majesty's customs but it's the national debt? Why isn't the debt his majesty's?" It always brought the house down.

Such was my baptism into the notion of a kingdom of Heaven on earth, into what I was going to understand ultimately to be the great liberal death wish. Inevitably, my father's heroes were the great intellectuals of the time, who banded themselves together in what was called the Fabian Society, of which he was a member—a very active member. For instance, Bernard Shaw, H. G. Wells, Harold Laski, people of that sort. All the leftist elite, like Sydney and Beatrice Webb, belonged to this Fabian Society, and in my father's eyes they were princes among men. I accepted his judgment.

Once I had a light shock when he took me to a meeting of the Fabian Society where H. G. Wells was speaking, and I can remember vividly his high squeaky voice as he said—and it stuck in my mind long afterward—"We haven't got time to read the Bible. We haven't got time to read the history of this obscure nomadic tribe in the Middle East." Subsequently, when I learned of the things that Wells *had* got time for, the observation broke upon me in all its richness.

Anyway, that for me was how my impression of life began. I was sent to Cambridge University, which of course in those days consisted very largely of boys from what we call public schools, and you call private schools. Altogether, it was for me a quite different sort of milieu, where the word *socialist* in those days—this was in 1920 when I went to Cambridge at 17— was almost unknown. We who had been to a government secondary school and then to Cambridge were regarded as an extraordinary and rather distasteful phenomenon. But my views about how the world was going to be made better remained firmly entrenched in the talk of my father and his cronies. Of course, in the meantime had come the First World War, to be followed by an almost insane outburst of expectations that henceforth peace would prevail in the world, that we would have a League of Nations to ensure that there would be no more wars, and gradually everybody would get more prosperous and everything would be better and better. That rather lugubrious figure Woodrow Wilson arrived on the scene, to be treated with the utmost veneration. I can see him now, lantern-jawed, wearing his tall hat—somehow for me he didn't fill the bill of a knight in shining armor who was going to lead us to everlasting peace. Somehow the flavor of Princeton about him detracted from that picture, but still I accepted him as an awesome figure.

My time at Cambridge was a rather desolate time. I never much enjoyed being educated, and have continued to believe that education is a rather overrated experience. Perhaps this isn't the most suitable place in the world to say that, but such is my opinion. I think that it is part of the liberal dream that somehow or other—and it was certainly my father's view—people, in becoming educated, instead of on Sundays racing their dogs or studying racing forms, or anything like that, would take to singing madrigals or reading *Paradise Lost* aloud. This is another dream that didn't quite come true.

Anyway, from Cambridge I went off to India, to teach at a Christian college there, and I must say it was an extremely agreeable experience. The college was in a remote part of what was the Travancore, but is now Kerala. It was not one of the missionary colleges, but associated with the indigenous Syrian Church, which you may know is a very ancient church, dating back to the fourth century, and now there are a million or more Syrian Christians. In this way it was quite an idyllic existence, but of course one came up against naked power for the first time. I had never thought of power before as something separate from the rest of life. But in India, under the British raj, with a relatively few white men ruling over three or four hundred million Indians, I came face to face with power unrelated to elections or any other representative device in the great liberal dream that became the great liberal death wish. However, it was a pleasant time, and of course the Indian nationalist movement was beginning, and Gandhi came to the college where I was teaching. This extraordinary little gargoyle of a man appeared, and held forth, and everybody got tremendously excited, and shouted against Imperialism, and the Empire in which at that time the great majority of the British people firmly believed, and which they thought would continue forever. If you ventured to say, as I did on the boat going to India, that it might come to an end before long, they laughed you to scorn, being firmly convinced that God had decided that the British should rule over a quarter of the world, and that nothing could ever change this state of affairs. Which again opened up a new vista about what this business of power signified, and how it worked, not as a theory, but in practice. We used to boast in those days that we had an Empire on which the sun never set, and now we have a commonwealth on which it never rises, and I can't quite say which concept strikes me as being the more derisory.

That was India, and then I came back to England and for a time taught in an elementary school in Birmingham, and married my wife, Kitty. (I wish she were here today because she's very nice. We have been married now for fifty-one years, so I am entitled to speak well of her.) She was the niece of Beatrice and Sydney Webb, so it was like marrying into a sort of aristocracy of the Left. After our wedding, we went off to Egypt, where I taught at the University of Cairo, and it was there that the dreadful infection of journalism got into my system. Turning aside from the honorable occupation of teaching, I started writing articles about the wrongs of the Egyptian people, how they were clamoring, and rightly so, for a democratic set-up, and how they would never be satisfied with less than one-man/one-vote and all that went therewith. I never heard any Egyptian say that this was his position, but I used to watch those old pashas in Groppi's café smoking their hubble-bubble pipes, and imagined that under their tabooshes was a strong feeling that they would never for an instant countenance anything less than full representative government. That at least was what I wrote in my articles, and they went flying over to England, and, like homing pigeons, in through the windows of the *Guardian* office in Manchester, at that time a high citadel of liberalism. That was where the truth was being expounded, that was where enlightenment reigned. In due course I was asked to join the editorial staff of the *Guardian*, which to me was a most marvelous thing. I may say that the work of teaching at Cairo University was not an arduous job, essentially for three reasons. One was that the students didn't understand English; the second that they were nearly always on strike or otherwise engaged in political demonstrations; and thirdly they were often stupefied with hashish. So I had a lot of leisure on my hands.

Incidentally, to be serious for a moment, it seems to me a most extraordinary thing that at that time you wouldn't have found anybody, Egyptian or English or anybody else, who wasn't absolutely clear in his mind that hashish was a most appalling and disastrous addiction. So you can imagine how strange it was forty years later for me to hear life peeresses and people like that insisting that hashish didn't do any harm to anybody, and was even beneficial. I see that in Canada it is going to be legalized, which will mean one more sad, unnecessary hazard comes into our world.

Anyway, these were the golden days of liberalism when the *Manchester Guardian* was widely read, and even believed. Despite all its misprints, you could make out roughly speaking what it was saying, and what we typed out was quite likely, to our great satisfaction, to be quoted in some paper in Baghdad or Smyrna as being the opinion of our very influential organ of enlightened liberalism. I remember my first day I was there, and somehow it symbolizes the whole experience. I was asked to write a leader—a short leader of about 120 words—on corporal punishment. At some headmasters' conference, it seemed, words had been spoken about corporal punishment and I was to produce appropriate comment. So I put my head into the room next to mine, and asked the man who was working there: "What's our line on corporal punishment?" Without looking up from his typewriter, he replied: "The same as capital, only more so." So I knew exactly what to tap out, you see. That was how I got into the shocking habit of pontificating about what was going on in the world; observing that the Greeks did not seem to *want* an orderly government, or that one despaired sometimes of the Irish having any concern for law and order; weighty pronouncement tapped out on a typewriter, deriving from nowhere, and for all one knew, concerning no one.

We were required to end anything we wrote on a hopeful note, because liberalism is a hopeful creed. And so, however appalling and black the situation that we described, we would always conclude with some sentence like: "It is greatly to be hoped that moderate men of all shades of opinion will draw together, and that wiser councils may yet prevail." How many times I gave expression to such jejune hopes! Well, I soon grew weary of this, because it seemed to me that immoderate men were rather strongly in evidence, and I couldn't see that wiser councils were prevailing anywhere. The Depression was on by that time, I am talking now of 1932–1933. It was on especially in Lancashire, and it seemed as though our whole way of life was cracking up, and, of course, I looked across at the USSR with a sort of longing, thinking that there was an alternative, some other way in which people could live, and I managed to maneuver matters so that I was sent to Moscow as the *Guardian* correspondent, arriving there fully prepared to see in the Soviet regime the answer to all our troubles, only to discover in a very short time that though it might be an answer, it was a very unattractive one.

It is difficult to convey to you what a shock this was, realizing that what I had supposed to be the new brotherly way of life my father and his cronies had imagined long before, was simply on examination an appalling tyranny, in which the only thing that mattered, the only reality, was power. So again, like the British raj, in the USSR I was confronted with power as the absolute and ultimate arbiter. However, that was a thing that one could take in one's stride. How I first came to conceive the notion of the great liberal death wish was not at all in consequence of what was happening in the USSR, which, as I came to reflect afterward, was simply the famous lines in the *Magnificat* working out: "He hath put down the mighty from their seat and hath exalted the humble and meek," whereupon, of course, the humble and meek become mighty in their turn and have to be put down. That was just history, something that happens in the world; people achieve power, exercise power, abuse power, and are booted out of power, and then it all begins again. The thing that impressed me, the thing that touched off my awareness of the great liberal death wish, my sense that Western man was, as it were, sleepwalking into his own ruin, was the extraordinary performance of the liberal intelligentsia, who, in those days, flocked to Moscow like pilgrims to Mecca. And they were one and all utterly delighted and excited by what they saw there. Clergymen walked serenely and happily through the anti-God museums, politicians claimed that no system of society could possibly be more equitable and just, lawyers admired Soviet justice, and economists praised the Soviet economy. They all wrote articles in this sense which we resident journalists knew were completely nonsensical. It is impossible to exaggerate to you the impression that this made on me. Mrs. Webb had said to Kitty and me: "You'll find that in the USSR Sydney and I are icons." As a matter of fact they were, Marxist icons.

How could this be? How could this extraordinary credulity exist in the minds of people who were adulated by one and all as maestros of discernment and judgment? It was from that moment that I began to get the feeling that a liberal view of life was not what I had supposed it to be—a creative movement which would shape the future—but rather a sort of death wish. How otherwise could you explain how people, in their own country ardent for equality, bitter opponents of capital punishment and all for more humane treatment of people in prison, supporters, in fact, of every good cause, should in the USSR prostrate themselves before a regime ruled over brutally and oppressively and arbitrarily by a privileged

party oligarchy? I still ponder over the mystery of how men displaying critical intelligence in other fields could be so astonishingly deluded. I tell
you, if ever you are looking for a good subject for a thesis, you could get a
very fine one out of a study of the books that were written by people like
the Dean of Canterbury, Julian Huxley, Harold Laski, Bernard Shaw, or the
Webbs about the Soviet regime. In the process you would come upon a
compendium of fatuity such as has seldom, if ever, existed on earth. And I
would really recommend it; after all, the people who wrote these books
were, and continue to be regarded as, pundits, whose words must be very,
very seriously heeded and considered.

I recall in their yellow jackets a famous collection in England called
the Left Book Club. You would be amazed at the gullibility that was expressed. We foreign journalists in Moscow used to amuse ourselves, as a
matter of fact, by competing with one another as to who could wish upon
one of these intelligentsia visitors to the USSR the most outrageous fantasy. We would tell them, for instance, that the shortage of milk in Moscow
was entirely due to the fact that all milk was given to nursing mothers—
things like that. If they put it in the articles they subsequently wrote, then
you would score a point. One story I floated myself, for which I received
considerable acclaim, was that the huge queues outside food shops came
about because the Soviet workers were so ardent in building socialism that
they just wouldn't rest, and the only way the government could get them to
rest for even two or three hours was organizing a queue for them to stand
in. I laugh at it all now, but at the time you can imagine what a shock it was
to someone like myself, who had been brought up to regard liberal intellectuals as the samurai, the absolute elite of the human race, to find that
they could be taken in by deceptions which a half-witted boy would see
through in an instant. I never got over that; it always remained in my mind
as something that could never be erased. I could never henceforth regard
the intelligentsia as other than credulous fools who nonetheless became
the media's prophetic voices, their heirs and successors remaining so still.
That is when I began to think seriously about the great liberal death wish.

In due course, I came back to England to await the Second World
War, in the course of which I found myself engaged in intelligence duties.
And let me tell you that if there is one thing more fantastical than news, it
is intelligence. News itself is a sort of fantasy; and when you actually go

collecting news, you realize that this is so. In a certain sense, you create news; you dream news up yourself and then send it. But that is nothing to the fantasy of intelligence. Of the two, I would say that news seems really quite a sober and considered commodity compared with your offerings when you are an intelligence agent.

Anyway, when in 1945 I found myself a civilian again, I tried to sort out my thoughts about the great wave of optimism that followed the Second World War—for me, a repeat performance. It was then that I came to realize how, in the name of progress and compassion, the most terrible things were going to be done, preparing the way for the great humane holocaust, about which I have spoken. There was, it seemed to me, a built-in propensity in this liberal world-view whereby the opposite of what was intended came to pass. Take the case of education. Education was the great mumbo-jumbo of progress, the assumption being that educating people would make them grow better and better, more and more objective and intelligent. Actually, as more and more money is spent on education, illiteracy is increasing, and I wouldn't be at all surprised if it didn't end up with virtually the whole revenue of the Western countries being spent on education, and a condition of almost total illiteracy resulting there from. It is quite on the cards.

Now I want to try to get to grips with this strange states of affairs. Let us look again at the humane holocaust. What happened in Germany was that long before the Nazis got into power, a great propaganda was undertaken to sterilize people who were considered to be useless or a liability to society, and after that to introduce what they called "mercy killing." This happened long before the Nazis set up their extermination camps at Auschwitz and elsewhere, and was based upon the highest humanitarian considerations. You see what I am getting at? On a basis of liberal–humanism, there is no creature in the universe greater than man, and the future of the human race rests only with human beings themselves, which leads infallibly to some sort of suicidal situation. It is to me quite clear that that is so, the evidence is on every hand. The efforts that men make to bring about their own happiness, their own ease of life, their own self-indulgence, will in due course produce the opposite, leading me to the absolutely inescapable conclusions that human beings cannot live and operate in this world without some concept of a being greater than themselves, and of a purpose which transcends their own egotistic or greedy desires. Once you eliminate the notion of a God, a creator, once you eliminate the notion that the creator has a purpose for us, and that life consists essentially in fulfilling that purpose, then you are abound, as Pascal points out, to induce the megalomania of which we have seen so many manifestations in our time—in the crazy dictators, as in the lunacies of people who are rich, or who consider themselves to be important or celebrated in the Western world. Alternatively, human beings relapse into mere carnality, into being animals. I see this process going on irresistibly, of which the holocaust is only just one example. If you envisage men as being only men, you are bound to see human society, not in Christian terms as a family, but as a factory-farm in which the only consideration that matters is the well-being of the livestock and the prosperity or productivity of the enterprise. That is where you land yourself. And it is in that situation that Western man is increasingly finding himself.

This might seem to be a despairing conclusion, but it isn't, you know, actually. First of all, the fact that we can't work out the liberal dream in practical terms is not bad news, but good news. Because if you could work it out, life would be too banal, too tenth-rate to be worth bothering about. Apart from that, we have been given the most extraordinary sign of the truth of things, which I continually find myself thinking about. This is that the most perfect and beautiful expressions of man's spiritual aspirations come, not from the liberal dream in any of its manifestations, but from people in the forced labor camps of the USSR. And this is the most extraordinary phenomenon, and one that of course receives absolutely no attention in the media. From the media point of view it is not news, and in any case the media do not want to know about it. But this is the fact for which there is a growing amount of evidence. I was reading about it in a long essay by a Yugoslav writer, Mihajlo Mihajlov,[2] who spent some years in a prison in Yugoslavia. He cites case after case of people who, like Solzhenitsyn, say that enlightenment came to them in the forced labor camps. They understood what freedom was when they had lost their freedom, they understood what the purpose of life was when they seemed to have no future. They say, moreover, that when it is a question of choosing whether to save your soul or your body, the man who chooses to save his soul gathers strength thereby to go on living, whereas the man who chooses to save his body at the expense of his soul loses both body and soul. In other words, fulfilling exactly what our Lord said, that he who hates his life in this world shall keep his life for all eternity, as those who love their lives in this world will assuredly lose them. Now, that is where I see the light in our darkness. There is an image I love—if the whole world were to be covered with concrete, there still would be some cracks in it, and through these cracks green shoots would come. The testimonies from the labor camps are the green shoots we can see in the world, breaking out from the monolithic power now dominating ever greater areas of it. In contradistinction, this is the liberal death wish, holding out the fallacious and ultimately destructive hope that we can construct a happy, fulfilled life in terms of our physical and material needs, and in the moral and intellectual dimensions of our mortality.

I feel so strongly at the end of my life that nothing can happen to us in any circumstances that is not part of God's purpose for us. Therefore, we have nothing to fear, nothing to worry about, except that we should rebel against His purpose, that we should fail to detect it and fail to establish some sort of relationship with Him and His divine will. On that basis, there can be no black despair, no throwing in of our hand. We can watch the institutions and social structures of our time collapse—and I think you who are young are fated to watch them collapse—and we can reckon with what seems like an irresistibly growing power of materialism and materialist societies. But, it will not happen that that is the end of the story. As St. Augustine said—and I love to think of it—when he received the news in Carthage that Rome had been sacked: Well, if that has happened, it is a great catastrophe, but we must never forget that the earthly cities that men build they destroy, but there is also the City of God which men didn't build and can't destroy. And he devoted the next seventeen years of his life to working out the relationship between the earthly city and the City of God—the earthly city where we live for a short time, and the City of God whose citizens we are for all eternity.

You know, it is a funny thing, but when you are old, as I am, there are all sorts of extremely pleasant things that happen to you. One of them is, you realize that history is nonsense, but I won't go into that now. The pleasantest thing of all is that you wake up in the night at about, say, three a.m., and you find that you are half in and half out of your battered old carcass. And it seems quite a toss-up whether you go back and resume full occupancy of your mortal body, or make off toward the bright glow you see in the sky, the lights of the City of God. In this limbo between life and death, you know beyond any shadow of doubt that, as an infinitesimal particle of God's creation, you are a participant in God's purpose for His creation, and that that purpose is loving and not hating, is creative and not destructive, is everlasting and not temporal, is universal and not particular. With this certainty comes an extraordinary sense of comfort and joy.

Nothing that happens in this world need shake that feeling; all the happenings in this world, including the most terrible disasters and suffering, will be seen in eternity as in some mysterious way a blessing, as a part of God's love. We ourselves are part of that love, we belong to that scene, and only insofar as we belong to that scene does our existence here have any reality or any worth. All the rest is fantasy—whether the fantasy of power which we see in the authoritarian states around us, or the fantasy of the great liberal death wish in terms of affluence and self-indulgence. The essential feature, and necessity of life, is to know reality, which means knowing God. Otherwise our mortal existence is, as Saint Teresa of Avila said, no more than a night in a second-class hotel.

Notes

1. Sometimes translated as *The Possessed*.
2. "Mystical Experience of the Labor Camps," included in Mihajlo Mihajlov's excellent book *Underground Notes*.

❏ ❏ ❏

Born in 1903, MALCOLM MUGGERIDGE was at various times the Moscow correspondent for the *Manchester Guardian*, a British intelligence agent in Africa during World War II, a liaison officer with the Free French, Deputy Editor of the *Daily Telegraph*, editor of *Punch*, and book reviewer for *Esquire*. Among his several books are *Something Beautiful for God* (1971), a two-volume memoir titled *Chronicles of Wasted Time* (1973), and *Confessions of a 20th-Century Pilgrim* (1988). In England he worked extensively with the BBC, starred in countless documentary films, and hosted a weekly discussion series that was immensely popular. Mr. Muggeridge passed away in 1990.

A New Vision of Man:
How Christianity Has Changed
Political Economy

Michael Novak

May 1995
Mr. Novak delivered the following speech at a Hillsdale College seminar, "God and Man: Perspectives on Christianity in the 20th Century," on the Hillsdale campus.

❏ ❏ ❏

For centuries, scholars and laymen have studied the Bible's impact on our religion, politics, education, and culture, but very little serious attention has been devoted to its impact on our economics. It is as if our actions in the marketplace have nothing to do with our spiritual beliefs. Nothing could be further from the truth. My aim here is to demonstrate how Judeo-Christianity, and Jesus, in particular, revolutionized the political economy of the ancient world and how that revolution still profoundly affects the world today.

I wish to propose for your consideration the following thesis: At least seven contributions made by Christian thinkers, meditating on the words and deeds of Jesus Christ, altered the vision of the good society proposed by the classical writers of Greece and Rome and made certain modern conceptions of political economy possible. Be warned that we are talking about foundational issues. The going won't be entirely easy.

Be warned, also, that I want to approach this subject in a way satisfying to secular thinkers. You shouldn't have to be a believer in Jesus in order to grasp the plausibility of my argument. In that spirit, let me begin, first, by citing Richard Rorty, who once wrote that as a progressive philosopher he owes more to Jesus for certain key progressive notions, such as compassion and equality, than to any of the classical writers. Analogously, in his book, *Why I am Not a Christian*, Bertrand Russell conceded that, although he took Jesus to be no more than a humanistic moral prophet, modern progressivism is indebted to Christ for the ideal of compassion.

In short, in order to recognize the crucial contributions that the coming of Christ brought into modern movements of political economy, one does not have to be a Christian. One may take a quite secular point of view and still give credit where credit is due.

Here, then, are the seven major contributions made by Jesus to our modern conceptions of political economy.

To Bring Judaism to the Gentiles

From Jerusalem, that crossroads between three continents open to the East and West, North and South, Jesus brought recognition of the One God, the Creator. The name this God gave to Himself is "I AM WHO AM"—He *is*, as opposed to the rest of us, who have no necessary or permanent hold on being. He is the One who IS; other things are those who are, but also are not. H*e* is the Creator of all things. All things that are depend upon Him. As all things spring from His action in creating them, so they depend upon Him for their being maintained in existence, their "standing out from" nothingness [E*x* + *sistere*, L., to stand out from].

The term "Creator" implies a free person; it suggests that creation was a free act, an act that did not flow from necessity. It was an act of intelligence, it was a choice, and it was willed. The Creator knew what He was doing, and He willed it; that is, "He saw that it is good." From this notion of the One God/Creator, three practical corollaries for human action follow.

Be *intelligent*. Made in the image of God, we should be attentive and intelligent, as our Creator is.

Trust liberty. As God loved us, so it is fitting for us to respond with love. Since in creating us He knew what He was doing and

He willed it, we have every reason to trust His will. He created us with understanding and free will; creation was a free act. Since He made us in His image, well ought we to say with Jefferson: "The God who gave us life gave us liberty."

Understand that history has a beginning, and an end. At a certain moment, time was created by God. Time is directed toward "building up the Kingdom of God . . . on earth as in heaven." Creation is directed toward final union with its Creator.

As many scholars have noted, the idea of "progress," like the idea of "creation," are not Greek ideas—nor are they Roman. The Greeks preferred notions of the necessary procession of the world from a First Principle. While in a limited sense they understood the progress of ideas, skills, and technologies and also saw how these could be lost, in general, they viewed history as a cycle of endless return. They lacked a notion of historical progress. The idea of history as a category distinct from nature is a Hebrew rather than a Greek idea.

Analogously, as Lord Acton argued in the essays he prepared for his *History of Liberty*, liberty is an idea coincident with the spread of Christianity. Up to a point, the idea of liberty is a Jewish idea. Every story in the Bible is about a drama involving the human will. In one chapter, King David is faithful to his Lord; in another unfaithful. The suspense always lies in what he will choose next. Nonetheless, Judaism is not a missionary religion; normally one receives Judaism by being born of a Jewish mother; in this sense, Judaism is rooted in genealogy rather than in liberty. Beyond this point, Christianity expanded the notion of liberty and made it universal. The Christian idea of liberty remains rooted in the liberty of the Creator, as in Judaism. Through Christianity, this Jewish idea becomes the inheritance of all the other peoples on earth.

Recognition of the One God/Creator means that the fundamental attitude of human beings toward God is, and ought to be, receptivity. All that we are we have received from God. This is true both of our creation and our redemption. God acts first. We respond. Everything is a gift. "Everything we look upon is blessed" (Yeats). "Grace is everywhere" (Bernanos). Thus, offering thanksgiving is our first moral obligation.

It is difficult to draw out, in brief compass, all the implications for political economy of the fact that history begins in the free act of the Creator, who made humans in His image and who gave them both existence and an impulse toward communion with their first breath. In this act of creation, in any case, Jefferson properly located (and it was the sense of the American people) not only the origin of the inner core of human rights: "... and endowed by their Creator with certain inalienable rights, including ... ," but also the perspective of providential history: "When in the course of human events. ..." The Americans were aware of creating something "new": a new world, a new order, a new science of politics. As children of the Creator, they felt no taboo against originality; on the contrary, they thought it their vocation.

Father, Son, and Holy Spirit

When Jesus spoke of God, He spoke of the communion of three persons in one. This means that, in God, the *mystery of being* and the *mystery of communion* are one. Unlike the Greeks such as Parmedides, Plato, and Aristotle, who thought of God or the N*ous* as One, living in solitary isolation, the Christian world was taught by Jesus to think of God as a communion of three. In other words, the mystery of communion, or community, is one with the very mystery of being. The sheer fact that we are alive sometimes comes over us at dusk on an autumn day, as we walk across a cornfield and in the tang of the evening air hear a crow lift off against the sky. We may pause then to wonder, in admiration and gratitude. We could so easily have not been, and yet we *are*, at least for these fragile moments. Soon another generation will take our place, and tramp over the same field. We experience wonder at the sheer fact: At this moment, we *are*. And we also apprehend the fact that we are part of a long procession of the human community in time; and that we are, by the grace of God, one with God. To exist is already something to marvel at; so great a communion is even more so. Our wonder is not so much doubled; it is squared, infinitely multiplied.

This recognition of the Trinity is not without significance for political economy. First, it inspires us with a new respect for an ideal of community not often found on this earth, a community in which each person is separate, distinct, and independent, and yet in which there is, nonetheless, communion. It teaches us that the relation between community and person is deeper and richer than we might have imagined. Christians should not simply lose themselves in community, having their personality and independence merge into an undifferentiated mass movement. On the contrary, Christianity teaches us that in true community the distinctness and independence of each person are also crucial. Persons reach their full development only in community with others. No matter how highly developed in himself or herself, a totally isolated person, cut-off from others, is regarded as something of a monster. In parallel, a community that refuses to recognize the autonomy of individual persons often uses individuals as means to "the common good," rather than treating persons as ends in themselves. Such communities are coercive and tyrannical.

Christianity, in short, opens up the ideal of catholicity which has always been a mark of true Christianity. *Katholike* means all of humanity, the whole human world. In this world, persons, and even cultures, are distinct, and have their own autonomy and claim on our respect. E *pluribus unum*. The many form one; but the one does not melt the many into the lowest common denominator. The many retain their individual vitality, and for this they show gratitude to the community that allows them, in fact encourages them, to do so. Person and community must be defined in terms of each other.

The Children of God

In Plato's *Republic*, citizens were divided in this way: A few were of gold, a slightly larger body of silver, and the vast majority of lead. The last had the souls of slaves and, therefore, were properly enslaved. Only persons of gold are truly to be treated as ends in themselves. For Judaism and Christianity, on the contrary, the God who made every single child gave worth and dignity to each of them, however weak or vulnerable. "What you do unto the least of these, you do unto me." God identified Himself with the most humble and most vulnerable.

Our Creator knows each of us by name, and understands our own individuality with a far greater clarity that we ourselves do; after all, He made us. (Thomas Aquinas once wrote that God is infinite, and so when He creates human beings in His image, He must in fact create an infinite number of them to mirror back His own infinity.) Each of us reflects only a small fragment of God's identity. If one of us is lost, the image of God intended to be reflected by that one is lost. The image of God reflected in the human becomes distorted.

In this respect, Judaism and Christianity grant a fundamental equality in the sight of God to all human beings, whatever their talents or station. This equality arises because God penetrates *below* any artificial rank, honor, or station that may on the surface differentiate one from another. He sees past those things. He sees *into* us. He sees us as we are in our uniqueness, and it is that uniqueness that He values. Let us call this form of equality by the clumsy but useful name, *equality-as-uniqueness*. Before God, we have equal weight in our *uniqueness*, not because we are *the same*, but because each of us is *different*. Each is made by God after an original design.

This conception of *equality–uniqueness* is quite different from the modern "progressive" or socialist conception of equality–sameness. The Christian notion is not a levelling notion. Neither does it delight in uniformity. On the contrary, it tries to pay heed to, and give respect to, the unique image of God in each person.

For most of its history, Christianity, like Judaism, flourished in hierarchical societies. While recognizing that every single person lives and moves in sight of God's judgment and is equally a creature of God, Christianity has also rejoiced in the differences among us and between us. God did not make us equal in talent, ability, character, office, calling, or fortune.

Equality–uniqueness is not the same as equality–sameness. The first recognizes our claim to a unique identity and dignity. The second desires to take away what is unique and to submerge it in uniformity. Thus, modern movements such as socialism have taken the original Christian impulse of equality, which they inherited, and disfigured it. Like Christianity, modern socialist movements reject the stratification of citizens into gold, silver, and lead, as in Plato's scheme. But, since they are materialistic at root, their traditional impulse has been to pull people down, to place all on the same level, to enforce uniformity. This program is inexorably coercive, unlovely, and depressing.

Compassion

It is true that virtually all peoples have traditions of compassion for the suffering, care for those in need, and concern for others. However, in most religious traditions, these movements of the heart are limited to one's own family, kin, nation, or culture. In some cultures, young males in particular have to be hard and insensitive to pain, so that they will be sufficiently cruel to enemies. Terror is the instrument intended to drive outsiders away from the territory of the tribe. In principle (though not always in practice), Christianity opposes this limitation on compassion. It teaches people the impulse to reach out, especially to the most vulnerable, to the poor, the hungry, the wretched, those in prison, the hopeless, the sick, and others. It tells humans to love their enemies. It teaches a universal compassion. It teaches people to see the dignity even of those who in the eyes of the world have lost their dignity, and those who are helpless to act on their own behalf. This is the "solidarity" whose necessity for modernity Rorty perceives.

In the name of compassion, Christianity tries to humble the mighty and to prod the rich into concern for the poor. It does not turn the young male away from being a warrior, but it does teach him to model himself on Christ, and thus to become a new type of male in human history: the knight bound by a code of compassion, the gentleman. It teaches him to learn, to be meek, humble, peaceable, kind, and generous. It introduces a new and fruitful tension between the warrior and the gentlemen, magnanimity and humility, meekness and fierce ambition.

A Universal Family

Christianity has taught human beings that an underlying imperative of history is to bring about a law-like, peaceable community among all people of good will on the entire earth. For political economy, Christianity proposes a new ideal: the entire human race is a universal family, created by the one same God, and urged to love that God. Yet at the same time, Christianity (like Judaism before it) is also the religion of a particular kind of God: not the Deity who looks down on all things from an olympian height but, in Christianity's case, a God who became *incarnate*. The Christian God, incarnate, was carried in the womb of a single woman, among a particular people, at a precise intersection of time and space, and nourished in a local community then practically unknown to the rest of the peoples on this planet. Christianity is a religion of the concrete and the universal. It pays attention to the flesh, the particular, the concrete, and each single intersection of space and time; its God is the God who made and cares for every lily of the field, every blade of grass, every hair on the head of each of us. Its God is the God of singulars, the God who Himself became a singular man. At the same time, the Christian God is the Creator of all.

In a sense, this Christian God goes beyond contemporary conceptions of "individualism" and "communitarianism." With 18th-century British statesman and philosopher Edmund Burke, Christianity sees the need for proper attention to every "little platoon" of society, to the immediate neighborhood, to the immediate family. Our social policies must be incarnate, must be rooted in the actual flesh of concrete people in their actual local, intimate worlds. At the same time, Christianity directs the attention of these little communities toward the larger communities of which they are a part. On the one hand, Christianity forbids them to be merely parochial or xenophobic. On the other hand, it warns them against becoming premature universalists, one-worlders, gnostics pretending to be pure spirits, and detached from all the limits and beauties of concrete flesh. Christianity gives warning against both extremes. It instructs us about the precarious balance between concrete and universal in our own nature. This is the mystery of catholicity.

"I Am the Truth"

The Creator of all things has total insight into all things. He knows what He has created. This gives the weak, modest minds of human beings the vocation to use their minds relentlessly, in order to penetrate the hidden layers of intelligibility that God has written into His creation. Everything in creation is in principle understandable: In fact, at every moment everything is understood by Him, who is eternal and therefore simultaneously present to all things. (In God there is no history, no past–present–future. In His insight into reality, all things are as if simultaneous. Even though in history they may unfold sequentially, they are all at once, that is, simultaneously, open to His contemplation.)

Our second president, John Adams, wrote that in giving us a notion of God as the Source of all truth, and the Judge of all, the Hebrews laid before the human race the possibility of civilization. Before the undeceivable Judgment of God, the Light of Truth cannot be deflected by riches, wealth, or worldly power. Armed with this conviction, Jews and Christians are empowered to use their intellects and to search without fear into the causes of things, their relationships, their powers, and their purposes. This understanding of Truth makes humans free. For Christianity does not teach that Truth is an illusion based upon the opinions of those in power, or merely a rationalization of powerful interests in this world. Christianity is not deconstructionist, and it is certainly not totalitarian. Its commitment to Truth beyond human purposes is, in fact, a rebuke to all totalitarian schemes and all nihilist cynicism.

Moreover, by locating Truth (with a capital T) in God, beyond our poor powers fully to comprehend, Christianity empowers human reason. It does so by inviting us to use our heads as best we can, to discern the evidences that bring us as close to Truth as human beings can attain. It endows human beings with a vocation to inquire endlessly, relentlessly, to give play to the unquenchable *eros* of the desire to understand—that most profoundly restless drive to know that teaches human beings their own finitude while it also informs them of their participation in the infinite.

The notion of Truth is crucial to civilization. As Thomas Aquinas held, civilization is constituted by conversation. Civilized persons persuade one another through argument. Barbarians club one another into submission. Civilization requires citizens to recognize that they do not possess the truth, but must be possessed by it, to the degree possible to them. Truth matters greatly. But Truth is greater than any one of us. We do not possess it; it possesses us. Therefore, humans must learn such civilizing habits as being respectful and open to others, listening attentively, trying to see aspects of the Truth that they do not as yet see. Because the search for Truth is vital to each of us, humans must argue with each other, urge each other onward, point out deficiencies in one another's arguments, and open the way for greater participation in the Truth by every one of us.

In this respect, the search for Truth makes us not only humble but also civil. It teaches us *why* we hold that every single person has an inviolable dignity: Each is made in the image of the Creator to perform noble acts, such as to understand, to deliberate, to choose, to love. These noble activities of human beings cannot be repressed without repressing the Image of God in them. Such an act would be doubly sinful. It violates the other person, and it is an offense against God.

One of the ironies of our present age is that the great philosophical advocates of the Enlightenment no longer believe in Reason (with a capital R). They have surrendered their confidence in the vocation of Reason to cynics such as to the postmodernists and deconstructionists. Such philosophers (*Sophists*, Socrates called them) hold that there is no Truth, that all things are relative, and that the great realities of life are power and interest. So we have come to an ironic pass. The children of the Enlightenment have abandoned Reason, while those they have considered unenlightened and living in darkness, the people of Jewish and Christian faith, remain today reason's (without a capital R) best defenders. For believing Jews and Christians ground their confidence in reason in the Creator of all reason, and their confidence in understanding in the One who understands everything He made—and loves it, besides.

There can be no civilization of reason, or of love, without this faith in the vocation of reason.

The Name of God: Mercy

Christianity teaches realistically not only the glories of human beings—their being made in the image of God—but also their sins, weaknesses, and evil tendencies. Judaism and Christianity are not utopian; they are quite realistic about human beings. They try to understand humans as they are, as God sees them both in their sins and in the graces that He grants them. This sharp awareness of human sinfulness was very important to the American founding.

Without ever using the term "original sin," the Founders were, in such documents as *The Federalist*, eloquent about the flaws, weaknesses, and evils to which human beings are prone. Therefore, they designed a republic that would last, not only among saints, but also among sinners. (There is no point in building a Republic for saints; there are too few of them; besides, the ones who do exist are too difficult to live with.) If you want to make a Republic that will last, you must construct it for sinners, because sinners are not just a moral majority, they are virtually a moral unanimity.

Christianity teaches that at every moment the God who made us is judging how well we make use of our liberty. And the first word of Christianity in this respect is: "Fear not. Be not afraid." For Christianity teaches that Truth is ordered to mercy. Truth is not, thank God, ordered first of all to justice. For if Truth were ordered to strict justice, not one of us would stand against the gale.

God is just, true, but the more accurate name for Him is not justice, but rather mercy. (The Latin root of this word conveys the idea more clearly: Misericordia comes from miseris + cor—give one's heart to les miserables, the wretched ones.) This name of God, Misericordia, according to St. Thomas Aquinas, is God's most fitting name. Toward our misery, He opens His heart. Precisely as sinners, He accepts us. "At the heart of Christianity lies the sinner," Charles Péguy wrote.

Yet mercy is only possible because of Judgment. Judgment Day is the Truth on which civilization is grounded. No matter the currents of opinion in our time, or any time, may be; no matter what the powers and principalities may say or do; no matter the solicitations pressing upon us from our families, friends, associates, and larger culture; no matter what the pressures may be—we will still be under the Judgment of the One who is undeceivable, who knows what is in us, and who knows the movements of our souls more clearly than we know them ourselves. In His Light, we are called to bring a certain honesty into our own lives, into our dealings with others, and into our respect for the Light that God has imparted to every human being. It is on this basis that human beings may be said to have inalienable rights, and dignity, and infinite worth.

Jesus, the Teacher

These seven recognitions lie at the root of Jewish-Christian civilization, the one that is today evasively called "Western civilization." From them, we get our deepest and most powerful notions of truth, liberty, community, person, conscience, equality, compassion, mercy, and virtue. These are the deepest ideals and energies working in our culture, as yeast works in dough, as a seed falling into the ground dies and becomes a spreading mustard tree.

These are practical recognitions. They have effects in every person and in every moment of life, and throughout society. If you stifle these notions, if you wipe them out, the institutions of the free society become unworkable. In this sense, a U.S. Supreme Court Justice once wrote, "Our institutions presuppose a Supreme Being." They do not presuppose *any* Supreme Being. They presuppose the God of Judaism and Christianity. And not only our institutions presuppose these realities. So do our conceptions of our own identity, and the daily actions of our own lives. Remove these religious foundations from our intellects, our lives, and the free society—in its complex checks and balances, and its highly articulated divisions of power—becomes incoherent to understanding and unworkable in practice.

For the present form of the free society, therefore, we owe a great deal to the intervention of Jesus Christ in history. In bringing those of us who are not Jewish the Word that brings life, in giving us a nobler conception of what it is to be human, and in giving us insight into our own weaknesses and sins, Jesus shed light available from no other source. Better than the philosophers, Jesus Christ is the teacher of many lessons indispensable for the working of the free society. These lessons may be, and have been secularized—but not without losing their center, their coherence, and their long-term persuasive power.

But that alone would be as nothing, of course, if we did not learn from Jesus that we, all of us, participate in His life, and in living with Him, live in, with and through the Father and the Holy Spirit in a glorious community of love. For what would it profit us, if we gained the whole world, and all the free institutions that flourish with it, and lost our own souls?

❑ ❑ ❑

MICHAEL NOVAK holds the George Frederick Jewett Chair in Religion, Philosophy, and Public Policy at the American Enterprise Institute. He received B.A. degrees from Stonehill College and the Gregorian University in Rome, and an M.A. in history and the philosophy of religion from Harvard University. From 1981 to 1982 he was Ambassador of the U.S. Delegation to the UN Human Rights commission in Geneva, and from 1984 to 1994 he was a member of the Board for International Broadcasting. Among his twenty-five books are *Belief and Unbelief* (1965), *Will It Liberate? Questions About Liberation Theology* (1986), *This Hemisphere of Liberty* (1990), and *On Two Wings: Humble Faith and Common Sense at the American Founding* (2001). In 1994 he received the Templeton Prize for Progress in Religion, which carries with it a million-dollar purse. Among his other awards are the International Prize of the Institution for World Capitalism (with Milton Friedman and Václav Klaus) and the Antony Fisher Prize for his classic book, *The Spirit of Democratic Capitalism*.

Religion and Democracy

Ralph Reed

April 1996

Dr. Reed delivered this speech at a Hillsdale College seminar, "Educating for Virtue," in Coeur d'Alene, Idaho.

❏   ❏   ❏

A New World

America is a nation unique in the history of the world. It is not the product of an accident or evolution. In spite of its tenuous connection to Great Britain, it is not a natural extension of an empire. America is literally, in the words of 17th-century European explorers, a "New World."

Its founders were free to decide its future, and they decided, with conscious purpose, to invent a nation the like of which had never been seen. Thus America is a nation with no kings, no royalty, and no privileged classes. It is a nation held together by a common bond and a common vision—a bond of common experience and a vision of uncommon greatness. America is George Washington's "common country," John Adams' "glorious morning," and Abraham Lincoln's "inestimable jewel."

America is also a nation in which one becomes American not by accident of birth or by ethnic heritage, but by *subscribing to an idea*. No one truly becomes a Frenchman merely by moving to France. No one becomes a Spaniard merely by moving to Spain. But America has lifted its lamp beside the golden door of entry to immigrants of all races and all nations and bids them welcome to what Irving Howe called "the good country."

It is not blood or marriage that counts but a vision—a vision of a society based on two fundamental beliefs. The first belief is that all men, created equal in the eyes of God with certain unalienable rights, are free to pursue the longings of their heart. The second belief is that the sole purpose of government is to protect those rights.

The first Americans shared this deeply spiritual vision. Most Americans still do. That is why, in the words of a remarkable cover story on religion in America that appeared last year in U.S. *News and World Report*, the United States is—with the sole exception of Israel—the most devoutly religious nation in the entire world. It is a fact borne out in experience, not simply in magazine cover stories. According to public opinion surveys, 92 percent of all Americans believe in God; 83 percent believe that the Bible is the infallible word of God; and 57 percent pray daily. Nearly 130 million attend church every Sunday. That means, thank goodness, that there are more people worshipping God on Sunday morning than are watching 60 *Minutes* on Sunday night.

There can be no better testimony to the faith of our nation than the reception that Pope John Paul II received when he came to the United States recently. Millions of Protestants and Catholics welcomed his message of spiritual renewal. Americans of every faith and no faith at all watched and listened as this remarkable man of God called on us to remember that there is more to life than ourselves.

The Faith of Our Founders

The Pope's message was far from new. It was the same message delivered by our founders. The American Revolution, which established a new nation, was not merely a revolution inspired by political or economic oppression but was a revolution of faith, arising from a great spiritual awakening that was sweeping the world in the 18th century. It should be of little surprise to us, then, to find the affirmation in the Declaration of Independence that there are certain truths that are "self-evident, that all men are created equal, that they are endowed by their Creator with certain unalienable rights." The founding fathers were certain that these rights are granted by God, are afforded His protection, and are not to be infringed upon by government.

The "father of our country," George Washington, wrote, "I am sure there never was a people who had more reason to acknowledge a divine interposition in their affairs, than those of the U.S. I should be pained to believe . . . that they failed to consider the omnipotence of God, who is alone able to protect them."

Our nation's second president, John Adams, added, "Our Constitution was designed for a moral and religious people only. It is wholly inadequate for any other." By this, President Adams did not mean that the Constitution was meant for people of any specific faith. He opposed religious tests for public office, as do I and all Americans. The point Adams made was far more profound. He meant that to create a nation where government was small, limited, and confined to enumerated functions, one must have a virtuous citizenry animated by faith in God and moral values.

Our founders possessed a view of the world and government that necessarily presupposed a people obedient to an internalized code of conduct—based upon that first, and best, code of law found in the books of Moses—that made a large central government superfluous. It was this view that the great French observer Alexis de Tocqueville wrote about in the early 19th century: "The Americans combine the notions of [religion] and liberty so intimately in their minds, that it is impossible to make them conceive of one without the other."

From the Quakers in Pennsylvania to the Congregationalists in New England and the Catholics in Maryland and the Baptists in Virginia, America is a nation undergirded by faith, built by faith, and enlivened by faith. And it is not a faith in word alone—it is an active, transforming faith. Look around today and what you will see are the fruits of our national faith. Throughout our history, America's faithful millions have founded orphanages, hospitals, lending libraries, and charities. America's first public schools were founded by clergymen. Her first colleges were divinity schools.

Children learned to read by using the Bible as a textbook. *McGuffey's Readers*, which sold 120 million copies during the 19th century, contained lessons drawn directly from Scripture. Historian David Herbert Donald points out that Abraham Lincoln, one of the most well-read presidents in our history, enjoyed only a single year of formal schooling. On the dirt floor of a log cabin, young Lincoln learned how to read by poring over the pages of his mother's Bible. The first lesson in his first spelling book read as follows: "No man can put off the law of God."

When Noah Webster published the first American dictionary in 1828, he used Bible verses as definitions. There was no false wall dividing private faith and public service in Webster's day. He was an author, teacher, and preacher who founded a college and served in Congress.

The Fourth Great Awakening

Lincoln and Webster understood what too many today have forgotten: The importance of faith to the public institutions in a democratic republic. Yet that connection today is a source of vigorous controversy. As we prepare for the 1996 presidential election, a crucial debate rages in the land over the role of religion in our public life and the role that religious believers should play in our politics.

The religious conservative vote, so vital to the Republican landslide in 1994, is now one of the largest, if not the largest, single voting bloc in the electorate. According to exit polls taken during the 1994 election, fully one-third of all voters were self-identified evangelicals and pro-family Roman Catholics. They cast 70 percent of their ballots for Republicans and only 24 percent for Democrats. The pendulum swing of evangelical voters has transformed the South into a virtually one-party region again, this time favoring the Republicans. The Catholic vote went Republican in 1994 for the first time since Irish Catholics landed on these shores more than a century and a half ago. The 1996 election will not be decided by the union vote, the feminist vote, the minority vote, or the third party vote. It will be decided by the religious vote.

What we are witnessing is nothing less than the largest mobilization of active religious believers in recent memory. And if history is any guide, this mobilization is the sign of another period of great transformation in America, for political change in the United States has always been rooted in religious upheaval. Nobel Prize-winning economic historian Robert Fogel argues that the current rightward shift in American politics can be traced to a new American religious revival, a "Fourth Great Awakening." The First Great Awakening, which began in 1730, helped bring on the revolutionary movement, the second in 1800 sparked the anti-slavery movement, and the third in 1890 gave rise to the progressive impulse. Now, Fogel suggests, the tectonic plates of a religious culture have shifted again, with vast political consequences.

Since the mid-1960s, mainline church membership has declined by one-fourth. That decline, however, is not indicative of a general decline in American faith. And it has been more than made up for by the skyrocketing popularity of conservative and evangelical churches in which membership has more than doubled. Pentecostal and fundamentalist revivals have converted millions of people. Nesting baby boomers are returning in droves to the churches and synagogues of their youth. With 15.2 million members, the Southern Baptist Convention has become the largest Protestant denomination in the world.

Religious Bigotry

The result is a complete transformation of America 's churchgoing population. Today, the typical American churchgoer is orthodox in faith, traditionalist in outlook, and conservative on cultural and political issues. Yet as active religious believers move beyond the pews and into public life, a strange and disturbing hostility greets them. Instead of being welcomed into the political arena and into a culture generally acknowledged to be in crisis, they are confronted by an intolerance that frequently curdles into religious bigotry.

This bigotry is manifested in many different settings. In a South Carolina race in 1994, a political candidate said of his opponent, "[H]is only qualifications for office are that he handles snakes and speaks fluently in tongues." In 1995, one candidate for the presidency denounced the nation's religious conservatives as "fringe" and "extremist." And in a bizarre twist, a candidate for the U.S. Senate in Massachusetts in 1995 was denounced not because of his stand on issues or ethical problems, but because he had once been an elder in a conservative church. The candidate was Mitt Romney. The accuser was Senator Edward M. Kennedy.

It was ironic that Senator Kennedy was making his accusations almost thirty-five years to the day after his brother, then-Senator John F. Kennedy, Jr., was fending off charges that his Roman Catholicism disqualified him from seeking the office of president of the United States. In a speech to the Greater Houston Ministerial Association in 1960, Kennedy said, "The issue in this campaign should be not what kind of church I believe in, for that should matter only to me. It should be what kind of America I believe in."

What Kind of America?

What kind of America do religious conservatives believe in? It is an America in which we would all like to live, a nation of safe streets, strong families, schools that work, marriages that stay together, with a smaller government, lower taxes, and civil rights for all. Religious conservatives do not countenance discrimination—or special rights—for anyone. Our faith is simple, and our agenda is direct.

For either political party to attack persons holding these views as "fanatics," "extremists," or worse, violates a basic American spirit of fairness. More than that, it runs counter to all we are as a nation and all we aspire to be as a people. For 200 years, America has pursued its vision, maintained its firm foundation, and achieved greatness because it honors God and welcomes people of faith into its public life. But in the thirty-five years since John F. Kennedy uttered his eloquent warning, we have lost our way. People of faith have become victims of the worst forms of stereotyping, marginalization, and demonology.

In the words of Yale law professor Stephen L. Carter, "a culture of disbelief" threatens our society. In the place of core beliefs and time-honored values many of our elites in the academy, the media, and government have promoted a different sort of value system—a system that presupposes the inability of Americans to care for themselves through a culture of compassion. This system is based not on the relevance and benevolence of God but on the ability of government to meet every need and provide every solution.

It is not a workable system. Witness the welfare state, once measured by the height of its aspirations and now measured by the depth of its failures. We read about them every morning in newspapers and see them every evening on television. Social pathologies once imagined only in our darkest nightmares are a daily reality. In 1960 only 5 percent of all children born in America were born out of wedlock. Today that figure is 33 percent and rising. In our largest cities as many as 67 percent of the children born today can claim no father.

The Carnegie Institute recently released a study detailing the carnage that is afflicting our young people. One in three adolescents has used illegal drugs before the age of thirteen. Since 1985, the murder and suicide rates for ten- to fourteen-year-olds have doubled. Former education secretary Bill Bennett has said that what we do to our children, they will do to society as adults. That is only partly true; many are not waiting until adulthood before turning to crime and forms of violence that were once unthinkable for children. A television correspondent recently asked a group of children what their greatest concern in life was. A seven-year-old African American boy raised his hand and said, "Gangs." Imagine that. A seven-year-old boy who goes to bed every night worrying about whether he will be cut down by gangs the next day.

Reaffirming the Role of Faith in Public Life

Not too long ago, the novelist John Updike wrote, "The fact that we live better than our counterparts in Eastern Europe and the former Soviet Union cannot ease the pain that we no longer live nobly." Our culture is testimony to the awful truth of his words. We may erect skyscrapers of silver that rise from streets paved with gold, but if our inner cities resemble Beirut, our children pass through metal detectors into schools that are war zones, and one out of every four high school graduates cannot read his diploma, then we will have failed ourselves, failed our nation, and failed our God. We cannot and must not fail. There is too much at stake.

What is the answer? We must begin by reaffirming the role of faith in our public life.

First Amendment Rights for Religious Believers

Let me be clear: I support the separation of church and state. I believe in a nation that is not officially Christian, Jewish, or Muslim. But I also believe in the right under the First Amendment to freedom of speech, including speech with religious content.

Yet the same Congress that begins every session with an organized prayer denies that right to students in our public schools. The same Supreme Court that issues rulings from a bench beneath an inscription of the Ten Commandments carved in granite has ruled that those commandments cannot be placed on a bulletin board in a public building.

These rulings have real consequences. Recently, a fourth grader in St. Louis, Raymond Raines, received a week-long detention. His crime? Bowing his head and praying before lunch. On at least three different occasions, school officials interrupted the intransigent Raymond in the middle of his prayer and hauled him off to the principal's office. Finally, the school attempted to extinguish this politically incorrect behavior by punishing Raymond with detention.

In southern California, students at a public high school were forbidden from handing out leaflets inviting other students to their Bible study group, even though California has a statute specifically allowing students to distribute petitions and literature. In another case, a fifth-grade public school teacher was told by the assistant principal that he could not have a Bible on top of his desk, that he could not read the Bible during silent reading period, and that he could not have two illustrated books of Bible stories in the classroom library of over 350 volumes. And in a scene repeated hundreds of times throughout the country every May and June, nervous administrators censor high school students and forbid all references to God and the Bible in graduation speeches.

Re-Entering Politics

If we are to reaffirm the role of religion in public life, we must also encourage those with strong spiritual values to re-enter politics after too many years of self-imposed retreat. Religious believers must become full citizens, with a place at the table and a voice in the conversation we call democracy. Their involvement should be a source of celebration, not fear. Their participation is not a threat to democracy but is essential to it. And as they enter the political arena, people of faith should not be asked to leave their moral convictions at the door. On issues such as strengthening the family and protecting human life, they are a voice for the voiceless, a defender of the defenseless, and a protector of the innocent.

Let me communicate not with code words but with clarity, not with ambiguity but with honesty and candor. For Republicans, who have welcomed religious conservatives into their party in recent years, this is a time of decision—a time to decide whether to be the party of Lincoln and Reagan or the party of retreat and accommodation. A time to stand for or to blur the distinction between what is just and unjust. A time to choose between reaffirming moral commitments or succumbing to the timid voices of compromise lurking in the wilderness. I do not speak of a debate over taxes, the budget, or trade. I speak of the most basic and defining issue of all: the sanctity of innocent human life. The Republican Party will not and cannot, in my view, remain the majority party that it became in 1994 if it tears from the fabric of its cherished history its noble heartfelt affirmation of the value of every single human being, including the aged, the infirm, and the unborn.

I freely acknowledge that not all share this view or the faith that inspires it. That is one of the great privileges of a democracy; I am confident that our views will be tested and our proposals improved by vigorous and open debate. But what must be acknowledged is the affirming and healing role that faith plays in society. Just as we acknowledge that at times in the past religion has been twisted to evil ends—such as when the Nazis trumpeted their horrific belief in the superiority of the Aryan race and when Muslim terrorists committed unspeakable acts of terrorism against innocent civilians while invoking the name of God—we must acknowledge the good ends and the enormous blessings of religion. If we can look without prejudice at the real historical record, then together we can bridge the differences that separate us and heal our land.

Recognizing the Limits of Politics

We must also recognize the limits of politics. As important as civic involvement is to a restoration of values, it cannot legislate what can only spring from the heart and soul. Politics alone cannot restore a land of loving parents, of strong marriages, of lullabies sung to sleeping babies and bedtime stories read to wide-eyed children. That work is too important to be left to the government. It is best done by mothers and fathers, churches and synagogues, home and hearth.

It is my hope that in the days and weeks and months and years to come that this will be an agenda and a vision shared by all Americans. We are a people of many faiths and many races. That is the genius of America. Our motto translated means, "Out of many, one." May it be so in our time.

❏ ❏ ❏

RALPH REED, JR. heads up Century Strategies, a political consulting firm. He received his B.A. from the University of Georgia and his Ph.D. in American history from Emory University. From 1982 to 1984 he served as Executive Director of the College Republican National Committee, where he supervised a grassroots network of 100,000 members on 1,000 campuses with a $600,000 budget. In 1984, he founded Students for America, of which he became Executive Director and built a grassroots conservative student network of 10,000 members on 200 campuses in 41 states. He was the Executive Director of the Christian Coalition from its inception in 1989 until the summer of 1997, at which time it had over 1.7 million members and supporters organized in 1,700 local chapters in all 50 states. His columns have appeared in the *New York Times*, *The Wall Street Journal*, *National Review*, and *Policy Review*. He is the author of *Politically Incorrect: The Emerging Faith Factor in American Politics* (1994).

CULTURE

❑ ❑ ❑

Television: The Cyclops That Eats Books

Larry Woiwode

February 1992

Mr. Woiwode delivered the following speech at a Hillsdale College seminar, "Freedom, Responsibility, and the American Literary Tradition," on the Hillsdale campus.

❏ ❏ ❏

What is destroying America today is not the liberal breed of one-world politicians, or the IMF bankers, or the misguided educational elite, or the World Council of Churches; these are largely symptoms of a greater disorder. If there is any single institution to blame, it is, to use the cozy diminutive, "TV."

TV is more than a medium; it has become a full-fledged institution, backed by billions of dollars each season. Its producers want us to sit in front of its glazed-over electronic screen, press our clutch of discernment through the floorboards, and sit in a spangled, zoned-out state ("couch potatoes," in current parlance) while we are instructed in the proper liberal tone and attitude by our present-day Plato and Aristotle—Dan Rather and Tom Brokaw. These television celebrities have more temporal power than the teachings of Aristotle and Plato have built up over the centuries.

Television, in fact, has greater power over the lives of most Americans than any educational system or government or church. Children are particularly susceptible. They are mesmerized, hypnotized, and tranquilized by TV. It is often the center of their world; even when the set is turned off, they continue to tell stories about what they've seen on it. No wonder, then, that as adults they are not prepared for the front line of life; they simply have no mental defenses to confront the reality of the world.

The Truth About TV

One of the most disturbing truths about TV is that it eats books.

Once out of school, nearly 60 percent of all adult Americans have *never read a single book,* and most of the rest read only one book a year. Alvin Kernan, author of *The Death of Literature,* says that reading books "is ceasing to be the primary way of knowing something in our society." He also points out that bachelor's degrees in English literature have declined by 33 percent in the last twenty years and that in many universities the courses are largely reduced to remedial reading. American libraries, he adds, are in crisis, with few patrons to support them.

Thousands of teachers at the elementary, secondary, and college levels can testify that their students' writing exhibits a tendency toward a superficiality that wasn't seen, say, ten or fifteen years ago. It shows up not only in the students' lack of analytical skills but in their poor command of grammar and rhetoric. I have been asked by a graduate student what a semicolon is. The mechanics of the English language have been tortured to pieces by TV. Visual, moving images—which are the venue of television—cannot be held in the net of careful language. They want to break out. They really have nothing to do with language. So language, grammar, and rhetoric have become fractured.

Recent surveys by dozens of organizations also suggest that up to 40 percent of the American public is functionally illiterate; that is, our citizens' reading and writing abilities, if they have any, are so seriously impaired as to render them, in that handy jargon of our times, "dysfunctional." The problem isn't just in our schools or in the way reading is taught: TV teaches people *not* to read. It renders them incapable of engaging in an art that is now perceived as *strenuous,* because it is an active art, not a passive hypnotized state.

Passive as it is, television has invaded our culture so completely that you see its effects in every quarter, even in the literary world. It shows up in supermarket paperbacks, from Stephen King (who has a certain clever skill) to pulp fiction. These are really forms of verbal TV—literature that is so superficial that those who read it can revel in the same sensations they experience when they are watching TV.

Even more importantly, the growing influence of television has, Kernan says, changed people's habits and values and affected their assumptions about the world. The sort of reflective, critical, and value-laden thinking encouraged by books has been rendered obsolete. In this context, we would do well to recall the Cyclopes—the race of giants that, according to Greek myth, predated man.

Here is a passage from the well-known classicist Edith Hamilton's summary of the encounter between the mythic adventurer Odysseus and the Cyclops named Polyphemus, as Odysseus is on his way home from the Trojan Wars. Odysseus and his crew have found Polyphemus's cave:

> At last he came, hideous and huge, tall as a great mountain crag. Driving his flock before him he entered and closed the cave's mouth with a ponderous slab of stone. Then looking around he caught sight of the strangers, and cried out in a dreadful booming voice, "Who are you who enter unbidden the house of Polyphemus? Traders or thieving pirates?" They were terror-stricken at the sight and sound of him, but Odysseus made shift to answer, and firmly too: "Shipwrecked warriors from Troy are we, and your suppliants, under the protection of Zeus, the suppliants' god." But Polyphemus roared out that he cared not for Zeus. He was bigger than any god and feared none of them. With that, he stretched out his mighty arms and in each great hand seized one of the men and dashed his brains out on the ground. Slowly he feasted off them to the last shred, and then, satisfied, stretched himself out across the cavern and slept. He was safe from attack. None but he could roll back the huge stone before the door, and if the horrified men had been able to summon courage and strength enough to kill him they would have been imprisoned there forever.

To discover their fate, read the book, preferably Robert Fitzgerald's masterful translation if you don't know Greek. What I find particularly appropriate about this myth as it applies today is that, first, the Cyclops imprisons these men in darkness, and that, second, he beats their brains out before he devours them. It doesn't take much imagination to apply this to the effects of TV on us and our children.

TV's Effect on Learning

Quite literally, TV *affects the way people think*. In *Four Arguments for the Elimination of Television* (1978), Jerry Mander quotes from the Emery Report, prepared by the Center for Continuing Education at the Australian National University, Canberra, that when we watch television, "our usual processes of thinking and discernment are semi-functional at best." The study also argues ". . . that while television appears to have the potential to provide useful information to viewers—and is celebrated for its educational function—the technology of television and the inherent nature of the viewing experience actually inhibit learning as we usually think of it." And its final judgment is: "The evidence is that television not only destroys the capacity of the viewer to attend, it also, by taking over a complex of direct and indirect neural pathways, decreases vigilance—the general state of arousal which prepares the organism for action should its attention be drawn to a specific stimulus."

We have all experienced this last reaction:

"Dad, it's time to—"
"Go on, get out of here!"
"But Dad, Mom just fell down the—"
"Leave me alone, can't you see I'm watching the Super Bowl?"

How are our neural pathways taken over? We think we are looking at a picture, or an image of something, but what we are actually seeing is thousands of dots of light blinking on and off in a strobe effect that is calculated to happen rapidly enough to keep us from recognizing the phenomenon. More than a decade ago, Mander and others pointed to instances of "TV epilepsy," in which those watching this strobe effect overextended their capacities, and the *New England Journal of Medicine* recently honored this affliction with a medical classification: video game epilepsy.

Shadows on the Screen

Television also teaches that people aren't quite real; they are images–gray-and-white shadows or technicolor little beings who move in a medium no thicker than a sliver of glass, created by this bombardment of electrons.

Unfortunately, the tendency is to start thinking of them in the way children think when they see too many cartoons: that people are merely objects that can be zapped. Or that can fall over a cliff and be smashed to smithereens and pick themselves up again. This contentless violence of cartoons has no basis in reality. Actual people aren't images but substantial, physical, corporeal beings with souls.

And, of course, the violence on television engenders violence; there have been too many studies substantiating this to suggest otherwise. One that has been going on for thirty years, begun by the psychologist Leonard Eron, began research on 875 eight-year-olds in New York state. Analyzing parental childrearing practices and aggressiveness in school, Eron discovered that the determining factor is the amount of TV parents permit their children to watch.

Eron's present partner in this extensive ongoing study, University of Illinois professor of psychology Rowell Huesmann, has written:

> When the research was started in 1960, television viewing was not a major focus. But in 1970, in the 10-year follow-up, one of the best predictions we could find of aggressive behavior in a teenage boy was how much violence he watched as a child. In 1981, we found that the adults who had been convicted of the most serious crimes were those same ones who had been the more aggressive teen-agers, and who had watched the most television violence as children.

Where is this report? Buried in an alumni publication of the University of Illinois. In 1982, the National Institute of Mental Health published its own study: "Television and Behavior: Ten Years of Scientific Progress and Implications for the '80s." This report stated that there is "overwhelming" evidence that violence on TV lends to aggressive behavior in children and teenagers. Those findings were duly reported by most of the major media in the early 1980s and then were forgotten.

Why do such reports sink into oblivion? Because the American audience does not want to face the reality of TV. They are too consumed by their love for it.

TV: Eating Out Our Substance

TV eats books. It eats academic skills. It eats positive character traits. It even eats family relationships. How many families do you know spend the dinner hour in front of the TV, seldom communicating with one another? How many have a television on while they have breakfast or prepare for work or school?

And what about school? I have heard college professors say of their students, "Well, you have to entertain them." One I know recommends using TV and film clips instead of lecturing, "throwing in a commercial every ten minutes or so to keep them awake." This is not only a patronizing attitude, it is an abdication of responsibility: A teacher should teach. But TV eats the principles of people who are supposed to be responsible, transforming them into passive servants of the Cyclops.

TV eats out our substance. Mander calls this the mediation of experience: "[With TV] what we see, hear, touch, smell, feel and understand about the world has been processed for us." And, when we "cannot distinguish with certainty the natural from the interpreted, or the artificial from the organic, then all theories of the ideal organization of life become equal." In other words, TV teaches that all lifestyles and all values are equal, and that there is no clearly defined right and wrong. In his *Amusing Ourselves to Death*, one of the more brilliant recent books on the tyranny of television, the author Neil Postman wonders why nobody has pointed out that television possibly oversteps the injunction in the Decalogue against making graven images.

In the 1960s and 1970s, many of the traditional standards and mores of society came under heavy assault; indeed, they were blown apart, largely with the help of television, which was just coming into its own. There was an air of unreality about many details of daily life. Even the "big" moral questions suffered distortion when they were reduced to TV images. During the Vietnam conflict there was graphic violence—soldiers and civilians actually dying—on screen. One scene that shocked the nation was an execution in which the victim was shot in the head with a pistol on prime-time TV. People "tuned in" to the war every night, and their opinions were largely formed by what they viewed, as if the highly complex and controversial issues about the causes, conduct, and resolution of the war could be summed up in these superficial broadcasts.

You saw the same phenomena again in the recent war in the Gulf. With stirring background music and sophisticated computer graphics, each network's banner script read across the screen, "WAR IN THE GULF," as if it were just another TV program. War isn't a program. It is a dirty, bloody mess. People are killed daily. Yet, television all but teaches that this carnage is merely another diversion, a form of blockbuster entertainment—the big show with all the international stars present.

In the last years of his life, Malcolm Muggeridge, a pragmatic and caustic TV personality and print journalist who embraced religion in later life, warned:

> From the first moment I was in the studio, I felt that it was far from being a good thing. I felt that television [would] ultimately be inimical to what I most appreciate, which is the expression of truth, expressing your reactions to life in words. I think you'll live to see the time when literature will be quite a rarity because, more and more, the presentation of images is preoccupying.

Muggeridge concluded:

> I don't think people are going to be preoccupied with ideas. I think they are going to live in a fantasy world where you don't need any ideas. The one thing that television can't do is express ideas. . . . There is a danger in translating life into an image, and that is what television is doing. In doing it, it is falsifying life. Far from the camera's being an accurate recorder of what is going on, it is the exact opposite. It cannot convey reality nor does it even want to.

❏ ❏ ❏

Larry Woiwode is the author of several novels, including *What I'm Going to Do, I Think* (1973), *Beyond the Bedroom Wall* (1975), *Poppa John* (1981), and *The Neumiller Stories* (1991). Three of these have been chosen "Best Books of the Year" by the *New York Times Book Review*. A former college professor who lives on a working ranch in North Dakota, Mr. Woiwode has also written short stories and poems for publications such as *Atlantic Monthly*, the *New Yorker*, and *Harper's*, and nonfiction books such as *Acts* (1993) and *What I Think I Did* (2001).

The New Segregation

Shelby Steele

August 1992

Dr. Steele delivered this speech at a Hillsdale College seminar, "Thought Police on Campus: Is Academic Freedom in Danger?," on the Hillsdale campus.

❑   ❑   ❑

The civil rights movement of the 1950s and 1960s culminated in the 1964 Civil Rights Act and the 1965 Voting Rights Act—two monumental pieces of legislation that have dramatically altered the fabric of American life. During the struggle for their passage, a new source of power came into full force. Black Americans and their supporters tapped into the moral power inspired by a 300-year history of victimization and oppression and used it to help transform society, to humanize it, to make it more tolerant and open. They realized, moreover, that the victimization and oppression that blacks had endured came from one "marriage"—a marriage of race and power. They had to stop those who said, "merely because we are white, we have the power to dominate, enslave, segregate and discriminate."

Race should not be a source of power or advantage or disadvantage for anyone in a free society. This was one of the most important lessons of the original civil rights movement. The legislation it championed during the 1960s constituted a new "emancipation proclamation." For the first time segregation and discrimination were made illegal. Blacks began to enjoy a degree of freedom they had never experienced before.

Delayed Anger

This did not mean that things changed overnight for blacks. Nor did it ensure that their memory of past injustice was obliterated. I hesitate to borrow analogies from the psychological community, but I think this one does apply: Abused children do not usually feel anger until many years after the abuse has ended, that is, after they have experienced a degree of freedom and normalcy. Only after civil rights legislation had been enacted did blacks at long last begin to feel the rage they had suppressed. I can remember that period myself. I had a tremendous sense of delayed anger at having been forced to attend segregated schools. (My grade school was the first school to be involved in a desegregation suit in the North.) My rage, like that of other blacks, threatened for a time to become all-consuming.

Anger was both inevitable and necessary. When suppressed, it eats you alive; it has got to come out, and it certainly did during the 1960s. One form was the black power movement in all of its many manifestations, some of which were violent. There is no question that we should condemn violence, but we should also understand why it occurs. You cannot oppress people for over three centuries and then say it is all over and expect them to put on suits and ties and become decent attaché-carrying citizens and go to work on Wall Street.

Once my own anger was released, my reaction was that I no longer had to apologize for being black. That was a tremendous benefit and it helped me come to terms with my own personal development. The problem is that many blacks never progressed beyond their anger.

The Politics of Difference

The black power movement encouraged a permanent state of rage and victimhood. An even greater failing was that it rejoined race and power—the very "marriage" that civil rights legislation had been designed to break up. The leaders of the original movement said, "Anytime you make race a source of power you are going to guarantee suffering, misery and inequity." Black power leaders declared: "We're going to have power because we're black."

Well, is there any conceivable difference between black power and white power? When you demand power based on the color of your skin, aren't you saying that equality and justice are impossible? Somebody is going to be in, somebody is going to be out. Somebody is going to win, somebody is going to lose, and race is once again a source of advantage for some and disadvantage for others. Ultimately, black power was not about equality or justice; it was, as its name suggests, about power.

And when blacks began to demand entitlements based on their race, feminists responded with enthusiasm, "We've been oppressed, too!" Hispanics said, "We're not going to let this bus pass us by," and Asians said, "We're not going to let it pass us by either." Eskimos and American Indians quickly hopped on the bandwagon, as did gays, lesbians, the disabled, and other self-defined minorities.

By the 1970s, the marriage of race and power was once again firmly established. Equality was out: The "politics of difference" was in. From then on, everyone would rally around the single quality that makes them different from the white male and pursue power based on that quality. It is a very simple formula. All you have to do is identify that quality, whatever it may be, with victimization. And victimization is itself, after all, a tremendous source of moral power.

The politics of difference demanded shifting the entire basis of entitlement in America. Historically, entitlement was based on the rights of citizenship elaborated in the Declaration of Independence and the U.S. Constitution. This was the kind of entitlement that the original civil rights movement leaders claimed for blacks: recognition of their rights as American citizens to equal treatment under the law. They did not claim, "We deserve rights and entitlements because we are black," but, "We deserve them because we are citizens of the United States and like all other citizens are due these rights." The politics of difference changed all that. Blacks and other minorities began demanding entitlement solely based on their history of oppression, their race, their gender, their ethnicity, or whatever quality that allegedly made them victims.

Grievance Identities

By the 1980s, the politics of difference had, in turn, led to the establishment of "grievance identities." These identities are not about such things as the great contributions of women throughout history or the rich culture of black Americans. To have a strong identity as a woman, for example, means that you are against the "oppressive male patriarchy"—period. To have a strong identity as a black means that you are against racist white America—period. You have no choice but to fulfill a carefully defined politically correct role: (1) you must document the grievance of your group; (2) you must testify to its abiding and ongoing alienation; and (3) you must support its sovereignty. As a black who fails any of these three requirements you are not only politically incorrect, you are a traitor, an "Uncle Tom." You are blaming the victim, you are letting whites off the hook, and you are betraying your people.

In establishing your grievance identity, you must turn your back on the enormous and varied fabric of life. There is no legacy of universal ideas or common human experience. There is only one dimension to your identity: anger against oppression. Grievance identities are thus "sovereignties" that compete with the sovereignties of the nation itself. Blacks, women, Hispanics, and other minorities are not even American citizens anymore. They are citizens of sovereignties with their own right to autonomy.

The New Segregation on Campus

The marriage of race and power, the politics of difference, and grievance identities—these are nurtured by the American educational establishment. They have also acted on that establishment and affected it in significant ways. After a talk I gave recently at a well-known university, a woman introduced herself as the chairperson of the women's studies department. She was very proud of the fact that the university had a separate degree-granting program in women's studies. I stressed that I had always been very much in favor of teaching students about the contributions of women. But I asked her what it was that students gained from segregated women's studies that could not be gained from studying within the traditional liberal arts disciplines. Her background was in English, as was mine, so I added, "What is a female English professor in the English department doing that is different from what a female English professor in the women's studies department is doing? Is she going to bring a different methodology to bear? What is it that academically justifies a segregated program for women, or for blacks, or any other group? Why not incorporate such studies into the English department, the history department, the biology department, or into any of the other regular departments?"

As soon as I began to ask such questions I noticed a shift in her eyes and a tension in her attitude. She began to see me as an enemy and quickly made an excuse to end the conversation. This wasn't about a rational academic discussion of women's studies. It was about the *sovereignty of the feminist identity,* and unless I tipped my hat to that identity by saying, "Yes, you have the right to a separate department," no further discussion or debate was possible.

Meanwhile, the politics of difference is overtaking education. Those with grievance identities demand separate buildings, classrooms, offices, clerical staff—even separate photocopiers. They all want to be segregated universities within the universities. They want their own space—their sovereign territory. Metaphorically, and sometimes literally, they insist that not only the university but society at large must pay tribute to their sovereignty.

Today there are some 500 women's studies departments. There are black studies departments, Hispanic studies departments, Jewish studies departments, Asian studies departments. They all have to have space, staff, and budgets. What are they studying that can't be studied in other departments? They don't have to answer this question, of course, but when political entitlement shifted away from citizenship to race, class and gender, a shift in cultural entitlement was made inevitable.

Those with grievance identities also demand *extra* entitlements far beyond what should come to us as citizens. As a black, I am said to "deserve" this or that special entitlement. No longer is it enough just to have the right to attend a college or university on an equal basis with others or to be treated like anyone else. Schools must set aside special money and special academic departments just for me, based on my grievance. Some campuses now have segregated dorms for black students who demand to live together with people of their "own kind." Students have lobbied for separate black student unions, black yearbooks, black homecoming dances, black graduation ceremonies—again, all so that they can be comfortable with their "own kind."

One representative study at the University of Michigan indicates that 70 percent of the school's black undergraduates have never had a white acquaintance. Yet, across the country, colleges and universities like Michigan readily and even eagerly continue to encourage more segregation by granting the demands of every vocal grievance identity.

White Guilt

A great contributing factor is, of course, white guilt—specifically a knowledge of ill-gotten advantage. Ignorance is innocence, knowledge is guilt. Whites in America generally know that there is at least a slight advantage in being white. If a white person walks into a department store, chances are he or she is not going to be followed by the security guard as I am. This kind of knowledge makes whites vulnerable. (Incidentally, I do not mean to deride all forms of guilt. Guilt can be a wonderful thing, a truly civilized emotion. Prisons are full of people incapable of feeling guilt.)

A member of a grievance identity points a finger and says, "Hey whitey, you've oppressed my people! You have had generations to build up wealth and opportunity while I've had nothing." Almost automatically, the white person's first reaction is: "Am I guilty? Am I a racist?"

The second reaction is escapism: "All right, what do you want? What is it going to take to prove to you that I am not racist?" White college and university administrators say, "You want a black student lounge? You got it. We have a little extra money, so we can pay for a black yearbook. We can hold a separate graduation just for you. What else do you want?"

The third reaction is blindness. Obviously, when you are preoccupied with escaping your own feelings of guilt, you are utterly blind to the people causing it. So college and university administrators blindly grant black students extra entitlements, from dorms to yearbooks, and build an entire machinery of segregation on campus while ignoring the fact that 72 percent of black American college students are dropping out.

Black students have the lowest grade point average of any student group. If whites were not so preoccupied with escaping their own guilt, they would see that the real problem is not racism; it is that black students are failing in tragic numbers. They don't need separate dorms and yearbooks. They need basic academic skills. But instead they are taught that extra entitlements are their due and that the greatest power of all is the power that comes to them as victims. If they want to get anywhere in American life, they had better wear their victimization on their sleeve, they had better tap into white guilt, making whites want to escape by offering money, status, racial preferences—something, anything—in return. Is this the way for a race that has been oppressed to come into its own? Is this the way to achieve independence?

A Return to a Common Culture

Colleges and universities are not only segregating their campuses, they are segregating learning. If only for the sake of historical accuracy, we should teach all students—black, white, female, male—about many broad and diverse cultures. But those with grievance identities use the multicultural approach as an all-out assault on the liberal arts curriculum, on the American heritage, and on Western culture. They have made our differences, rather than our common bonds, sacred. Often they do so in the name of building the "self-esteem" of minorities. But they are not going to build anyone's self-esteem by condemning our culture as the product of "dead white males."

We *do* share a common history and a common culture, and that must be the central premise of education. If we are to end the new segregation on campus, and everywhere else it exists, we need to recall the spirit of the original civil rights movement, which was dedicated to the "self evident truth" that all men are created equal.

Even the most humble experiences unite us. We have all grown up on the same sitcoms, eaten the same fast food, and laughed at the same jokes. We have practiced the same religions, lived under the same political system, read the same books, and worked in the same marketplace. We have the same dreams and aspirations as well as fears and doubts for ourselves and for our children. How, then, can our differences be so overwhelming?

❑   ❑   ❑

SHELBY STEELE is a research fellow at the Hoover Institution. He received his B.A. from Coe College, his M.A. from Southern Illinois University, and his Ph.D. in English from the University of Utah. He received the National Book Critic's Circle Award in 1990 for his book *The Content of Our Character: A New Vision of Race in America* (1990). His most recent book is *A Dream Deferred: The Second Betrayal of Black Freedom in America* (1998). In 1991, his work on the documentary *Seven Days in Bensonhurst* was recognized with an Emmy Award, the Writer's Guild Award for television documentary writing, and the San Francisco Film Festival Award for television documentary writing. He is a member of the National Association of Scholars, the national board of the American Academy for Liberal Education, the University Accreditation Association, and the national board at the Center for the New American Community at the Manhattan Institute.

Saving Childhood

Michael Medved

September 1998

Mr. Medved delivered the following speech at a Hillsdale College seminar, "Heroes for a New Generation and a New Century," in Scottsdale, Arizona.

❏ ❏ ❏

To Frighten and Corrupt Our Young

In every corner of contemporary culture childhood innocence is under assault. The very idea of parental protectiveness has been overwhelmed by relentless pressure from a society that seems perversely determined to frighten and corrupt its own young in a misguided effort to "prepare" them for a harsh, dangerous future.

From the bleakest ghettos to the most privileged suburbs, families face the same fears. We worry not only about what might happen to our kids on the way to school but about what values they will learn once they get there. We are concerned not only with the threat of physical assault but with the emotional and moral battering that our children endure from peers and the media. In short, we feel powerless to counteract the implacable social forces that push our own flesh and blood to grow up too soon—and too cynical. We may shower youngsters with every sort of material blessing and glitzy diversion, but we can't seem to give them the greatest gift of all—a secure, optimistic, and reasonably sheltered childhood.

Nihilistic messages now come at our kids from so many directions at once that childhood innocence doesn't stand a chance. Consider:

- In Philadelphia, a four-year-old keeps squirming away when embraced by a favorite uncle who has come for his weekly visit. When asked by her puzzled relative what is wrong, she tells him that her nursery school teacher warned her against any adults who "touch her too hard." If he persists in squeezing her, she tearfully informs him, she will have to call the police.

- In Dallas, a three-year-old returns from a play group to regale his disbelieving parents with an earnest, straight-faced singing and dancing rendition of "Mama's Got a Great Big Butt."

- In Salt Lake City, a first-grader begins compulsively throwing away her previously cherished dolls, much to the horror of her parents. It takes several hours to get an explanation: Her teacher showed the class that the world was so bad—and so crowded— that nobody should have children. The sensitive and solemn girl didn't even want to pretend to raise babies of her own.

- And in our own home, in the winter of 1994, our daughter, Shayna, joins her excited kindergarten classmates for an after-school field trip to the botanical gardens. As these neatly uniformed parochial school kids squeal and giggle in the back seat of a van, the adults listen to the hourly news on the radio, which includes a graphic description of Lorena Bobbitt cutting off her husband's penis and throwing it out the window of her car. Hearing this, our daughter covers her ears in horror and begins sobbing, soon joined by two of her frightened classmates.

Admittedly, such anecdotes represent relatively minor upsets in a world scarred by youth violence, widespread substance abuse, teen pregnancy, and adolescent suicide. Nevertheless, such small examples illustrate the depth—and breadth—of the problem. Today, even the most conscientious and protective parents feel helpless when it comes to shielding the innocence of their children.

"They're Trying to Kidnap My Kids"

The most visible assault on that innocence involves the omnipresent messages of the mass media. As one anguished mother commented to me years ago: "My resentment toward Hollywood [filmakers] is entirely personal—because I can't escape the feeling that they're trying to kidnap my kids." The big entertainment conglomerates continue to churn out jaded and cynical diversions that seem to go out of their way to undermine the most important values parents want to impart to their own offspring. Aging boomers look back nostalgically to the innocent TV offerings of their youth, from I Love Lucy to Leave It to Beaver, and lament the fact that "the Beaver" has transmogrified into "Beavis." Meanwhile, the wildly popular cable cartoon show South Park is so crude and offensive (and, yes, inventive) that its characters make even Beavis and Butthead look, by comparison, like Will and Henry James. In this new show, a group of Colorado third-graders exemplify the current vision of childhood, demonstrating every imaginable antisocial and self-destructive attitude, while cheering violent wrestling matches between Santa and Jesus, or interacting with fanciful characters such as a talking pile of feces known as "Mr. Hanky, the Christmas Poo."

South Park highlights the fact that in today's media culture, even material about children—or aimed specifically at a youthful audience—attempts to develop an "edge" by exploring risky or disturbing content. The rating "PG" now seems to signify "Profanity Guaranteed." Even gorgeously animated feature films pitched at five-year-olds, such as Disney's Mulan or Pocahontas, feature dark and politically correct preaching about persecution of Native Americans or the liberating impact of cross-dressing.

These messages matter because, for most American kids, media images represent their chief source of information about the larger world beyond the home. TV alone occupies today's youngsters for some twenty-five hours a week—not even counting the additional time lavished on films, videos, pop music, and video games. In a typical year, the average American child will invest more hours digesting the products of the entertainment industry than he will spend in a classroom—because kids don't take summer vacations, Christmas breaks, or weekends off when it comes to their media consumption. This immersion in artificiality erodes childhood innocence through its inevitable emphasis on the bitter and the bizarre, emphasizing dysfunction and danger that is inherently dramatic.

Counselors, Condoms, and "Enlightened" Attitudes

Unfortunately, the time children spend in school seldom serves to counteract this malign media influence; far more often it reinforces it. Contemporary curricula warn kids about global warming and overpopulation in the name of environmental awareness and impose guilt concerning slavery or Japanese internment or Native American genocide or oppression of women —all in the interests of sensitivity and multiculturalism. Anti-drug, anti-smoking, and "safe sex" instruction (targeted at children as early as kindergarten) serve to advance the idea that it is not the home but the school—with its counselors, condoms, and "enlightened" attitudes—that represents a safe haven in a child's life.

Parents themselves too frequently collaborate in prematurely terminating childhood innocence. In order to provide some elusive edge in the pursuit of academic glory, even preschool kids are hurried into competitive, high pressure situations and find themselves rushed from one demanding (but theoretically "enriching") activity to another. Through it all, mother and father prefer the role of pal to that of protector, striving to become good friends rather than guides. With self-absorbed parents trapped in perpetual adolescence and refusing to accept adulthood, children cannot enjoy the sheltered, solid, and predictable atmosphere traditionally associated with childhood.

Preparation Replaces Protection

The assault on innocence from the media, schools, and parents themselves comes cloaked in the best of intentions and with an aura of utter inevitability. As Marie Winn observed in her wise 1981 book, *Children Without Childhood*, society has abandoned its old emphasis on "protection" of kids and embraced a new priority of "preparation." According to this thinking, children cannot afford the luxury of sweetness and simplicity in some sort of golden age of innocence but rather must equip themselves to confront a bitter, dangerous world—and the sooner the better.

The new preparation model may seem to make logical sense, but the sad fact is that it doesn't work. Rather than reducing the levels of teenage drug addiction, sexually transmitted diseases, gang violence, depression, and suicide, all efforts to confront kids with life's bleak realities at ever earlier ages appear to have made the situation worse.

The first step in saving childhood involves a clear rejection of the failed and bankrupt notion that terrifying and pressuring kids somehow helps them cope with the world's challenges. Feeling helpless and hopeless promotes neither success nor happiness. Instead of abandoning our young to today's trendy cynicism, American families should exalt childhood innocence, not just as an absence of information or an enforced ignorance but as a positive value in its own right, featuring three indispensable elements: security, optimism, and a sense of wonder.

Security and the World's Best Instinctive Conservatives

All kids crave security and predictability. If you doubt that proposition for a moment, just pause to consider their culinary preferences. As a child, I wanted to eat hot dogs at every single meal; my own daughters and my own son express an unswerving preference for macaroni and cheese. When it comes to the contents of the daily lunch box, children hardly crave surprises or exotic choices. Even in the most sophisticated households, they seem to prefer the old reliables like peanut-butter-and-jelly sandwiches to adventuresome fare like Cajun shrimp or sushi. And you can forget about trying new restaurants. Children want to eat at the same neighborhood joints over and over again.

Rearrange the furniture in your daughter's room lately? That's the sort of minor change that's likely to produce a major revolt. Our girls not only insist that the dresser, desk, and bed remain in precisely the same position but that their Barbies are arranged in their familiar rows. Even a pleasant family milestone such as buying a new car to replace some beloved old clunker may provoke tearful protest from youngsters who in-stinctively resist all change.

My wife and co-author, Diane Medved, a clinical psychologist, be-lieves it is easy to understand these profoundly conservative instincts among nearly all kids. Young people go through such intense and dra-matic change in their bodies and their emotional makeup that they inevi-tably want as little alteration as possible in their surroundings. If I go off on a business trip and return three days later, I look at the kids and know they are different—noticeably grown and transformed in just that brief time away. No wonder these constantly changing children yearn to be en-veloped by predictable patterns!

That is why family ritual can play such an important and constructive role in children's lives. These traditions may include Sunday outings, Mon-day night parents-and-kids basketball games, or just the simple but crucial habit of tucking in the youngsters and saying prayers at bedtime. Each fam-ily develops its own unique and sometimes quirky ways of observing birth-days, meals, and other occasions. Older rituals, rooted in religious faith, involve more timeless, universal elements, providing children with a solid sense of their place in the family and in the world.

We saw religious ritual perform its protective function with our kids when they faced the greatest challenge of their young lives—moving, for the first time, to a new home. After twenty years in the same house in Los Angeles, we made a decisive—and for our children, devastating—break and relocated in Seattle. During the first six days in the Northwest we rattled around a strange and empty house, waiting for the moving van to arrive with our possessions. Living in sleeping bags, the three children complained almost constantly; they missed their friends and wondered why we had to disrupt their lives to come to this different and disorienting place.

Then on Friday evening we welcomed the Jewish Sabbath. As the sun went down over Lake Washington, Diane and I set out paper plates and food that we had bought at a nearby market. We lit the candles and said the traditional blessings over the wine and bread. Then we blessed each of the children and sang some of the songs that they had heard every week from the time they were infants. Finally, our older daughter, Sarah, then nine years old, came over to hug her mother and said: "You know what? Maybe it won't be so bad here after all."

Children appreciate the power of ritual. That is one of many reasons that seemingly small gestures, such as reciting the Pledge of Allegiance in the morning or thanking God before a meal, can provide significant benefits. Children deserve to know what to expect from life, and they also deserve to know what is expected of them. In other words, they need to feel a sense of predictability when it comes to the consequences of their actions. Even if those consequences involve punishment or other unpleasantness, consistency and reliability contribute to a belief in an ordered world that makes sense—helping to rescue childhood.

Hard-Wired for Optimism

Nearly all kids seem to be hard-wired for optimism—an attitude that represents the second key element of childhood innocence. It is possible that pseudo-sophistication, media assaults, trendy cynicism, and a misguided educational system can eventually shatter this natural hopefulness, but, in so doing, these forces must overcome a child's healthy instincts.

Have you noticed, for instance, that children inevitably prefer stories with happy endings? My daughters have been studying Shakespeare in the home school cooperative Diane has organized, and so far they have covered *Twelfth Night* (their favorite), *Much Ado About Nothing, A Midsummer Night's Dream, As You Like It, Taming of the Shrew*, and *The Tempest*. Over dinner, I recently asked them why they hadn't tried to tackle *Hamlet* or *Julius Caesar*, and the girls looked at me as if I were an imbecile. They declared in unison, "Why would we want to? Those stories are so sad!"

I am sure there will come a time when they confront the tragedies of Shakespeare and the tragedies of life, but I am gratified that they feel no inclination to do so when they are nine and eleven, respectively. It hardly helps children to depress them in the name of preparation and to convince them at an early age that life is random, chaotic, or doomed. Unless kids look forward to the future with anticipation and joy, the process of growing up will seem merely pointless and painful.

Educators spend a great deal of time and energy today trying to build "self-esteem." But far more important than implanting the notion that "I'm a great kid" is establishing the conviction that "It's a great world." If a feeling of amazement and joy at this vast and dazzling universe escapes our offspring in childhood, it will likely be denied to them for a lifetime.

What is the best way to counteract the whining self-pity that plays such a prominent role in politically correct thinking and pop culture? The true antidote to pessimism isn't some forced Pollyanna optimism—it is gratitude, expressed fervently and frequently. Anyone fortunate enough to be born in the United States, this blessed island of sanity and decency in the midst of the dark, bloody, turbulent ocean of historic human misery, should make every day Thanksgiving Day and the Fourth of July.

We need to acknowledge our appreciation for our country, for its founders and heroes, and for our own parents and grandparents. Above all, however, we owe a debt of gratitude to the Almighty, who has showered us with gifts and opportunities of an altogether unprecedented nature. The refusal to recognize that debt sours our present and threatens our future. We all know what happens in our own lives if a parent, a spouse, or a business associate deserves our appreciation but some spirit of stubbornness or pride prevents us from expressing it. The resulting sense of ingratitude can become an acid that corrodes our very soul. At the moment, public and private ingratitude in America has become an acid that is corroding the soul of our society.

Recapturing a Sense of Wonder

The vast majority of American parents have consciously misled their children and felt no guilt whatever about the deception. Even the most hip, educated, and fashionable families tend to tell kids at one point in their lives about Santa Claus or the Tooth Fairy. Why do we go to such great lengths to persuade them to accept these farfetched fantasies? We do so because we instinctively, and most often unconsciously, understand the importance of the third fundamental aspect of childhood innocence: a sense of wonder.

Any parent who has watched a child's wide, excited eyes glimpsing the miraculous presents that appear on Christmas morning under the tree, or reading the note left under the pillow by the fast-moving and elusive Tooth Fairy, comprehends the priceless nature of this sense of wonder. A belief in magic, in goodness, in angelic protection, in well-deserved miracles —these are the very essence of childhood. Such attitudes encourage the imagination and foster an appreciation of the world. They are precious precisely because they are so fleeting. If a four-year-old passionately believes in Santa Claus, then he and his family can revel in the messages of supernatural generosity and kindness involved in his belief. If he still believes in Santa Claus at age 24, then his parents will feel less proud: They have either raised a young adult who is deeply disturbed—or a die-hard liberal.

The point is that childhood should remain fundamentally different from adulthood, with kids reveling in the freshness and fun of their experience. In his great poem about vanished childhood, "Fern Hill," Dylan Thomas writes,

> . . . it was all
> Shining, it was Adam and maiden,
> The sky gathered again
> And the sun grew round that very day.
> So it must have been after the birth of the
>   simple light
> In the first, spinning place. . . .

In this spinning place we all inhabit, we can best protect a sense of wonder in our kids by nurturing a sense of wonder in ourselves. Pausing to rejoice in everyday delights—especially in the company of those we love most—can promulgate the important awareness that life is always precious, always new.

And it is, without question, much too precious to waste so much of it on TV. When it comes to defending childhood innocence, we have inexplicably invited the principal enemy and potential destroyer into our own living rooms. By the age of six, the average American child has spent more hours watching the tube than he will spend speaking to his father in his lifetime. This is madness and, in a very real sense, child abuse. And the old parental excuse, "My kids only watch the quality programs," does not carry any weight at all. The underlying problem with television and kids isn't quality. It is *quantity*.

If you are unconvinced, try the following thought experiment. Imagine that William Bennett, former drug czar, becomes our new TV czar, and he is granted special authority so that every television show must pass a "Bill Bennett virtue test" before it is broadcast. In this fantasy world, the tube would become considerably less destructive, but it would hardly be transformed into a benign factor in our lives. As long as our kids watched twenty-five hours a week, television would still harm family relationships, physical health, moral development, attention span, reading ability, and communal life.

Regardless of programming content, our hurried, overscheduled kids still need to get up off the couch, join softball games with neighbors, read books for fun, joke with friends, interact with family, or just play by themselves in the yard to stretch their imagination. Every family can benefit by turning off, or turning down, the TV set, and eliminating, or at least reducing, the impact of this dominating influence. If you worry that a decision to get rid of the boob tube would make your child stand out from some of his peers, please remember: One of the greatest gifts that parents can give their offspring is the courage to be different.

Our chance to influence, for better or for worse, the children that God has entrusted to our care is always too brief. Last year, on my daughter Shayna's eighth birthday, we celebrated with a Sabbath meal. Our guests all helped serenade her with the traditional "Happy Birthday" over the cake—without candles, since we refrain from creating fire on the Sabbath. Our daughter enjoyed every minute of the occasion, but toward the end of the day as the Sabbath was ending and the sun was going down, she came over to me to cuddle. "Well, I want to say good-bye," she said sweetly. This alarmed me, and I asked her why she felt the need to say good-bye.

"Because," she explained, "after today, you're never going to see a seven-year-old daughter again." She was right, of course. After today, the precious gift of your child—at this unique moment in his life—is gone forever.

In his incomparable book of poems, A *Child's Garden of Verses*, Robert Louis Stevenson declares,

The world is so full of a number of things,
I'm sure we should all be as happy as kings.

In that spirit, may all our children linger in the garden.

❏ ❏ ❏

MICHAEL MEDVED is a film critic, a best-selling author, and a nationally syndicated radio talk show host. His daily three-hour program, emphasizing the intersection of politics and pop culture, reaches more than 1.8 million listeners in 140 markets, coast to coast. He graduated with honors from Yale University, and then attended Yale Law School. After working as a screenwriter in Hollywood, he reviewed movies for CNN, later becoming chief film critic for the *New York Post*. He also served for twelve years as co-host of *Sneak Previews*, the nationally televised weekly movie review show on PBS-TV. He is the author of eight nonfiction books, including the national bestseller *What Really Happened to the Class of '65?* (1976) and *Hollywood vs. America* (1993). His columns on media and society appear regularly in *USA Today*, where he serves as a member of the Board of Contributors. Mr. Medved and his wife, clinical psychologist and author Diane Medved, are Hillsdale College Associates.

Does Honor Have a Future?

William J. Bennett

December 1998

Dr. Bennett delivered the following speech at a Hillsdale College seminar, "Heroes for a New Century and a New Generation," in Scottsdale, Arizona.

❑ ❑ ❑

The modern age brings to mind Christian apologist C. S. Lewis's chilling words in *The Abolition of Man*: "We make men without chests and expect of them virtue and enterprise. We laugh at honour and are shocked to find traitors in our midst."

America is the greatest nation in the history of the world—the richest, most powerful, most envied, most consequential. And yet America is the same nation that leads the industrialized world in rates of murder, violent crime, imprisonment, divorce, abortion, sexually transmitted diseases, single-parent households, teen suicide, cocaine consumption, and pornography production and consumption.

America is a place of heroes, honor, achievement, and respect. But it is also a place where heroism is often confused with celebrity, honor with fame, true achievement with popularity, individual respect with political correctness. Our culture celebrates self-gratification, the crossing of all moral boundaries, and now even the breaking of all social taboos. And on top of it all, too often the sound heard is whining—the whining of America

—which can be heard only as the enormous ingratitude of we modern men toward our unprecedented good fortune.

Despite our wonders and greatness, we are a nation that has experienced so much social regression, so much decadence, in so short a period of time, that we have become the kind of place to which civilized countries used to send missionaries.

Casting Stones

Social regression and decadence are glaringly obvious in the current presidential administration. Now, whenever I make a comment these days criticizing Bill Clinton, someone inevitably asks, "Aren't you casting stones?" It shows how far we have fallen that calling upon the president of the United States to account for charges of adultery, lying to the public, perjury, and obstruction of justice is regarded as akin to stoning.

It is also an example of what sociologist Alan Wolfe refers to as America's new 11th Commandment: "Thou shalt not judge." In *One Nation After All*, Wolfe writes, "Middle-class Americans are reluctant to pass judgment on how other people act and think." Of course, all of us are in favor of tolerance and forgiveness. But the moral pendulum has swung too far in the direction of relativism. If a nation of free people can no longer make pronouncements on fundamental matters of right and wrong—for example, that a married fifty-year-old commander-in-chief ought not to have sexual relations with a young intern in his office and then lie about it—it has lost its way.

The problem is not with those who are withholding judgment until all the facts are in, but with the increasing number of people who want to avoid judgment altogether. Firm moral convictions have been eroded by tentativeness, uncertainty, diffidence. The new relativist consensus Wolfe describes is not surprising. During the last thirty years we have witnessed a relentless assault on traditional norms and a profound shift in public attitudes. The tectonic plates have moved.

Why have we been drawn toward such permissiveness? My former philosophy professor John Silber was correct when he spoke of an "invitation to mutual corruption." We are hesitant to impose upon ourselves a common moral code because we want our own exemptions. This modern allergy to judgments and standards, of which attitudes toward the Clinton scandals are but a manifestation, is deeply problematic, for a defining mark of a good republic is precisely the willingness to make judgments about things that matter.

In America, we do not defer to kings, cardinals, or aristocrats; we rely instead on the people's capacity to make reasonable judgments based on moral principles. Our form of government requires of us not moral perfection but modest virtues and adherence to some standards.

Those who constantly invoke the sentiment of "Who are we to judge?" should consider the anarchy that would ensue if we adhered to this sentiment in, say, our courtrooms. What would happen if those sitting on a jury decided to be "nonjudgmental" about rapists and sexual harassers, embezzlers and tax cheats? Justice would be lost. Without being "judgmental," Americans would never have put an end to slavery, outlawed child labor, emancipated women, or ushered in the civil rights movement. Nor would we have prevailed against Nazism and communism, or known how to explain our opposition.

Mr. Clinton himself admitted in a judgment-laden 1996 proclamation he signed during National Character Week: "[I]ndividual character involves honoring and embracing certain core ethical values: honesty, respect, responsibility. . . . Parents must teach their children from the earliest age the difference between right and wrong. But we must all do our part."

How do we judge a wrong—any wrong whatsoever—when we have gutted the principle of judgment itself? What arguments can be made after we have stripmined all the arguments of their force, their power, and their ability to inspire public outrage? We all know that there are times when we will have to judge others, when it is both right and *necessary* to judge others. If we do not confront the soft relativism that is currently disguised as a virtue, we will find ourselves morally and intellectually disarmed.

Corruption

In living memory, the chief threats to American democracy have come from without: first Nazism and Japanese imperialism, and later, Soviet communism. But these wars, hot and cold, ended in spectacular American victories. The threats we now face are from within. They are far different, more difficult to detect, more insidious: decadence, cynicism, and boredom.

Writing about corruption in democratic government, Alexis de Tocqueville warned about "not so much the immorality of the great as the fact that immorality may lead to greatness." When private citizens impute a ruler's success "mainly to some of his vices . . . an odious connection is thus formed between the ideas of turpitude and power, unworthiness and success, utility and dishonor." The rulers of democratic nations, Tocqueville said, "lend the authority of the government to the base practices of which they are accused. They afford dangerous examples, which discourage the struggles of virtuous independence."

Tocqueville recognized, too, that democratic citizens would not be conscious of this tendency, and in fact would probably disagree that it even existed. This is what makes it all the more dangerous; the corrupt actions of democratic leaders influence the public in subtle ways that often go unnoticed among citizens. This sort of decay is gradual and hard to perceive over a short period of time.

Which brings us back to Bill Clinton. If there is no consequence to the president's repeated betrayal of public trust and his abuses of power, it will have a profound impact on our political and civic life. Bill Clinton and his defenders are defining personal morality down, radically lowering the standards of what we expect from our president, and changing for the worse the way politics is and will be practiced. Recall the words of John Dean: "If Watergate had succeeded, what would have been put into the system for years to come? People thinking the way Richard Nixon thought and thinking that is the way it should be. It would have been a travesty; it would have been frightening."

We find ourselves at this familiar juncture today. It would be a travesty, and frightening, to legitimize Mr. Clinton's ethics and arguments made on their behalf. But we are getting close, disconcertingly close, to doing just that. "He's strictly one of a kind," *Washington Post* columnist Mary McGrory wrote, "our first president to be strengthened by charges of immorality."

You will often hear Clinton apologists argue that to take a stand against the president's misconduct will send the signal that anyone who is not a saint need not apply for the job. Nonsense. We do not expect our presidents to be men of extraordinary virtue, who have lived lives of near perfection. We should not even expect all our presidents to have the sterling character of, say, a Washington or a Lincoln, although we should hope for it, and certainly honor it on those rare occasions when we find it.

We have every right, however, to expect individuals who, taken in the totality of their acts, are decent and trustworthy. This is not an impossible standard; there are many examples we can look to—Truman, Eisenhower, Carter, and Reagan, to name just four men who served six terms since World War II. These are men, like all of us, who had an assortment of flaws and failings. They made mistakes. But at the end of the day, they were men whose character, at least, we could count on.

Bill Clinton's is not. The difference between these men and Mr. Clinton is the difference between common human frailty and corruption. That we accept the latter as common is a measure of how low our standards have dropped. We have to aim higher—and expect more—from our presidents and ourselves.

The Value-Free Culture

Our most exalted leader, a man who once proudly boasted that he would head the most ethical administration in history, is now saying to the American people, in effect, "My political enemies are to blame for all the scandals that surround me. I have nothing more to say. The rules don't apply to me. There are no consequences to my actions. It's irrelevant. My private life has nothing to do with my public life. My only responsibility is to do the people's business."

This is moral bankruptcy, and it is damaging our country, our standards, and our self-respect. It is also jeopardizing the future of the next generation of American leaders. A year ago, I delivered an address at the U.S. Naval Academy in which I told the Annapolis cadets that I was well aware of the fact that even among their ranks—among the military's brightest and best young men and women—there is widespread confusion of purpose and attenuation of belief. After all, if the character and personal conduct of the acknowledged leader of the free world is "irrelevant," then what is relevant? Why should anyone feel compelled to make sacrifices for the sake of an abstract principle like honor?

Young people just don't seem to be finding the answers to these troubling questions in the value-free culture of the 1990s. Please allow me to use two major historical events as reference points to describe this culture. In 1999, the famous New York rock festival, Woodstock, will celebrate its thirtieth anniversary. In its first 24 hours, Woodstock attracted 300,000 young people. It was characterized by rowdiness, drinking, drug use, promiscuity, and even death.

But back in the summer of '69, Woodstock was hailed uncritically as the "defining event of a generation." It was undoubtedly the high point of the counterculture movement in America. "If it feels good, do it" was the unofficial banner under which the participants paraded. It is worth noting, however, that most of those who attend Woodstock reunions today were not even at the original festival. Evidently, the memories are just not worth rekindling. The boys and girls have grown up—and grown beyond what Woodstock stood for. As adults, they consider it to have been childish, utopian, irrelevant, irresponsible, or worse.

But their children and grandchildren are receiving a very different impression from countless magazine articles, books, television specials, music videos, and movies that claim Woodstock was the greatest—the hippest—event ever and that the psychedelic pioneers should be envied for their brave and mocking defiance of everyone and everything that went before.

The year 1999 will also mark the 54th anniversary of Operation Overlord. This secret Normandy invasion under the command of Dwight D. Eisenhower was the largest amphibious landing in history. In its first 24 hours, it involved about 170,000 young people. What D-Day veterans, as well as their families and friends, continue to celebrate in huge numbers at *their* reunions is something far different than is celebrated at Woodstock.

Poignancy and dignity surround their gatherings, if only because the stakes during the dark days of World War II were so high, the heroism so manifest, the examples so inspiring. The participants can well recall President Roosevelt's moving radio broadcast on June 6, 1944, which called the nation to pray:

> Almighty God: Our sons, Pride of our nation, this day have set on a mighty endeavor. . . . They will need thy blessings. Their road will be long and hard. For the enemy is strong. He may hurl back our forces. . . . They will be sorely tried, by night and day. . . . The darkness will be rent by noise and flame. Men's souls will be shaken with the violence of war.

As at Woodstock, there were deaths. But they were different, in numbers and in cause. In one ten-minute period on Omaha Beach, a single rifle company of 205 men lost 197, including every officer and sergeant. These were not pointless or avoidable deaths. The price was very high—but that for which the soldiers died was sacred. We remember. Their comrades-in-arms remember. And so do those who come back again and again to the battlefields to commemorate what has come to be called the "longest day."

What do today's youth learn about Operation Overlord from the present culture? With a few notable exceptions, like the recent film *Saving Private Ryan*, they learn that it was just an unfortunate episode in our history that happened a long time ago and that only interests "old-timers" like their grandparents and great-grandparents. Young people don't feel they need to know much about D-Day, unless it is going to be covered on a test in school, and they certainly don't regard it as relevant to their own lives.

What Endures

In both cases, we can easily change young people's minds, but first we need to take on the much more difficult task of changing the present culture. Properly speaking, a value-laden culture should take heed of the fact that ephemeral things are the flies of summer. They drift away with the breeze of time. They are as wind and ashes. An event like Woodstock cannot hold the affections of the heart, or command respect, or win allegiance, or make men and women proud. It may be remembered by the media, but it leaves no lasting impression on the soul. It is forgotten. It is meant to be forgotten. Few people make pilgrimages to Woodstock, for it can give them nothing of worth.

Plato reminds us that what is real is what endures. That is why events like Operation Overlord will, in a value-laden culture, remain vivid and meaningful. War has always been the crucible—that is, the vessel as well as the severest test—for our core beliefs. The battles of Trenton, Midway, and Tarawa; those who served with John Paul Jones on the *Bonhomme Richard* and the crews of *Taffey Three* in Leyte Gulf; the Marines and brave Navy officers at "Frozen Chosin"—these things endure.

But it is not only these things that provide us with the opportunity to remember and revere our past. In the peaceful pursuits of business, politics, religion, culture, and education, we can strive to understand and to pass on to our children the common principles and common virtues that make us essentially American. We can also introduce the next generation to ancient concepts of honor, which have been cheapened for far too long.

In the *Funeral Oration*, the great Athenian statesman Pericles said two thousand years ago, "For it is only love of honor that never grows old; and honor it is, not gain as some would have it, that rejoices the heart of age and helplessness."

Honor never grows old, and honor gives the greatest joy, because honor is, finally, about defending noble and worthy things that deserve to be defended, even at a high cost. In our time, the cost may be social disapproval, public scorn, hardship, persecution, or even death.

Does honor have a future? Like all things human, it is always open to question. As free citizens, we can always fail to live up to the "better angels of our nature." After the conclusion of the Constitutional Convention in 1787, a lady reportedly asked Benjamin Franklin, "Well, Doctor, what have we got—a republic or a monarchy?" Franklin replied, "A republic, if you can keep it."

And so honor has a future, if we can keep it. And we keep it only if we continue to esteem it, value those who display it, and refuse to laugh at it.

❑ ❑ ❑

WILLIAM J. BENNETT is a Distinguished Fellow in Cultural Policy Studies at the Heritage Foundation and co-director of Empower America. He holds a B.A. from Williams College, a Ph.D. in philosophy from the University of Texas, and a law degree from Harvard. In 1981, President Reagan chose him to head the National Endowment for the Humanities, and in 1985 he was named Secretary of the Department of Education. In 1989, President Bush appointed him director of the Office of National Drug Control Policy. He has written or edited numerous books, including *The Book of Virtues* (1993), *Children's Book of Virtues* (1995), *The Death of Outrage: Bill Clinton and the Assault on American Ideals* (1998), and *Why We Fight: Moral Clarity and the War on Terrorism* (2002).

Modesty Revisited

Wendy Shalit

March 2001

Miss Shalit delivered the following speech at a Hillsdale College seminar, "The Morality of Civility," on the Hillsdale campus.

❏ ❏ ❏

This afternoon I was reading a magazine for brides in which a woman had submitted the following question: "My fiancé wants us to move in together, but I want to wait until we're married. Am I doing our marriage an injustice?" The editor responded: "Your fiancé should understand why you want to wait to share a home. Maybe you're concerned about losing your identity as an individual. Or maybe you're concerned about space issues."

Space issues? Losing her identity? If this woman cared about those things she wouldn't want to get married in the first place. Her question was a moral one. She wanted to know what would be best for her marriage. And on this—however unbeknownst to the magazine's new-agey editor—the evidence is in: Couples who live together before marriage are much less likely to get married; and if they do marry, they are more likely to get divorced. Yet the vocabulary of modesty has largely dropped from our cultural consciousness; when a woman asks a question that necessarily implicates it, we can only mumble about "space issues."

I first became interested in the subject of modesty for a rather mundane reason—because I didn't like the bathrooms at Williams College.

255

Like many enlightened colleges and universities these days, Williams houses boys next to girls in its dormitories and then has the students vote by floor on whether their common bathrooms should be coed. It's all very democratic, but the votes always seem to go in the coed direction because no one wants to be thought a prude. When I objected, I was told by my fellow students that I "must not be comfortable with [my] body." Frankly, I didn't get that, because I was fine with my body; it was *their* bodies in such close proximity to mine that I wasn't thrilled about.

I ended up writing about this experience in *Commentary* as a kind of therapeutic exercise. But when my article was reprinted in *Reader's Digest*, a weird thing happened: I got piles of letters from kids who said, "I thought I was the only one who couldn't stand these bathrooms." How could so many people feel they were the "only ones" who believed in privacy and modesty? It was troubling that they were afraid to speak up. When and why, I wondered, did modesty become such a taboo?

At Yale in 1997, a few years after my own coed bathroom protest, five Orthodox Jewish students petitioned the administration for permission to live off-campus instead of in coed dorms. In denying them, a dean with the Dickensian name of Brodhead explained that "Yale has its own rules and requirements, which we insist on because they embody our values and beliefs." Yale has no core curriculum, of course, but these coed bathrooms, according to Dean Brodhead, embody its beliefs. I would submit that as a result of this kind of "liberationist" ideology, we today have less, not more freedom, than in the pre-1960s era when modesty was upheld as a virtue. In this regard it is important to recall that when colleges had separate dorms for men and women, and all the visitation rules that went with them, it was also possible for kids to circumvent those rules. It was possible, for instance—now, I'm not advocating this—for students to sneak into each others' dorms and act immodestly. But in the new culture of "liberation," a student can't sneak into the dorms and be modest, or, more accurately, she can't sneak *out*. There is no "right of exit" in today's immodest society. If you don't participate, you're a weirdo. Hence students are not really free to develop their best selves, to act in accordance with their hopes.

Modesty's Loss, Social Pathology's Gain

Many of the problems we hear about today—sexual harassment, date rape, young women who suffer from eating disorders and report feeling a lack of control over their bodies—are all connected, I believe, to our culture's attack on modesty. Listen, first, to the words we use to describe intimacy: what once was called "making love," and then "having sex," is now "hooking up"—like airplanes refueling in flight. In this context I was interested to learn, while researching for my book, that the early feminists actually praised modesty as ennobling to society. Here I am not just talking about the temperance-movement feminists, who said, "Lips that touch liquor shall never touch mine." I am talking about more recent feminists like Simone de Beauvoir, who warned in her book, *The Second Sex*, that if society trivializes modesty, violence against women would result. And she was right. Since the 1960s, when our cultural arbiters deemed this age-old virtue a "hang-up," men have grown to expect women to be casual about sex, and women for their part don't feel they have the right to say "no." This has brought us all more misery than joy. On MTV I have seen a 27-year-old woman say she was "sort of glad" that she had herpes, because now she has "an excuse to say 'no' to sex." For her, disease had replaced modesty as the justification for exercising free choice.

In 1948 there was a song called "Baby, It's Cold Outside" by Frank Loesser, in which a boyfriend wants his girlfriend to sleep over. His argument is simple but compelling: Baby, it's cold outside, and if she doesn't sleep over, she could catch pneumonia and die, and that would cause him "lifelong sorrow." In response, the girl offers several counter-arguments: "My father will be waiting at the door, there's bound to be talk tomorrow," etc. It's a very cute song. And while postmodern intellectuals at progressive institutions like Yale would no doubt say this song proves how oppressed women were in 1948, I would argue that today's culture—in which fathers can't be counted on to be waiting at the door—is far creepier.

The counterpoint to "Baby, It's Cold Outside" is a story I read in a women's magazine, written by an ex-boyfriend of an eighteen-year-old girl whose father had decided that she was too old to be a virgin. After commiserating with the boyfriend, this father drove the pair to a hotel (he didn't trust the boyfriend with his *car*), where the girl became hysterical and the scheme fell apart. This article was called "My Ex-Girlfriend's Father: What a Man!" And although the story isn't typical, it is quite common these days for parents to rent hotel rooms for their kids on prom nights, which is essentially the same principle. So the father in "Baby, It's Cold Outside" waiting at the door, and the older culture that supported modesty, actually made women stronger. It gave them the right to say "no" until they met someone they wanted to marry. Today's culture of "liberation" gives women no ground on which to stand. And an immodest culture weakens men, too—we are all at the mercy of other people's judgment of us as sexual objects (witness the revolution in plastic surgery for men), which is not only tiring but also dishonest because we cannot be ourselves.

When I talk to college students, invariably one will say, "Well, if you want to be modest, be modest. If you want to be promiscuous, be promiscuous. We all have a choice, and that's the wonderful thing about this society." But the culture, I tell them, cannot be neutral. Nor is it subtle in its influence on behavior. In fact, culture works more like a Sherman tank. In the end, if it is not going to value modesty, it will value promiscuity and adultery, and all our lives and marriages will suffer as a result.

Four Myths Exposed

A first step toward reviving respect for modesty in our culture is to strike at the myths that undermine it. Let me touch on four of these.

The first myth is that modesty is Victorian. But what about the story of Rebecca and Isaac? When Rebecca sees Isaac and covers herself, it is not because she is trying to be Victorian. Her modesty was the key to what would bring them together and develop a profound intimacy. When we cover up what is external or superficial—what we all share in common— we send a message that what is most important are our singular hearts and minds. This separates us from the animals, and always did, long before the Victorian era.

The second myth about modesty is that it is synonymous with prudery. This was the point of the dreadful movie *Pleasantville*, the premise of which was that nobody in the 1950s had fun or experienced love. It begins in black-and-white and turns to color only when the kids enlighten their parents about sex. This of course makes no sense on its face: If the parents didn't know how to do it, then how did all these kids get there in the first place? But it reflects a common conceit of baby boomers that passion, love, and happiness were nonexistent until modesty was overcome in the 1960s. In truth, modesty is nearly the opposite of prudery. Paradoxically, prudish people have more in common with the promiscuous. The prudish and the promiscuous share a disposition against allowing themselves to be moved by others, or to fall in love. Modesty, on the other hand, invites and protects the evocation of real love. It is erotic, not neurotic.

To illustrate this point, I like to compare photographs taken at Coney Island almost a century ago with photographs from nude beaches in the 1970s. At Coney Island, the beach-goers are completely covered up, but the men and women are stealing glances at one another and seem to be having a great time. On the nude beaches, in contrast, men and women hardly look at each other—rather, they look at the sky. They appear completely bored. That is what those who came after the 1960s discovered about this string of dreary hook-ups: Without anything left to the imagination, sex becomes boring.

The third myth is that modesty isn't natural. This myth has a long intellectual history, going back at least to David Hume, who argued that society invented modesty so that men could be sure that children were their own. As Rousseau pointed out, this argument that modesty is a social construct suggests that it is possible to get rid of modesty altogether. Today we try to do just that, and it is widely assumed that we are succeeding. But are we?

In arguing that Hume was wrong and that modesty is rooted in nature, a recently discovered hormone called oxytocin comes to mind. This hormone creates a bonding response when a mother is nursing her child, but is also released during intimacy. Here is physical evidence that women become emotionally bonded to their sexual partners even if they only intend a more casual encounter. Modesty protected this natural emotional vulnerability; it made women strong. But we don't really need to resort to physiology to see the naturalness of modesty. We can observe it on any windy day when women wearing slit skirts hobble about comically to avoid showing their legs—the very legs those fashionable skirts are designed to reveal. Despite trying to keep up with the fashions, these women have a natural instinct for modesty.

The fourth and final myth I want to touch on is that modesty is solely a concern for women. We are where we are today only in part because the feminine ideal has changed. The masculine ideal has followed suit. It was once looked on as manly to be faithful to one woman for life, and to be protective toward all women. Sadly, this is no longer the case, even among many men to whom modest women might otherwise look as kindred spirits. Modern feminists are wrong to expect men to be gentlemen when they themselves are not ladies, but men who value "scoring" and then lament that there are no modest women around anymore—well, they are just as bad. And of course, a woman can be modestly dressed and still be harassed on the street. So the reality is that a lot depends on male respect for modesty. It is characteristic of modern society that everyone wants the other guy to be nice to him without having to change his own behavior, whether it is the feminists blaming the men, the men blaming the feminists, or young people blaming their role models. But that is an infantile posture.

Restoring a Modest Society

Jews read a portion of the Torah each week, and in this week's portion there is a story that shows us beautifully, I think, how what we value in women and men are inextricably linked. Abraham is visited by three men, really three angels, and he is providing them with his usual hospitality, when they ask him suddenly, "Where is Sarah your wife?" And he replies, famously, "Behold! In the tent!" Commentators ask, why in the world are the angels asking where Sarah is? They know she is in the tent. They are, after all, angels. And one answer is, to remind *Abraham* of where she is, in order to increase his love for her. This is very interesting, because in Judaism the most important work takes place, so to speak, "in the tent"—keeping kosher, keeping the Sabbath, keeping the laws of marital purity. Torah is only passed on to the next generation because of what the woman is doing in the home. Yet it is not enough for there to be a Sarah who is in the tent; it is also necessary that there be an Abraham who appreciates her. So I think the lesson is clear if we want to reconstruct a more modest, humane society, we have to start with ourselves.

I don't think it is an accident that the most meaningful explication of modesty comes from the Bible. I was fascinated in my research to discover how many secular women are returning to modesty because they found, simply as a practical matter, that immodesty was not working for them. In short, they weren't successful finding the right men. For me this prompts an essentially religious question: Why were we created in this way? Why can't we become happy by imitating the animals? In the sixth chapter of *Isaiah* we read that the fiery angels surrounding the throne of God have six wings. One set is for covering the face, another for covering the legs, and only the third is for flying. Four of the six wings, then, are for modesty's sake. This beautiful image suggests that the more precious something is, the more it must conceal and protect itself. The message of our dominant culture today, I am afraid, is that we are not precious, that we weren't created in the divine image. I am saying to the contrary that we were, and that as such we deserve modesty.

❏ ❏ ❏

WENDY SHALIT was born in Milwaukee, Wisconsin, and received her B.A. in philosophy from Williams College. Her essays have appeared in *The Wall Street Journal*, *Commentary*, *City Journal*, and other publications. Her book, *A Return to Modesty*, was published by The Free Press in 1999, and was reissued in paperback in 2001 by Touchstone Books in an edition that includes questions for classroom use.

INTERNATIONAL
RELATIONS

❏ ❏ ❏

Words of Warning to America

Aleksandr I. Solzhenitsyn

September 1975

The following was Alexsandr Solzhenitsyn's first major public
address following his expulsion from the Soviet Union in 1974.
It was reprinted in **Imprimis** with permission of the AFL–CIO,
which invited him to speak in Washington, D.C.

❏ ❏ ❏

Let me remind you of a recent incident which some of you may have seen
in the newspapers, although others might have missed it: Certain of your
businessmen, on their own initiative, established an exhibition of crimi-
nological technology in Moscow. This was the most recent and elaborate
technology, which here, in your country, is used to catch criminals, to bug
them, to spy on them, to photograph them, to tail them, to identify criminals. This was taken to Moscow to an exhibition in order that the Soviet
KGB agents could study it, as if not understanding what sort of criminals,
who would be hunted by the KGB.

The Soviet government was extremely interested in this technology,
and decided to purchase it. And your businessmen were quite willing to sell
it. Only when a few sober voices here raised an uproar against it was this
deal blocked. Only for this reason it didn't take place. But you have to realize
how clever the KGB is. This technology didn't have to stay two or three weeks
in a Soviet building under Soviet guard. Two or three nights were enough for
the KGB there to look through it and copy it. And if today, persons are being

hunted down by the best and most advanced technology, for this, I can also thank your Western capitalists.

This is something which is almost incomprehensible to the human mind: that burning greed for profit which goes beyond all reason, all self-control, all conscience, only to get money.

I must say that Lenin foretold this whole process. Lenin, who spent most of his life in the West and not in Russia, who knew the West much better than Russia, always wrote and said that the Western capitalists would do anything to strengthen the economy of the USSR. They will compete with each other to sell us goods cheaper and sell them quicker, so that the Soviets will buy from one rather than from the other. He said: They will bring it themselves without thinking about their future. And, in a difficult moment, at a party meeting in Moscow, he said: "Comrades, don't panic, when things go very hard for us, we will give a rope to the bourgeoisie, and the bourgeoisie will hang itself."

Then, Karl Radek, whom you may have heard of, who was a very re-sourceful wit, said: "Vladimir Ilyich, but where are we going to get enough rope to hang the whole bourgeoisie?"

Lenin effortlessly replied, "They'll supply us with it."

Through the decades of the 1920s, the 1930s, the 1940s, the 1950s, the whole Soviet press wrote: Western capitalism, your end is near.

But it was as if the capitalists had not heard, could not understand, could not believe this.

Nikita Khrushchev came here and said, "We will bury you!" They didn't believe that, either. They took it as a joke.

Now, of course, they have become more clever in our country. Now they don't say "we are going to bury you" anymore, now they say "détente."

Nothing has changed in communist ideology. The goals are the same as they were, but instead of the artless Khrushchev, who couldn't hold his tongue, now they say "détente."

In order to understand this, I will take the liberty of making a short his-toric survey—the history of such relations, which in different periods have been called "trade," "stabilization of the situation," "recognition of realities," and now "détente." These relations now are at least forty years old.

Let me remind you with what sort of system they started.

The system was installed by armed uprising.

It dispersed the Constituent Assembly.

It capitulated to Germany—the common enemy.

It introduced execution without trial.

It crushed workers' strikes.

It plundered the villagers to such an unbelievable extent that the peasants revolted, and when this happened it crushed the peasants in
the bloodiest possible way.

It shattered the Church.

It reduced twenty provinces of our country to a condition of famine. This was in 1921, the famous Volga famine. A very typical communist tech-nique: To seize power without thinking of the fact that the productive forces will collapse, that the fields will not be sown, the factories will stop, that the country will decline into poverty and famine—but when poverty and hunger come, then they request the humanitarian world to help them. We see this in North Vietnam today, perhaps Portugal is approaching this also. And the same thing happened in Russia in 1921. When the three-year civil war, started by the communists—and "civil war" was a slogan of the communists, civil war was Lenin's purpose; read Lenin, this was his aim and his slogan—when they had ruined Russia by this civil war, then they asked America, "America, feed our hungry." And indeed, generous and magnanimous America did feed our hungry.

The so-called American Relief Administration was set up, headed by your future President Hoover, and indeed many millions of Russian lives were saved by this organization of yours.

But what sort of gratitude did you receive for this? In the USSR not only did they try to erase this whole event from the popular memory—it is almost impossible today in the Soviet press to find any reference to the American Relief Administration—but they even denounce it as a clever spy organization, a clever scheme of American imperialism to set up a spy network in Russia. I repeat, it was a system that introduced concentration camps for the first time in the history of the world.

A system that, in the 20th century, was the first to introduce the use of hostages, that is to say, not to seize the person whom they were seeking, but rather a member of his family or someone at random, and shoot that person.

This system of hostages and persecution of the family exists to this day. It is still the most powerful weapon of persecution, because the bravest person, who is not afraid for himself, still shivers at the threat to his family.

It is a system which was the first—long before Hitler—to employ false registration, that is to say: "Such and such people have to come in to register." People would comply and then they were taken away to be annihilated.

We didn't have gas chambers in those days. We used barges. A hundred or a thousand persons were put into a barge and then it was sunk.

It was a system which deceived the workers in all of its decrees—the decree on land, the decree on peace, the decree on factories, the decree on freedom of the press.

It was a system which exterminated all additional parties, and let me make it clear to you that it not only disbanded the party itself, but destroyed its members. All members of every other party were exterminated. It was a system which carried out genocide of the peasantry; fifteen million peasants were sent off to extermination.

It was a system which introduced serfdom, the so-called "passport system."

It was a system which, in time of peace, artificially created a famine, causing six million persons to die in the Ukraine in 1932 and 1933. They died on the very edge of Europe. And Europe didn't even notice it. The world didn't even notice it—six million persons!

I could keep on enumerating these endlessly, but I have to stop because I have come to the year 1933 when, with all I have enumerated behind us, your President Roosevelt and your Congress recognized this system as one worthy of diplomatic recognition, of friendship, and of assistance.

Let me remind you that the great Washington did not agree to recognize the French Convention because of its savagery. Let me remind you that in 1933, voices were raised in your country objecting to recognition of the Soviet Union. However, the recognition took place and this was the beginning of friendship and ultimately of a military alliance.

Let us remember that in 1904, the American press was delighted at the Japanese victories and everyone wanted Russia's defeat because it was a conservative country. I want to remind you that in 1914 reproaches were directed at France and England for having entered into an alliance with such a conservative country as Russia.

The scope and the direction of my speech today do not permit me to say more about prerevolutionary Russia. I will just say that information about prerevolutionary Russia was obtained by the West from persons who were either not sufficiently competent or not sufficiently conscientious. I will just cite for the sake of comparison a number of figures which you can read for yourself in *Gulag Archipelago*, Volume 1, which has been published in the United States, and perhaps many of you may have read it. These are the figures.

According to calculations by specialists, based on the most precise objective statistics, in prerevolutionary Russia, during the eighty years before the revolution—years of the revolutionary movement when there were attempts on the Tsar's life, assassination of a Tsar, revolution—during these years about seventeen persons a year were executed. The famous Spanish Inquisition, during the decades when it was at the height of its persecution, destroyed perhaps ten persons a month. In the Archipelago—I cite a book which was published by the Cheka in 1920, proudly reporting on its revolutionary work in 1918 and 1919 and apologizing that its data were not quite complete—in 1918 and 1919 the Cheka executed, without trial, more than a thousand persons a month! This was written by the Cheka itself, before it understood how this would look to history.

At the height of Stalin's terror in 1937–1938, if we divide the number of persons executed by the number of months, we get more than 40,000 persons shot per month! Here are the figures: 17 a year, 10 a month, more than 1,000 a month, more than 40,000 a month! Thus, that which had made it difficult for the democratic West to form an alliance with prerevolutionary Russia had, by 1941, grown to such an extent and still did not prevent the entire united democracy of the world—England, France, the United States, Canada, Australia, and small countries—from entering into a military alliance with the Soviet Union. How is this to be explained? How can we understand it? Here we can offer a few explanations. The first, I think, is that the entire united democracy of the world was too weak to fight against

Hitler's Germany alone. If this is the case, then it is a terrible sign. It is a terrible portent for the present day. If all these countries together could not defeat Hitler's little Germany, what are they going to do today, when more than half the globe is flooded with totalitarianism? I don't want to accept this explanation.

The second explanation is perhaps that there was simply an attack of panic—of fear—among the statesmen of the day. They simply didn't have sufficient confidence in themselves, they simply had no strength of spirit, and in this confused state decided to enter into an alliance with Soviet totalitarianism. This is also not flattering to the West.

Finally, the third explanation is that it was a deliberate device. Democracy did not want to defend itself. For defense it wanted to use another totalitarian system, the Soviet totalitarian system.

I am not talking now about the moral evaluation of this, I am going to talk about that later. But in terms of simple calculation, how shortsighted, what profound self-deception!

We have a Russian proverb: "Do not call a wolf to help you against the dogs." If dogs are attacking and tearing at you, fight against the dogs, but do not call a wolf for help. Because when the wolves come, they will destroy the dogs, but they will also tear you apart.

World democracy could have defeated one totalitarian regime after another, the German, then the Soviet. Instead, it strengthened Soviet totalitarianism, helped bring into existence a third totalitarianism, that of China, and all this finally precipitated the present world situation.

Roosevelt, in Teheran, during one of his last toasts, said the following: "I do not doubt that the three of us"—meaning Roosevelt, Churchill, and Stalin—"lead our peoples in accordance with their desires, in accordance with their aims." How are we to explain this? Let the historians worry about that. At the time, we listened and were astonished. We thought, "when we reach Europe, we will meet the Americans, and we will tell them." I was among the troops that were marching toward the Elbe. A little bit more and I would have reached the Elbe and would have shaken the hands of your American soldiers. But just before that happened, I was taken off to prison and my meeting did not take place.

But now, after all this great delay, the same hand has thrown me out of the country and here I am, instead of the meeting at the Elbe. After a delay of thirty years, my Elbe is here today. I am here to tell you, as a friend of the United States, what, as friends, we wanted to tell you then, but which our soldiers were prevented from telling you on the Elbe.

There is another Russian proverb: "The yes-man is your enemy, but your friend will argue with you." It is precisely because I am the friend of the United States, precisely because my speech is prompted by friendship, that I have come to tell you: "My friends, I'm not going to tell you sweet words. The situation in the world is not just dangerous, it isn't just threatening, it is catastrophic."

Something that is incomprehensible to the ordinary human mind has taken place. We over there, the powerless, average Soviet people, could not understand, year after year and decade after decade, what was happening. How were we to explain this? England, France, the United States, were victorious in World War II. Victorious states always dictate peace; they receive firm conditions; they create the sort of situation which accords with their philosophy, their concept of liberty, their concept of national interest.

Instead of this, beginning in Yalta, your statesmen of the West, for some inexplicable reason, have signed one capitulation after another. Never did the West or your President Roosevelt impose any conditions on the Soviet Union for obtaining aid. He gave unlimited aid, and then unlimited concessions. Already in Yalta, without any necessity, the occupation of Mongolia, Moldavia, Estonia, Latvia, Lithuania was silently recognized. Immediately after that, almost nothing was done to protect Eastern Europe, and seven or eight more countries were surrendered.

Stalin demanded that the Soviet citizens who did not want to return home be handed over to him, and the Western countries handed over 1.5 million human beings. How was this done? They took them by force. English soldiers killed Russians who did not want to become prisoners of Stalin, and drove them by force to Stalin to be exterminated. This has recently come to light—just a few years ago—a million and a half human beings. How could the Western democracies have done this?

And after that, for another thirty years, the constant retreat, the surrender of one country after another, to such a point that there are Soviet satellites even in Africa; almost all of Asia is taken over by them; Portugal is rolling down the precipice.

During those thirty years, more was surrendered to totalitarianism than any defeated country has ever surrendered after any war in history. There was no war, but there might as well have been.

For a long time we in the East couldn't understand this. We couldn't understand the flabbiness of the truce concluded in Vietnam. Any average Soviet citizen understood that this was a sly device which made it possible for North Vietnam to take over South Vietnam when it so chose. And suddenly, this was rewarded by the Nobel Prize for Peace—a tragic and ironic prize.

A very dangerous state of mind can arise as a result of this thirty years of retreat: give in as quickly as possible, give up as quickly as possible, peace and quiet at any cost.

This is what many Western papers wrote: "Let's hurry up and end the bloodshed in Vietnam and have national unity there." But at the Berlin Wall no one talked of national unity. One of your leading newspapers, after the end of Vietnam, had a full headline: "The Blessed Silence." I would not wish that kind of "blessed silence" on my worst enemy. I would not wish that kind of national unity on my worst enemy.

I spent eleven years in the Archipelago, and for half of my lifetime I have studied this question. Looking at this terrible tragedy in Vietnam from a distance, I can tell you, a million persons will be simply exterminated, while four to five million (in accordance with the scale of Vietnam) will find themselves in concentration camps and will be rebuilding Vietnam. And what is happening in Cambodia you already know. It is genocide. It is full and complete destruction but in a new form. Once again their technology is not up to building gas chambers. So, in a few hours, the entire capital city—the guilty capital city—is emptied out: old people, women, children are driven out without belongings, without food. "Go and die!"

This is very dangerous for one's view of the world when this feeling comes on: "Go ahead, give it up." We already hear voices in your country and in the West—"Give up Korea and we will live quietly. Give up Portugal, of course; give up Japan, give up Israel, give up Taiwan, the Philippines, Malaysia, Thailand, give up ten more African countries. Just let us live in peace and quiet. Just let us drive our big cars on our splendid highways; just let us play tennis and golf, in peace and quiet; just let us mix our cocktails in peace and quiet as we are accustomed to doing; just let us see the beautiful toothy smile with a glass in hand on every advertisement page of our magazines."

But look how things have turned out: Now in the West this has all turned into an accusation against the United States. Now, in the West, we hear very many voices saying, "It's your fault, America." And, here, I must decisively defend the United States against these accusations.

I have to say that the United States, of all the countries of the West, is the least guilty in all this and has done the most in order to prevent it. The United States has helped Europe to win the First and the Second World Wars. It twice raised Europe from postwar destruction—twice—for ten, twenty, thirty years it has stood as a shield protecting Europe while European countries were counting their nickels, to avoid paying for their armies (better yet to have none at all) to avoid paying for armaments, thinking about how to leave NATO, knowing that in any case America will protect them anyway. These countries started it all, despite their thousands of years of civilization and culture, even though they are closer and should have known better.

I came to your continent—for two months I have been travelling in its wide open spaces and I agree: here you do not feel the nearness of it all, the immediacy of it all. And here it is possible to miscalculate. Here you must make a spiritual effort to understand the acuteness of the world situation. The United States of America has long shown itself to be the most magnanimous, the most generous country in the world. Wherever there is a flood, an earthquake, a fire, a natural disaster, disease, who is the first to help? The United States. Who helps the most and unselfishly? The United States.

And what do we hear in reply? Reproaches, curses, "Yankee Go Home." American cultural centers are burned, and the representatives of the Third World jump on tables to vote against the United States.

But this does not take the load off America's shoulders. The course of history—whether you like it or not—has made you the leaders of the world. Your country can no longer think provincially. Your political leaders can no longer think only of their own states, of their parties, of petty arrangements which may or may not lead to promotion. You must think about the whole world, and when the new political crisis in the world will arise (I think we have just come to the end of a very acute crisis and the next one will come any moment), the main decisions will fall anyway on the shoulders of the United States of America.

And while already here, I have heard some explanations of the situation. Let me quote some of them: "It is impossible to protect those who do not have the will to defend themselves." I agree with that, but this was said about South Vietnam. In one-half of today's Europe and in three-quarters of today's world the will to defend oneself is even less than it was in South Vietnam.

We are told, "We should not protect those who do not have full democracy." This is the most remarkable argument of the lot. This is the leitmotif I hear in your newspapers and in the speeches of some of your political leaders. Who in the world, ever, on the front line of defense against totalitarianism has been able to sustain full democracy? You, the united democracies of the world, were not able to sustain it. America, England, France, Canada, Australia together did not sustain it. At the first threat of Hitlerism, you stretched out your hands to Stalin. You call that sustaining democracy?

And there is more of the same (there were many of these speeches in a row): "If the Soviet Union is going to use détente for its own ends, then we. . . ." But what will happen then? The Soviet Union has used détente in its own interests, is using it now and will continue to use it in its own interests! For example, China and the Soviet Union, both actively participating in détente, have quietly grabbed three countries of Indochina. True, perhaps as a consolation, China will send you a ping-pong team. And the Soviet Union has sent you the pilots who once crossed the North Pole. In a few days you are flying into space together.

A typical diversion. I remember very well the year, this was June of 1937, when Chkalov, Baidukov, and Beliakov heroically flew over the North

Pole and landed in the State of Washington. This was the very year when Stalin was executing more than 40,000 persons a month. And Stalin knew what he was doing. He sent those pilots and aroused in you a naïve delight —the friendship of two countries across the North Pole. The pilots were heroic, nobody will say anything against them. But this was a show—a show to divert you from the real events of 1937. And what is the occasion now? Is it an anniversary—38 years? Is 38 years some kind of an anniversary? No, it is simply necessary to cover up Vietnam. And, once again, those pilots were sent here. The Chkalov memorial was unveiled in the State of Washington. Chkalov was a hero and is worthy of a memorial. But, to present the true picture, behind the memorial there should have been a wall and on it there should have been a bas relief showing the executions, showing the skulls and bones.

We are also told (I apologize for so many quotes, but there are many more in your press and radio): "We cannot ignore the fact that North Vietnam and the Khmer Rouge have violated the agreement, but we're ready to look into the future." What does that mean? It means: Let them exterminate people. But if these murderers, who live by violence, these executioners, offer us détente we will be happy to go along with them. As Willy Brandt once said: "I would even be willing to have détente with Stalin." At a time when Stalin was executing 40,000 a month he would have been willing to have détente with Stalin?

Look into the future. This is how they looked into the future in 1933 and 1941, but it was a shortsighted look into the future. This is how they looked into the future two years ago when a senseless, incomprehensible, nonguaranteed truce in Vietnam was arranged, and it was a shortsighted view. There was such a hurry to make this truce that they forgot to liberate your own Americans from captivity. They were in such a hurry to sign this document that some 1,300 Americans—"Well, they have vanished; we can get by without them." How is that done? How can this be? Part of them, indeed, can be missing in action, but the leaders of North Vietnam themselves have admitted that some of them are still being kept in prison. And do they give you back your countrymen? No, they are not giving them back, and they are always raising new conditions. At first they said, "Remove

Thieu from power." Now, they say, "Have the United States restore Vietnam, otherwise it is very difficult for us to find these people."

If the government of North Vietnam has difficulty explaining to you what happened with your brothers, with your American POWs who have not yet returned, I, on the basis of my experience in the Archipelago, can explain this quite clearly. There is a law in the Archipelago that those who have been treated the most harshly and who have withstood the most bravely, the most honest, the most courageous, the most unbending, never again come out into the world. They are never again shown to the world because they will tell such tales as the human mind cannot accept. A part of your returned POWs told you that they were tortured. This means that those who have remained were tortured even more, but did not yield an inch. These are your best people. These are your first heroes, who, in a solitary combat, have stood the test. And today, unfortunately, they cannot take courage from our applause. They can't hear it from their solitary cells where they may either die or sit thirty years, like Raoul Wallenberg, the Swedish diplomat who was seized in 1945 in the Soviet Union. He has been imprisoned for thirty years and they will not yield him up.

And you have some hysterical public figure who said: "I will go to North Vietnam. I will stand on my knees and beg them to release our prisoners of war." This isn't a political act—this is masochism.

To understand properly what détente has meant all these forty years—friendships, stabilization of the situation, trade, etc., I would have to tell you something, which you have never seen or heard, of how it looked from the other side. Let me tell you how it looked. Mere acquaintance with an American, and God forbid that you should sit with him in a café or restaurant, meant a ten-year term for suspicion of espionage.

In the first volume of *Archipelago* I tell of an event which was not told me by some arrested person, but by all of the members of the Supreme Court of the USSR during those short days when I was in the limelight under Khrushchev. One Soviet citizen was in the United States and on his return said that in the United States they have wonderful automobile roads. The KGB arrested him and demanded a term of ten years. But the judge said: "I don't object, but there is not enough evidence. Couldn't you find something else against him?" So the judge was exiled to Sakhalin because he dared to argue and they gave the other man ten years. Can you imagine what a lie he told? And what sort of praise this was of American imperialism—in America there are good roads? Ten years.

In 1945–1946 through our prison cells passed a lot of persons—and these were not ones who were cooperating with Hitler, although there were some of those, too. They were not guilty of anything, but rather persons who had just been in the West and had been liberated from German prison camps by the Americans. This was considered a criminal act: liberated by the Americans. That means he has seen the good life. If he comes back he will talk about it. The most terrible thing is not what he did but what he would talk about. And all such persons got ten-year terms.

During Nixon's last visit to Moscow your American correspondents were reporting in the Western way from the streets of Moscow. I am going down a Russian street with a microphone and asking the ordinary Soviet citizen: "Tell me please, what do you think about the meeting between Nixon and Brezhnev?" And, amazingly, every last person answered: "Wonderful. I'm delighted. I'm absolutely overjoyed!"

What does this mean? If I'm going down a street in Moscow and some American comes up to me with a microphone and asks me something, then I know that on the other side of him is a member of the state security, also with a microphone who is recording everything I say. You think that I'm going to say something that is going to put me in prison immediately? Of course I say: "It's wonderful; I'm overjoyed."

But what is the value of such correspondents if they simply transfer Western techniques over there without thinking things through?

You helped us for many years with Lend–Lease, but we have now done everything to forget this, to erase it from our minds, not to remember it if at all possible. And now, before I came into this hall, I delayed my visit to Washington a little in order to first take a look at some ordinary parts of America, going to various states and simply talking with people. I was told, and I learned this for the first time, that in every state during the war years there were Soviet–American friendship societies which collected assistance for Soviet people—warm clothes, canned food, gifts and sent them to the Soviet Union. But we not only never saw these, we not only never received them (they were distributed somewhere among the privileged circles), no one ever even told us that this was being done. I only learned about it for the first time here, this month, in the United States.

Everything poisonous which could be said about the United States was said in Stalin's days. And all of this is a heavy sediment which can be stirred up anytime. Any day the newspapers can come out with the headlines: "Bloodthirsty American imperialism wants to seize control of the world," and this poison will rise up from the sediment and many people in our country will believe this, and will be poisoned by it, and will consider you as aggressors. This is how détente has been managed on our side.

The Soviet system is so closed that it is almost impossible for you to understand from here. Your theoreticians and scholars write works trying to understand and explain how things occur there. Here are some naïve explanations which are simply funny to Soviet citizens. Some say that the Soviet leaders have now given up their inhumane ideology. Not at all. They haven't given it up one bit.

Some say that in the Kremlin there are some on the left, some on the right. And they are fighting with each other, and we've got to behave in such a way as not to interfere with those on the left side. This is all fantasy: left . . . right. There is some sort of a struggle for power, but they all agree on the essentials.

There also exists the following theory, that now, thanks to the growth of technology, there is a technocracy in the Soviet Union, a growing number of engineers and the engineers are now running the economy and will soon determine the fate of the country, rather than the party. I will tell you, though, that the engineers determine the fate of the economy just as much as our generals determine the fate of the Army. That means zero. Everything is done the way the party demands. That's our system. Judge it for yourself.

It is a system where for forty years there haven't been genuine elections but simply a comedy, a farce. Thus a system which has no legislative organs. It is a system without an independent press; a system without an independent judiciary; where the people have no influence either on external or internal policy; where any thought which is different from what the state thinks is crushed.

And let me tell you that electronic bugging in our country is such a simple thing that it is a matter of everyday life. You had an instance in the United States where a bugging caused an uproar which lasted for a year and a half. For us it is an everyday matter. Almost every apartment, every institution has got its bug and it doesn't surprise us in the least—we are used to it.

It is a system where unmasked butchers of millions, like Molotov, and others smaller than him, have never been tried in the courts but retire on tremendous pensions in the greatest comfort. It is a system where the show still goes on today and to which every foreigner is introduced surrounded by a couple of planted agents working according to a set scenario. It is a system where the very constitution has never been carried out for one single day; where all the decisions mature in secrecy, high up in a small irresponsible group and then are released on us and on you like a bolt of lightning.

And what are the signatures of such persons worth? How could one rely on their signatures to documents of détente? You yourselves might ask your specialists now and they will tell you that precisely in recent years the Soviet Union has succeeded in creating wonderful chemical weapons, missiles, which are even better than those used by the United States.

So what are we to conclude from that? Is détente needed or not? Not only is it needed, it is as necessary as air. It is the only way of saving the earth—instead of a world war to have détente, but a true détente, and if it has already been ruined by the bad word which we use for it—"détente"—then we should find another word for it.

I would say that there are very few, only three, main characteristics of such a true détente.

In the first place, there would be disarmament—not only disarmament from the use of war but also from the use of violence. We must stop using not only the sort of arms which are used to destroy one's neighbors, but the sort of arms which are used to oppress one's fellow countrymen. It is not détente if we here with you today can spend our time agreeably while over there people are groaning and dying and in psychiatric hospitals. Doctors are making their evening rounds, for the third time injecting people with drugs which destroy their brain cells.

The second sign of détente, I would say, is the following: that it be not one based on smiles, not on verbal concessions, but it has to be based on a firm foundation. You know the words from the Bible: "Build not on sand, but on rock." There has to be a guarantee that this will not be broken overnight and for this the other side—the other party to the agreement—must have its acts subject to public opinion, to the press, and to a freely elected parliament. And until such control exists there is absolutely no guarantee.

The third simple condition—what sort of détente is it when they employ the sort of inhumane propaganda which is proudly called in the Soviet Union "ideological warfare." Let us not have that. If we are going to be friends, let us be friends; if we are going to have détente, then let us have détente—and an end to ideological warfare.

The Soviet Union and the communist countries can conduct negotiations. They know how to do this. For a long time they don't make any concessions and then they give in a little bit. Then everyone says triumphantly, "Look, they've made a concession; it's time to sign." The European negotiators of the 35 countries for two years now have painfully been negotiating and their nerves were stretched to the breaking point and they finally gave in. A few women from the communist countries can now marry foreigners. And a few newspapermen are now going to be permitted to travel a little more than before. They give 1/1,000th of what natural law should provide. Matters which people should be able to do even before such negotiations are undertaken. And already there is joy. And here in the West we hear many voices, saying: "Look, they're making concessions; it's time to sign."

During these two years of negotiations, in all the countries of Eastern Europe, the pressure has increased, the oppression intensified, even in Yugoslavia and Romania, leaving aside the other countries. And it is precisely now that the Austrian chancellor says, "We've got to sign this agreement as rapidly as possible."

What sort of an agreement would this be? The proposed agreement is the funeral of Eastern Europe. It means that Western Europe would finally, once and for all, sign away Eastern Europe, stating that it is perfectly willing to see Eastern Europe be crushed and overwhelmed once and for all, but please don't bother us. And the Austrian chancellor thinks that if all these countries are pushed into a mass grave, Austria at the very edge of this grave will survive and not fall into it also.

And we, from our lives there, have concluded that violence can only be withstood by firmness.

You have to understand the nature of communism. The very ideology of communism, all of Lenin's teachings, is that anyone is considered to be a fool who doesn't take what is lying in front of him. If you can take it, take it. If you can attack, attack. But if there is a wall, then go back. And the communist leaders respect only firmness and have contempt and laugh at persons who continually give in to them. Your people are now saying—and this is the last quotation I am going to give you from the statements of your leaders—"Power, without any attempt at conciliation, will lead to a world conflict." But I would say that power with continual subservience is no power at all.

But from our experience I can tell you that only firmness will make it possible to withstand the assaults of communist totalitarianism. We see many historic examples, and let me give you some of them. Look at little Finland in 1939, which by its own forces withstood the attack. You, in 1948, defended Berlin only by your firmness of spirit, and there was no world conflict. In Korea in 1950 you stood up against the communists, only by your firmness, and there was no world conflict. In 1962 you compelled the rockets to be removed from Cuba. Again it was only firmness, and there was no world conflict. And the late Konrad Adenauer conducted firm negotiations with Khrushchev and thus started a genuine détente with Khrushchev. Khrushchev started to make concessions and if he hadn't been removed, that winter he was planning to go to Germany and to continue the genuine détente.

Let me remind you of the weakness of a man whose name is rarely associated with weakness—the weakness of Lenin. Lenin, when he came to power, in panic gave up to Germany everything Germany wanted. Just what it wanted. Germany took as much as it wanted and said, "Give Armenia to Turkey." And Lenin said, "Fine." It's almost an unknown fact but Lenin petitioned the Kaiser to act as intermediary to persuade the Ukraine and, thus, to make possible a boundary between the communist part of Russia and the Ukraine. It wasn't a question of seizing the Ukraine but rather of making a boundary with the Ukraine.

We, we the dissidents of the USSR, don't have any tanks, we don't have any weapons, we have no organization. We don't have anything. Our hands are empty. We have only a heart and what we have lived through in the half century of this system. And when we have found the firmness within ourselves to stand up for our rights, we have done so. It is only by firmness of spirit that we have withstood. And if I am standing here before you, it is not because of the kindness or the good will of communism, not thanks to détente, but thanks to my own firmness and your firm support. They knew that I would not yield one inch, not one hair. And when they couldn't do more they themselves fell back.

This is not easy. In our conditions this was taught to me by the difficulties of my own life. And if you yourselves—any one of you—were in the same difficult situation, you would have learned the same thing. Take Vladimir Bukovsky, whose name is now almost forgotten. Now, I don't want to mention a lot of names because however many I might mention there are more still. And when we resolve the question with two or three names it is as if we forget and betray the others. We should rather remember figures. There are tens of thousands of political prisoners in our country and—by the calculation of English specialists—7,000 persons are now under compulsory psychiatric treatment. Let us take Vladimir Bukovsky as an example. It was proposed to him, "All right, we'll free you. Go to the West and shut up." And this young man, a youth today on the verge of death said: "No, I won't go this way. I have written about the persons whom you have put in insane asylums. You release them and then I'll go West." This is what I mean by that firmness of spirit to stand up against granite and tanks.

Finally, to evaluate everything that I have said to you, I would say we need not have had our conversation on the level of business calculations. Why did such and such a country act in such and such a way? What were they counting on? We should rather rise above this to the moral level and, say: "In 1933 and in 1941 your leaders and the whole Western world, in an unprincipled way, made a deal with totalitarianism." We will have to pay for this, someday this deal will come back to haunt us. For thirty years we have been paying for it and we are still paying for it. And we are going to pay for it in a worse way.

One cannot think only in the low level of political calculations. It is necessary to think also of what is noble, and what is honorable—not only what is profitable. Resourceful Western legal scholars have now introduced the term "legal realism." By legal realism, they want to push aside any moral evaluation of affairs. They say, "Recognize realities; if such and such laws have been established in such and such countries by violence, these laws still must be recognized and respected."

At the present time it is widely accepted among lawyers that law is higher than morality—law is something which is worked out and developed, whereas morality is something inchoate and amorphous. That is not the case. The opposite is rather true! Morality is higher than law! While law is our human attempt to embody in rules a part of that moral sphere which is above us. We try to understand this morality, bring it down to earth and present it in a form of laws. Sometimes we are more successful, sometimes less. Sometimes you actually have a caricature of morality, but morality is always higher than law. This view must never be abandoned. We must accept it with heart and soul.

It is almost a joke now in the Western world, in the 20th century, to use words like "good" and "evil." They have become almost old-fashioned concepts, but they are very real and genuine concepts. These are concepts from a sphere which is higher than us. And instead of getting involved in base, petty, shortsighted political calculations and games, we have to recognize that the concentration of World Evil and the tremendous force of hatred is there and it is flowing from there throughout the world. And we have to stand up against it and not hasten to give to it, give to it, give to it, everything that it wants to swallow.

Today there are two major processes occurring in the world. One is the one which I have just described to you which has been in progress more than thirty years. It is a process of shortsighted concessions; a process of giving up and giving up and giving up and hoping that perhaps at some point the wolf will have eaten enough.

The second process is one which I consider the key to everything and which, I will say now, will bring all of us our future; under the cast-iron shell of communism—for twenty years in the Soviet Union and a shorter time in other communist countries—there is occurring a liberation of the human spirit. New generations are growing up which are steadfast in their struggle with evil; which are not willing to accept unprincipled compromises; which prefer to lose everything—salary, conditions of existence, and life itself—but are not willing to sacrifice conscience; not willing to make deals with evil.

This process has now gone so far that in the Soviet Union today, Marxism has fallen so low that it has become an anecdote, it is simply an object of contempt. No serious person in our country today, not even university and high school students, can talk about Marxism without smiling, without laughing. But this whole process of our liberation, which obviously will entail social transformations, is slower than the first one—the process of concessions. Over there, when we see these concessions, we are frightened. Why so quickly? Why so precipitously? Why yield several countries a year?

I started by saying that you are the allies of our liberation movement in the communist countries. And I call upon you: Let us think together and try to see how we can adjust the relationship between these two processes. Whenever you help the persons persecuted in the Soviet Union, you not only display magnanimity and nobility, you are defending not only them but yourselves as well. You are defending your own future.

So let us try and see how far we can go to stop this senseless and immoral process of endless concessions to the aggressor—these clever legal arguments for why we should give up one country after another. Why must we hand over to communist totalitarianism more and more technology—complex, delicate, developed technology which it needs for armaments and for crushing its own citizens? If we can at least slow down that process of concessions, if not stop it all together—and make it possible for the process of liberation to continue in the communist countries—ultimately these two processes will yield us our future.

On our crowded planet there are no longer any internal affairs. The communist leaders say, "Don't interfere in our internal affairs. Let us strangle our citizens in peace and quiet." But I tell you: Interfere more and more. Interfere as much as you can. We beg you to come and interfere.

❏ ❏ ❏

ALEXANDR I. SOLZHENITSYN was born in 1918 in Kislovodsk, Russia. After receiving a degree in mathematics, he served in the Red Army artillery during World War II. In 1945, he was arrested for criticizing Stalin in a letter and imprisoned in Soviet labor camps for eight years, during which time he began writing. In 1970, he was awarded the Nobel Prize for Literature. In 1974, he was arrested, tried for treason, and exiled, settling finally in the United States. He returned to his native Russia in 1994. Mr. Solzhenitsyn's several novels include *One Day in the Life of Ivan Denisovich* (1962), *The First Circle* (1968), *Cancer Ward* (1968), and *August 1914* (1971). His histories include the three-volume *The Gulag Archipelago* (1974).

Exit Communism, Cold War, and the Status Quo

Jeane J. Kirkpatrick

January 1991

Dr. Kirkpatrick delivered the following speech at Hillsdale College's FreedomQuest Gala on the Hillsdale campus.

❏ ❏ ❏

It is exciting to be here at Hillsdale College. I was pleased and honored when Hillsdale presented me with the Freedom Leadership Award in 1984. As a speaker for the College's off-campus programs for some years, I was also happy to share some of my views about the importance of Hillsdale on the College's recently released FreedomQuest campaign video, but this is my first visit to campus and, like Charlton Heston, who preceded me during this program, I am impressed with what I see. I am impressed with the hundreds of loyal and interested supporters who are here too, who share the sense that what goes on here—indeed, the very idea of this college—is important to our country, our values and our culture. So I congratulate you, Hillsdale, and I thank you for inviting me.

How 1989 Changed the World

I am here to talk a little bit about the world of the late 1980s and early 1990s. The year 1989, in particular, was one of the most extraordinary periods in modern history. The most important lessons this year has taught

287

are, first, that we must expect the unexpected, and second, that we must stand firm for what we believe. The old adage that if we have patience and persist, things will get better turned out to be true.

There was a very direct relationship between the patient and persistent policies from President Truman to President Reagan. With his rebuilding of American strength in the 1980s, and his unembarrassed defense of democratic ideals at home and abroad, Reagan encouraged the remarkable changes that have occurred in Eastern Europe and in the Soviet Union and are indeed still occurring.

In truth, 1989 changed the world. At the beginning of that year, the world was much as it had been for the previous four decades. It was the post-World War II status quo: Europe was divided by a cold war created by a real Soviet threat, as evidenced by the brutal occupation of Eastern Europe and by continuing Soviet expansion into five continents. Soviet dominance extended into our own backyard, not only in Nicaragua, but by the threat of its attempted expansion into El Salvador, Guatemala, Columbia, Peru, Grenada, and Jamaica.

It is difficult today even to recall the situation of the world in 1980, which remained nearly unchanged up until 1989, when there was what the Soviets call a "change of the world correlation of forces." This change had been brought about by the resurgence and renaissance of American strength, and by the continuing decline of the Soviet Union. The Soviet Union was and still is the only industrial power in the world whose living standards are declining rather than increasing, whose average life expectancy is declining (from seventy-four years for Soviet males to seventy-one years over a period of about five years in the last decade) while infant mortality rates are rising.

A "Crisis of the Soul"

By 1989, it was undeniable that the Soviet Union was in a decline that was incredible by any standards, and it was equally evident that such a decline had created a kind of "crisis of conscience," or, perhaps, that the crisis of conscience had created the decline. We don't usually talk about conscience when we talk about Soviet leaders and Soviet policy. I have been discovering of late some fascinating facets reading the speeches of some of Mikhail Gorbachev's principal advisors. Let me share with you a few words from the text of Aleksandr Yakovlev, for example. Yakovlev is the man whom almost everyone thinks is Mikhail Gorbachev's closest advisor. Yakovlev has emphasized intellectual and spiritual factors in Soviet changes. One of his statements about the Soviet people that has been widely quoted is: "We have suffered not only a crisis in economics but a crisis of the soul." This is Aleksandr Yakovlev on July 2, 1990:

> I am convinced that the time has come for truth. To speak of nobility, charity, honor, and conscience, even at a Congress of Communists, shaking from our feet the mud of enmity and suspicion that has built up over the decades. It is the very time for the party to take the initiative in the moral cleansing of our existence and our consciousness. This is why I am convinced of the historic correctness of the choice that was made in 1985 to establish perestroika.

He went on to remark on his activities in the years since 1985, which went beyond advising Mikhail Gorbachev:

> A special sphere of my work in recent years has been the Commission study of materials relating to the repressions visited on our country in the past. I will tell you honestly; it is heavy, spiritually exhausting work when the ashes of millions of people constantly haunt you. The good names of almost a million people have been returned. But there has been falsification of such a scale. Repressions could not have been a matter of chance and could not have been the consequence of an evil will alone. [By] whom and how is the mechanism of repression created and set in motion? How did it function? Why did nothing stand in its path?

Yakovlev then went on to discuss the Stalinist period. He paused over the collectivization in the Ukraine, that horror about which Robert Conquest has written movingly and accurately in books like *The Great Terror* and *The Genocide of the Ukraine*, in which a manmade famine was visited upon the people of the Ukraine. Starving men, women and children were driven off their land, scattered, and killed.

Yakovlev says, "In my view that was the most monstrous crime when hundreds of thousands of peasant families were driven out of the villages, not understanding why such a fate befell them. They were driven out by the authorities they themselves had established. The dead cannot be brought back but their good names may be restored in history." And then Yakovlev added a line that has since become famous among his countrymen: "Let us remember not the empty shelves but the empty souls who have brought a change to our country which demands revolutionary change."

The reaction of Yakovlev, one of the most well-known public figures in the Soviet Union, is worth our serious attention. Unfortunately, his comments and those of others like him are being largely ignored or discounted in the West.

Yakovlev quoted Kant in early September: "Long ago, the great philosopher Kant wrote that there are two prejudices: 'to believe everything and to believe nothing.' But then again, he wrote there are also mysteries, the scarlet sky above us, and the moral law within us."

Imagine the second most powerful man in the Soviet Union talking about the moral law within us—and then imagine virtually all the major media outlets in the West ignoring his extraordinary pronouncement! Both are remarkable.

Yakovlev added, "According to the moral law, our society that is transforming itself into a free society has yet . . . in the process of transforming itself to overcome the obstructions of falsehood." He goes on to charge that the confidence of the people had been abused in the old communist system, and that "the people wished us merely good and the State responded with the evil of prisons and camps."

Yakovlev ends this comment with an extraordinary appeal, "Preserve me, Almighty, from calls for vengeance, from a new round of intolerance, that our society must know the names of the people who committed these deeds in order to assess them according to moral criteria."

Soviet Reprisals: The Dog That Didn't Bark

I share these words of Aleksandr Yakovlev with you that I have been reading with growing surprise myself. I also want to share with you a sense of the depth of change that is taking place in the Soviet Union today. That change has, of course, already transformed the post-World War II world in which we had lived for over forty years. It was an uncomfortable world, because we were faced by continuous challenges, and because it imposed very heavy burdens on our country. Yet it was comfortable, because we knew it and were accustomed to it, and we knew what we should do—help defend the frontiers of freedom.

What happened in 1989 that was most remarkable was like the dog that didn't bark in Sherlock Holmes's famous mystery tale. What didn't happen was that the Soviet troops did not intervene to crush the liberation movements in Hungary, Poland, Czechoslovakia, and East Germany. I was in Poland in late August of that year. The first elected government since World War II had been installed. It was, naturally, largely Solidarity government, although you will recall that it included two communist ministers (who have only recently been fired). Those two communist ministers were in the defense ministry and in the interior. The newly elected Polish Solidarity government had agreed to give the communists, who had been clobbered in the elections, the control over the armed forces and the police. Why? Because they thought they had to; because they feared that Soviet troops would crush their democratic movement.

At the time I was there last August, Solidarity's victory was still uncertain. No one knew what to expect; every step toward independence was taken courageously enough, but was attended by great misgivings. Two Solidarity leaders, ministers in the new government, confessed privately to me: "None of us forgets our years in prison." After all, they had been in prison less than five years before when Poland was under martial law and no one's rights were protected. And it had been less than a decade since Father Popieluszko had been beaten to death for daring to speak about independence for his country.

The uncertainty existed for all Eastern Europe. No one knew what was going to happen in Hungary when its citizens announced that they were going to change the national constitution and open the border with Austria. Even though it was rumored that they had the approval of Mikhail Gorbachev, no one, not even Gorbachev, could predict the results of such unprecedented reform. We know now that when the border did open, East Germans began to surge through in a kind of human tidal wave. We also know that this mass exodus began the process of the reunification of Germany.

No one knew what would happen when the citizens of Czechoslovakia went into the streets for the first time since 1968. Miraculously, they did not encounter tanks—just each other—and there, too, freedom at last was realizable.

The Challenge of Normal Times

The most important event of 1989 was really a nonevent: the tanks that did not roll and the Soviet troops that stayed in their barracks. This was the end of the Soviet empire, and it disintegrated faster than any other empire in modern history. Obviously, the danger is not yet over—there are still Soviet tanks and troops in Eastern Europe, and there are tens of thousands of Soviet missiles. But the "will to empire" has disappeared. We can say of the year 1989 that history's most bold, daring, and ruthless experiment in social engineering was effectively abandoned by the heirs of the men who began it.

Now, the question is, what will replace that experiment? Some Soviets like Yakovlev, who lived in the West for nearly a decade, talk of building a free society. Gorbachev often says the same thing, and although I am not sure that he understands what such freedom really means, he is a very pragmatic man who understands that reform is in his and the Soviet Union's best interest. In the last few years he has begun to ask questions that the Soviet people were, to say the least, unaccustomed to hearing. For example, he asked if it were true old Bolsheviks were guilty of the crimes they had been executed for, and even went to the trouble of establishing two investigative commissions that discovered that some were wrongly accused.

"Is it true?"—that is not a Bolshevik question, as anyone knows who recalls the infamous Moscow show trials of the 1930s. And Gorbachev followed up with another uncharacteristic question about the Soviet economy. He asked, simply, "Does it work?" When Bolsheviks before him asked if the economy worked, what they really meant was, "Does it serve the Revolution?" To his credit, Gorbachev meant something quite different. He pointed to Soviet agriculture as an unworkable system and advocated following the practice of Hungary and China in leasing land to farmers. The state is still in control, of course, but once even half-measures of private ownership are introduced, the pressure for complete reform begins to build momentum.

Watching Soviet leaders like Gorbachev let go of power is a fascinating experience. The stops and starts, the infighting with other Soviets like Ligachev, the retrenchments and advances—these are all part of a historical drama. There has never been a totalitarian state quite like the Soviet Union, and there has never been one that was dismantled without great violence. Yet we seem to be witnessing a relatively peaceful transformation to a democratic political structure and a market economy in the USSR.

Ironically enough, our libraries are filled with books on the transformation from capitalism to socialism, but practically no books have been written about how to bring about the reverse. There are only one or two like the brilliant Peruvian Hernando de Soto's book about his country called *The Other Path*. They desperately need such books in Eastern Europe and the Soviet Union.

In the West, we need books that will remind us that it has been democratic capitalism, not socialism, that has won the Cold War, lest we allow the former's few remaining adherents to convince us that socialism is the wave of the future. We also need to be aware, as we have been vividly reminded by the Persian Gulf crisis, that the post-Cold War world is not necessarily a more peaceful world. Military power and national resolve still count. In this less predictable, less "connected" world, there are many centers of power, and international politics has become much more complicated. The challenge ahead is not the same as it was during the Cold War; it is, rather, the challenge of "normal times," times in which the future is still uncertain. Let us hope that we will see more years like 1989.

❏ ❏ ❏

JEANE J. KIRKPATRICK is the Leavey Professor at Georgetown University and a Senior Fellow and Director of Foreign and Defense Policy Studies at the American Enterprise Institute. She received her A.B. at Barnard College, and her M.A. and Ph.D. in comparative politics at Columbia University. From 1981 to 1985, she was the U.S. Representative to the United Nations and a member of President Reagan's cabinet. She served as a member of the President's Foreign Policy Advisory Board from 1985 to 1990, and of the Defense Policy Review Board from 1985 to 1993. She has published numerous articles in major publications such as the *New York Times*, the *Washington Post*, *Foreign Affairs*, and *Commentary*. Her books include *Legitimacy and Force: Political and Moral Dimensions* (1988) and *The Withering Away of the Totalitarian State . . . and Other Surprises* (1990).

Keeping the Faith: Religion, Freedom, and International Affairs

Paul Marshall

March 1999

Mr. Marshall delivered the following speech at a Hillsdale College seminar, "Faith and Freedom Around the World," on the Hillsdale campus.

❏ ❏ ❏

At the end of 1997, former *New York Times* executive editor A. M. Rosenthal confessed, "I realized that in decades of reporting, writing, or assigning stories on human rights, I rarely touched on one of the most important. Political human rights, legal, civil, and press rights, emphatically often; but the right to worship where and how God or conscience leads, almost never."

The habit of ignoring religious persecution is all too common in the West. On August 22, 1998, for example, seven leaders of underground churches in China released an unprecedented joint statement calling for dialogue with the communist government. The U.S. media virtually ignored the statement, despite the fact that these leaders represent the *only* nationwide group in China not under government control. Their membership of fifteen million is several times larger than the population of Tibet and hundreds of times larger than the number of China's democracy and human rights activists. But the press just isn't interested.

Nor is it interested in religious persecution in Sudan, the largest country in Africa, which still practices crucifixion. After enduring more than forty years of civil war, the predominantly Christian population in southern Sudan is subject to torture, rape, and starvation for its refusal to convert to Islam. Christian children are routinely sold into slavery. Muslims who dare to convert to Christianity are faced with the death penalty.

In the last fifteen years, Sudan's death toll of more than 1.9 million is far greater than Rwanda's (800,000), Bosnia's (300,000), and Kosovo's (1,000) *combined*. The United Nations' special rapporteur on Sudan, Gaspar Biro, produced five official reports documenting the carnage, declaring "abuses are past proving . . . these are the facts." He resigned when his reports were consistently ignored.

Not a week goes by that Freedom House's Center for Religious Freedom does not learn of major stories of religious persecution abroad. Christians are usually the victims, but so are many others, such as Buddhists in Vietnam, Baha'i's in Iran, and Shiite Muslims in Afghanistan. These stories rarely make headlines or penetrate the consciousness of journalists and foreign policy professionals.

Secular Myopia

One main cause for this ignorance is what I call "secular myopia," that is, "an introverted, parochial inability even to see, much less understand, the role of religion in human life." It is a condition that mainly afflicts the "chattering classes," which include diplomats, journalists, political commentators, and policy analysts. As strategic theorist Edward Luttwak has observed, the chattering classes are eager to examine economic causes, social differentiations, and political affiliations, but they generally disregard the impact of faith upon the lives of individuals and the lives of nations.

Secular myopia can have painful consequences. Remember how little the U.S. knew about the Ayatollah Khomeini and his followers in Iran during the late 1970s? Luttwak notes that there was only one proposal for the CIA to examine "the attitude and activities of the more prominent religious leaders" and that this proposal was vetoed as an irrelevant exercise in sociology.

As the Shah's regime was collapsing, U.S. political analysts kept insisting that everything was fine. True to their training, they focused on economic variables, class structure, and the military, and they concluded that, since businessmen, the upper classes, and the military supported the Shah, he was safe. There were, of course, many *mullahs* (religious teachers and leaders) arousing Islamic sentiment, but the analysts believed that religious movements drew only on folk memories, were destined to disappear with "modernization," and were irrelevant to the real forces and institutions of political power.

Consequently, the U.S. did not clear its embassy of important documents or staff. When Khomeini seized power, his followers captured both. They used the former to attack American personnel throughout the Middle East and the latter to precipitate a hostage crisis that paralyzed our nation for two years.

According to Luttwak, during the Vietnam War, "every demographic, economic, ethnic, social, and, of course, military aspect of the conflict was subject to detailed scrutiny, but the deep religious cleavages that afflicted South Vietnam were hardly noticed." He added that the "tensions between the dominant Catholic minority [and] a resentful Buddhist majority... were largely ignored until Buddhist monks finally had to resort to flaming self-immolations in public squares, precisely to attract the attention of Americans so greatly attentive to everything else in Vietnam that was impeccably secular."

Similar tales can be told of our myopic view of conflicts in Bosnia, Nicaragua, Israel, Lebanon, India, the Philippines, and Indonesia.

Misunderstanding Religion

Religion as Ethnicity

In 1997, when Malaysian Prime Minister Mahathir Mohamed railed against speculators with the outrageous claim, "We are Muslims, and the Jews are not happy to see the Muslims progress," the *Los Angeles Times* described him as "race-obsessed." Perhaps the *Times* took its cue from media descriptions of former Yugoslavia. In this tortured land, the war raging between the Orthodox, Catholics, and Muslims is always referred to as "ethnic" and attacks on Bosnian Muslims are always referred to as "ethnic cleansing."

There are many such examples of media misunderstanding. *The Economist* headlined a 1997 story about attacks on twenty-five churches and a temple in Eastern Java that were prompted by a Muslim heresy trial as "Race Riots." A 1998 *New York Times* editorial on rampant violence in Indonesia cited "tensions between Indonesia's Muslim majority and Chinese minority" as if there were no Chinese Muslims and no non-Muslims except for the Chinese.

Religion as Irrationality

Western opinionmakers and policymakers consider themselves the heirs of the "Enlightenment," an 18th-century intellectual movement that stressed rationalism and science over faith and other forms of "superstition." To them, all contemporary peoples, events, and issues fall into Enlightenment categories, which are most often political or ideological.

Muslims are identified as "right-wing," even when they advocate leftist economic controls. Hindus who propose to build a temple on the site of the Babri mosque in India and Jews who propose to build a Third Temple on the site of the Dome of the Rock in Jerusalem are also labeled "left-wing" or "right-wing" without any regard to religious context.

When the vocabulary of "left" and "right" has run its tired course, we are left with that old standby, "fundamentalist"—a word dredged up from the American past, despite dubious provenance. What "fundamentalist" means when applied to Christians, Buddhists, Hindus, or Muslims is hard to understand. Using the term is a sign of intellectual laziness. If what believers believe does not easily fall into an Enlightenment category, then it is assumed that they must be "irrational." Thus, "fundamentalist" is now merely shorthand for "religious fanatic"—for someone who is to be categorized rather than heard, observed rather than comprehended, dismissed rather than respected.

Religion as Sublimated Anxiety

When ethnicity and psychology fail to subsume religion, the alternative is to treat it, in quasi-Marxist fashion, as the sublimation of drives that supposedly can be explained by poverty, economic changes, or the stresses of modernity. Of course, these factors do play a role, but, all too often, what we encounter is an a priori methodological commitment to treating religion as secondary—as a mildly interesting phenomenon that can be explained, but that is never an explanation in and of itself.

So great is this bias that when the *Journal of International Affairs* devoted its 1996 edition to studies of religious influences, it apologized in part for even mentioning faith with the admission, "Religion may seem an unusual topic for an international affairs journal." The editors added that "it is hardly surprising that scholars . . . have, for the most part, ignored [religion]."

Taking Religion Seriously

Religion and War

If we *do* start to take religion seriously in international affairs, then we will learn a great deal about war, about democracy, and about freedom of all kinds.

It was pointed out by religion scholars long before political scientist Samuel Huntington's recent book, *The Clash of Civilizations and the Remaking of the World Order*, that chronic armed conflict is concentrated on the margins of the traditional religions, especially along the boundaries of the Islamic world. The Middle East, the Southern Sahara, the Balkans, the Caucasus, Central Asia, and Southern Asia are where Islam, Christianity, Judaism, Buddhism, and Hinduism intersect. It is also where most wars have broken out in the last fifty years.

These are not explicitly religious wars. But since religion shapes cultures, people in these regions have different histories and different views of human life. Regardless of the triggers for conflict, they are living in unstable areas where conflict is likely to occur—in religious fault zones that are also prone to political earthquakes.

Religion and Democracy

Religion also shapes governments. In Eastern Europe, authoritarian governments are finding it easier to hold on in areas where the Orthodox church, with its long history of association with the state, has had special influence. The new boundaries of Eastern and Western Europe are tending to fall along the old divide between Orthodox and Catholic/Protestant.

Huntington makes a strong case that in the 1970s to 1980s a "third wave of democracy" swept over Portugal, Spain, Eastern Europe, Latin America, and the Philippines, in part because of important changes in the dominant nongovernment institution—the Catholic church. (He concludes that changes made after the Second Vatican Council inspired a major movement toward democracy and human rights.)

The role of the church in the fall of communism may not be clear to Western observers afflicted with secular myopia, but it is all too clear to Chinese government officials. As brutal practitioners of communism, they are perversely aware of the power of human spirituality, and so they regard religion with deadly seriousness. In 1992, the Chinese press noted that "the church played an important role in the change" in Eastern Europe and the former Soviet Union and warned, "If China does not want such a scene to be repeated in its land, it must strangle the baby while it is still in the manger."

Underground church or "house church" leaders consistently report that the current government crackdown is due to fears prompted by religious events in the former Soviet bloc. Even Chinese government documents actually implementing the crackdown state that one of their purposes is to prevent "the changes that occurred in the former Soviet Union and Eastern Europe."

Each year, Freedom House conducts a comparative survey of political rights and civil liberties around the world. The 1998–1999 survey finds that, of the 88 countries rated as "free," 79 "are majority Christian by tradition or belief." Clearly, correlations are not causalities, so this does not imply any direct link between Christianity and democracy (the survey also finds a connection between Hinduism and democracy). However, the existence of such a relationship is significant, not least because it is far greater than material factors such as economic growth, on which theorists and analysts lavish attention.

Politics and the Nature of the Church

One reason for the modern correlation between Christianity and political freedom lies in the nature of the church. From the beginning Christians, while usually loyal citizens, necessarily have an attachment to "another king" and a loyalty to a divine order that is apart from and beyond the political order.

In the Latin churches of the West, the two realms of *sacerdotium* (church) and *regnum* (state) emerged. Henceforth, there were two centers of authority in society. As political philosopher George Sabine reminds us, the Christian church became a distinct institution, independent of the state, entitled to shape the spiritual concerns of mankind. This, he adds, "may not unreasonably be described as the most revolutionary event in the history of Western Europe, in respect both to politics and to political thought."

It is not that the church or the state directly advocated religious freedom or any other freedom—they did not, and often inquisitions were defended. But people in both realms always believed that there *should be* boundaries, and they struggled over centuries to define them. This meant that the church, whatever its lust for civil control, had always to acknowledge that there were forms of political power which it could and should not exercise. And the state, whatever its drive to dominate, had to acknowledge that there were areas of human life that were beyond its reach.

The very existence of the modern church denies that the state is the all-encompassing or ultimate arbiter of human life. Regardless of how the relationship between God and Caesar has been confused, it now at least means that, contra the Romans and modern totalitarians, *Caesar is not God.* This confession, however mute, sticks in the craw of every authoritarian regime and draws an angry and bloody response.

Faith and Freedom

This confession also suggests that people interested in democracy should heed religion. For example, attention to China's courageous prodemocracy activists is certainly deserved, but it must be remembered that their following is quite small.

Therefore, more attention should be paid to China's dissident churches, which, at a conservative estimate, number some twenty-five million members (apart from fifteen million members in official churches) and which are growing at a rate of 10 to15 percent a year.

In a 1997 cover story, "God Is Back," the *Far East Economic Review* quoted the words of one Beijing official: "If God had the face of a seventy-year-old man, we wouldn't care if he was back. But he has the face of millions of twenty-year-olds, so we are worried."

Clearly, the rapid growth of the only nationwide movement in China not under government control merits *political* attention.

Religion and International Relations

Apart from some of the horrific situations already described in Sudan, the Balkans, and elsewhere, the following religious trends also merit political reflection:

- •The rise of large, militant religious parties such as the Welfare Party in Turkey and the Bharatiya Janata Party (BJP) in India and the growth of radical Islam all over the world.

- •The rapid growth of charismatic Protestantism and Catholicism in Latin America. As Cambridge sociologist David Martin has shown, these indigenous developments represent one of the largest religious changes of the century. They also produce personal reform and provide a major impetus toward entrepreneurial activity.

- •The pattern of violence and warfare along the sub-Saharan boundary from Nigeria to Ethiopia. This constitutes a huge Christian/Muslim breach that must be addressed before peace is possible.

- •Massive rates of Christian conversions in Korea (now 25 percent of the population), China (a minimum of forty million, up from one million in 1980), Taiwan, and Indonesia.

- •Increasing religious tensions in trouble spots such as Nigeria and Indonesia. There is widespread religious violence in the northern and central regions of Nigeria, with thousands dead in recent years. There could be all-out religious war. In Indonesia, escalating religious strife precedes and has some separate dynamics from recent anti-Chinese violence: 200 churches were destroyed in Java alone in a recent fifteen-month period, and most of them were not attended by ethnic Chinese. Such incidents threaten to undermine what has been one of the world's best examples of interreligious toleration and cooperation.

In both of these regions, there is the possibility that instability and violence will spread far beyond the religious communities themselves.

•The exodus of Christians from the Middle East—some two million in the last five years. Currently some 3 percent of Palestinians are Christians, compared to an estimated 25 percent fifty years ago. Similar mass flight from Egypt, Syria, Lebanon, Turkey, and Iraq has occurred.

•The emergence of the Orthodox church as a unifying symbol in Russia, the Balkans, and other parts of the former Soviet Union.

•The increasing prominence of religion in the conflicts between India and Pakistan, which now possess nuclear weapons.

I am not making the absurd suggestion that religion—apart from other cultural, ethnic, economic, political, or strategic elements—is the only or the key factor in international affairs. Societies are complex. But I am saying that it is absurd to examine any political order *without* attending to the role of religion. We consistently need to deal with religion as an important independent factor. Analyses that ignore religion should be inherently suspect.

The Centrality of Religious Freedom

In the West there are now hopeful signs of a new awareness of the importance of religion and religious freedom. On October 9, 1998, the U.S. Senate passed the landmark International Religious Freedom Act. The following day, the House did the same. On October 27, President Clinton—a strong opponent—cut his losses and signed the act, which establishes a commission appointed by Congress and the White House to monitor global religious persecution and recommend responses. This is a small step, but it *is* a step, and in a vital area where few have trod. It is vital that *we* take similar steps—as concerned citizens.

We must support policies, programs, and organizations that promote and defend religious freedom.

We must support people such as Pope John Paul II, a man with no military or economic resources who is nonetheless daily aware of the spiritual dynamics of the world and who, for this reason, is perhaps its most important statesman.

We must make religious freedom a core element of "human rights." This is not a parochial matter. Historically, it is the first freedom in the growth of human rights, and it is the first freedom in the First Amendment to the U.S. Constitution.

While all human rights pressures make "geopolitical realists" nervous, religion carries the additional burdens of touching on deeply felt commitments, of facing confused domestic claims about "separation of church and state," and fears that the U.S. is an imperial Christian power. But this is no reason to hesitate. Religious rights must be at the forefront of any sound human rights policy. And unless we understand this, our ability to fight for any freedom at all is compromised.

❏ ❏ ❏

PAUL MARSHALL is a senior fellow at Freedom House's Center for Religious Freedom, an adjunct fellow at the Claremont Institute, and an adjunct professor at the Free University of Amsterdam and at Fuller Theological Seminary. He is the author (with Lela Gilbert) of the award-winning *Their Blood Cries Out* (1997) and the editor of *Religious Freedom in the World: A Global Report on Freedom and Persecution* (2000).

"All Beginnings Are Hopeful"
Challenges Facing the 21st Century

Margaret Thatcher

April 2001

Lady Thatcher delivered the following speech at a Hillsdale College seminar, "Taxes, Freedom, and America's Future," in Fort Myers, Florida.

❏ ❏ ❏

All beginnings are hopeful. That's what the principal of Somerville College, Oxford, said to those of us who arrived there in 1944, even in the midst of world war. It is an idea that has always stuck in my mind, and that has always seemed to me to be true. When I came to office in 1979, years of socialist policies had placed our country and our people in terrible shape. The top tax rate on earned income was 83 percent, and on investment income it was 98 percent. There were controls on prices, controls on income, controls on investment, and controls on foreign exchange. To get permission to do anything one had to go through a set of bureaucratic committees. Yet we were hopeful.

Right away I decided that we weren't going to go slowly in restoring the free and hardworking Britain I had known as a child. I determined that the only thing to do was to knock out these controls all at once, and return to being a free society. So in six weeks we got all the top rates of tax down to 40 percent. (And you know, when the Labour government finally got in again, it didn't put these rates back up. When you convert your opponents and make them electable, it's tough; but it's better than the alternative.) We also changed trade union law for the simple reason that the trade unions were almost running the country. So over a period of eighteen months, we had to change the rules and make certain that before the unions went on strike, they would have to place the issue on a ballot and obtain a majority vote by their members. This was not required before. And we privatized. Practically every major industry had been placed under state control, and there was no stimulus to work because these industries did not have to produce a dividend. We got something like fifteen of them back into private ownership rather quickly, and completed the lot the next year.

But these economic moves were only a part of our work. A more difficult task is to get people to work once they have gotten used to controls. History has taught us that freedom cannot long survive unless it is based on moral foundations. You can get the economics right, but in addition liberty must be cultivated as a moral quality. The right to liberty is fundamental. But it is what a person or a people does with it that tells their caliber and their fiber, and that decides whether they will continue to be free, and whether their nation will be prosperous. I like very much what John Adams, your second president, wrote in 1798: "Our Constitution was made only for a moral and religious people. It is wholly inadequate to the government of any other." That idea was right at the heart of your nation's founding. The virtues prized in free countries are honesty, self-discipline, a sense of responsibility to one's family, a sense of loyalty to one's employer and staff, and a pride in the quality of one's work. And these virtues only flourish in a climate of freedom.

Communism's Lingering Effects

Britain has now, despite its relatively small population, the fourth-largest economy in the world. This is a result of getting initiative and enterprise back, and of giving people an incentive to work. We must keep this in mind when we look at some of the problems that affect the world today. Look, for example, at the nations of the former Soviet Union. Russia, by far the biggest of these, has so many natural resources that it should be one of the richest countries in the world. It is communism and its lingering effects that have prevented Russia from becoming what it should, and from doing the best for its people. Of course Russia's political system has changed. But it is not easy for people who have acted for decades only under instruction or control to go about setting up small businesses. So what you tend to get during the transition from socialism to freedom is quite a lot of corruption. The International Monetary Fund was very generous and made considerable grants to Russia, but that money did not get to some of the places for which it was intended. Indeed, quite a bit of it ended up in bank accounts outside Russia. This, I am afraid, is what happens when you have a country in which integrity has very little meaning. You cannot have true liberty without a rule of law. We have not thought about this closely enough before. Any country coming to liberty must acquire a rule of law based on equity, fairness, and justice. It is something to which we must give the greatest attention. If you are going to have freedom, it must be under a rule of law that must apply to everyone.

The other great communist country, of course, is China. We in Britain had to deal with China because of the end of our leasehold on Hong Kong. The people of Hong Kong under British rule had an average income of about $28,000 a year, compared with $800 a year in China. These are the same people, with the same abilities and the same talents. The difference is that Hong Kong was a free society with a rule of law, and China was a total dictatorship. And I am afraid China's leaders have not yet learned the lesson. China, of all the countries in the world, is the most closed—much more so than Russia. Its leaders are willing to allow more economic liberty in order to achieve some of the prosperity they have seen elsewhere, but any suggestion of political freedom meets with total silence. I think one day that system will crack, partly as a result of people making more and more money. As people obtain one kind of freedom, other kinds of freedom will come too. Also it becomes increasingly difficult to keep the truth hidden from people, even in closed societies. It is difficult anymore to hide the fact that the number of people who lost their lives under communism in the last century—not in war, but simply because of the heavy handedness of government—approaches 100 million. Twenty million people lost their lives in the Soviet Union, sixty-five million people lost their lives in China, two million people lost their lives in North Korea, two million people lost their lives in Cambodia, and so on. This fact stands as an object lesson for the whole world, and trade only increases the tendency for this and other facts to become known. So we need to work as closely as we can with China. But again, of all the countries with which we should want to deal, China is the most difficult. Freeing up its rigid dictatorial system will take quite a long time.

Reason For Optimism

One of my favorite freedom fighters against communism, Václav Havel of the Czech Republic, has said that in everyone there is some longing for humanity's rightful dignity and for moral integrity. And indeed, in spite of all the terrors of communism, it could not crush the religious beliefs and the hopes of those suffering under it. This is why many of us were always certain that communism would eventually fail. It produces neither dignity nor prosperity. It takes all power away from the people and places it in the hands of a self-appointed elite. And because it distorts and manipulates the distinctive talents of individuals rather than letting those talents flourish, it prevents progress and prosperity.

I recall first hearing from Mr. Gorbachev that he would like to come and see us. He was on his way back to Russia from Canada on a Sunday and we were at Chequers, which is the lovely home of Britain's prime minister. So we collected him from the airport and brought him down to Chequers by car. He had been the Soviet Minister of Agriculture, and had soaked up the propaganda about the superiority of Soviet crops. Of course when he came from the airport through our lovely agricultural countryside and saw the prosperity of our crops, he was amazed. He studied our countryside carefully. Then in our meetings that afternoon, he was the first Russian I had ever met who, when you asked him a question, didn't pull a paper from a sheath and read whatever was on it, regardless of its relevance. Although he was due to go away at 4:30, we talked until about 6. It was an easy conversation, unlike any I had experienced with any communist before. So when Mr. Gorbachev left to fly home, I went straight to the telephone to ring up President Reagan, to tell him that there was something very unusual beginning to happen in the Soviet Union, that maybe it was beginning to crack.

Later, as you know, President Reagan went to see Mr. Gorbachev. And as an aside, it always fascinated me that people thought that Ronnie Reagan was not a detail man. If ever he was negotiating or going on a significant visit, he would have everything at his fingertips. He was the most thorough person in preparation that I ever knew. And of course those he met with were always most impressed. He knew all the answers, and would have a whole range of questions himself. President Reagan could dominate any meeting with two people. He is a very, very great man, and we are very fortunate that we had him when we did, because I think if it hadn't been for him, we would not have begun to get the cracking up of the Soviet Union.

Strength In Defense

Out of 150 states in the world, only 72 are free countries with democracy. So there is a long way to go yet. But as we get more and more communication and travel, and as more and more people come to see how we in the free countries run our affairs, one has to have great hope for the future. Yet there is a further thing I must say: We must always keep up our strength in defense. My generation remembers that we had such faith after World War I that there could never be another world war, we let our defenses down too far. They had to be restored very quickly when World War II began, and it was very difficult during the early stages. We must keep our defenses up and we must have equipment of the very latest technology. This is absolutely vital.

Partly here I have in mind the argument that is going on about missile defense. There is an old treaty we had with the Soviet Union that neither side would develop anti-ballistic missiles to knock the other side's missiles down. It was a treaty between the United States and the Soviet Union. You in the United States may, of course, choose to treat that treaty as if it is still in existence, but in fact the Soviet Union has ceased to exist. Therefore that treaty has ceased to be relevant, and we could legally build anti-ballistic missiles right away. I believe we should do that. It is a matter for the Russians to decide what they want to do, but I believe the first duty of any government is to protect the lives of its citizens under all circumstances. And we do that by having the latest technology in the United States.

My friends, you are citizens of a wonderful country. You have built the greatest country in the world in terms of establishing the rule of law, defending the freedoms of others, and building a most prosperous future for your people. If those who do not have liberty would be guided by your example, what a much better world it would be. In the meantime, what I call the English-speaking peoples, who have for so long defended liberty for the rest of the world, must continue to keep up that reputation, and to help those who still do not enjoy the liberty we take for granted.

❏ ❏ ❏

MARGARET THATCHER was born the daughter of a grocer in 1925, and went on to earn a degree in chemistry from Somerville College, Oxford, and a master of arts degree from the University of Oxford. Elected to the House of Commons in 1953, she held several ministerial appointments, including Minister of Education and Science from 1970 to 1974. She was elected leader of the opposition Conservative Party in 1975. In 1979 she was elected prime minister, and served in that position—winning re-election in 1983 and in 1987—until resigning in 1990. In 1992 she was elevated to the House of Lords, becoming Baroness Thatcher of Kesteven. She is the author of *The Downing Street Years* (1993), *The Path to Power* (1995), and *Statecraft: Strategies for a Changing World* (2002).

The Urgent Need for Ballistic Missile Defense

Brian T. Kennedy

November 2001

Mr. Kennedy delivered the following speech at a Hillsdale
College seminar, "Restoring the Constitution: America's First
Order of Business at the Dawn of a New Century," in Scotts-
dale, Arizona.

❏ ❏ ❏

On September 11, our nation's enemies attacked us using hijacked airlin-
ers. Next time, the vehicles of death and destruction might well be ballistic
missiles armed with nuclear, chemical, or biological warheads. And let us
be clear: The United States is defenseless against this mortal danger. We
would today have to suffer helplessly a ballistic missile attack, just as we
suffered helplessly on September 11. But the dead would number in the
millions and a constitutional crisis would likely ensue, because the survi-
vors would wonder—with good reason—if their government were capable
of carrying out its primary constitutional duty: to "provide for the common
defense."

The Threat is Real

The attack of September 11 should not be seen as a fanatical act of individuals like Osama bin Laden, but as a deliberate act of a consortium of
nations who hope to remove the U.S. from its strategic positions in the

Middle East, in Asia and the Pacific, and in Europe. It is the belief of such nations that the U.S. can be made to abandon its allies, such as Israel, if the cost of standing by them becomes too high. It is not altogether unreasonable for our enemies to act on such a belief. The failure of U.S. political leadership, over a period of two decades, to respond proportionately to terrorist attacks on Americans in Lebanon, to the first World Trade Center bombing, to the attack on the Khobar Towers in Saudi Arabia, to the bombings of U.S. embassies abroad, and most recently to the attack on the USS *Cole* in Yemen, likely emboldened them. They may also have been encouraged by observing our government's unwillingness to defend Americans against ballistic missiles. For all of the intelligence failures leading up to September 11, we know with absolute certainty that various nations are spending billions of dollars to build or acquire strategic ballistic missiles with which to attack and blackmail the United States. Yet even now, under a president who supports it, missile defense advances at a glacial pace.

Who are these enemy nations, in whose interest it is to press the U.S. into retreating from the world stage? Despite the kind words of Russian President Vladimir Putin, encouraging a "tough response" to the terrorist attack of September 11, we know that it is the Russian and Chinese governments that are supplying our enemies in Iraq, Iran, Libya, and North Korea with the ballistic missile technology to terrorize our nation. Is it possible that Russia and China don't understand the consequences of transferring this technology? Are Vladimir Putin and Jiang Zemin unaware that countries like Iran and Iraq are known sponsors of terrorism? In light of the absurdity of these questions, it is reasonable to assume that Russia and China transfer this technology as a matter of high government policy, using these rogue states as proxies to destabilize the West because they have an interest in expanding their power, and because they know that only the U.S. can stand in their way.

We should also note that ballistic missiles can be used not only to kill and destroy, but to commit geopolitical blackmail. In February of 1996, during a confrontation between mainland China and our democratic ally on Taiwan, Lt. Gen. Xiong Guang Kai, a senior Chinese official, made an implicit nuclear threat against the U.S., warning our government not to interfere because Americans "care more about Los Angeles than they do Taipei."

With a minimum of twenty Chinese intercontinental ballistic missiles (ICBMs) currently aimed at the U.S., such threats must be taken seriously.

The Strategic Terror of Ballistic Missiles

China possesses the DF-5 ballistic missile with a single four-megaton warhead. Such a warhead could destroy an area of 87.5 square miles, or roughly all of Manhattan, with its daily population of three million people. Even more devastating is the Russian SS-18, which has a range of 7,500 miles and is capable of carrying a single 24-megaton warhead or multiple warheads ranging from 550 to 750 kilotons.

Imagine a ballistic missile attack on New York or Los Angeles, resulting in the death of three to eight million Americans. Beyond the staggering loss of human life, this would take a devastating political and economic toll. Americans' faith in their government—a government that allowed such an attack—would be shaken to its core. As for the economic shock, consider that damages from the September 11 attack, minor by comparison, are estimated by some economists to be nearly 1.3 trillion dollars, roughly one-fifth of GNP.

Missile defense critics insist that such an attack could never happen, based on the expectation that the U.S. would immediately strike back at whomever launched it with an equal fury. They point to the success of the Cold War theory of Mutually Assured Destruction (MAD). But even MAD is premised on the idea that the U.S. would "absorb" a nuclear strike, much like we "absorbed" the attack of September 11. Afterward the president, or surviving political leadership, would estimate the losses and then employ our submarines, bombers, and remaining land-based ICBMs to launch a counterattack. This would fulfill the premise of MAD, but it would also almost certainly guarantee additional ballistic missile attacks from elsewhere.

Consider another scenario. What if a president, in order to avoid the complete annihilation of the nation, came to terms with our enemies? What rational leader wouldn't consider such an option, given the unprecedented horror of the alternative? Considering how Americans value human life, would a Bill Clinton or a George Bush order the unthinkable? Would *any* president launch a retaliatory nuclear strike against a country, even one as small as Iraq, if it meant further massive casualties to American citizens? Should we not agree that an American president ought not to have to make such a decision? President Reagan expressed this simply when he said that it would be better to prevent a nuclear attack than to suffer one and retaliate.

Then there is the blackmail scenario. What if Osama bin Laden were to obtain a nuclear ballistic missile from Pakistan (which, after all, helped to install the Taliban regime), place it on a ship somewhere off our coast, and demand that the U.S. not intervene in the destruction of Israel? Would we trade Los Angeles or New York for Tel Aviv or Jerusalem? Looked at this way, nuclear blackmail would be as devastating politically as nuclear war would be physically.

Roadblock to Defense: The ABM Treaty

Signed by the Soviet Union and the United States in 1972, the Anti-Ballistic Missile Treaty forbids a national missile defense. Article I, Section II reads: "Each Party undertakes not to deploy ABM systems for a defense of the territory of its country and not to provide a base for such a defense, and not to deploy ABM systems for defense of an individual region except as provided for in Article III of this Treaty." Article III allows each side to build a defense for an individual region that contains an offensive nuclear force. In other words, the ABM Treaty prohibits our government from defending the American people, while allowing it to defend missiles to destroy other peoples.

Although legal scholars believe that this treaty no longer has legal standing, given that the Soviet Union no longer exists, it has been upheld as law by successive administrations—especially the Clinton administration—and by powerful opponents of American missile defense in the U.S. Senate.

As a side note, we now know that the Soviets violated the ABM Treaty almost immediately. Thus the Russians possess today the world's only operable missile defense system. Retired CIA Analyst William Lee, in *The* ABM *Treaty Charade*, describes a 9,000-interceptor system around Moscow that is capable of protecting 75 percent of the Russian population. In other words, the Russians did not share the belief of U.S. arms-control experts in the moral superiority of purposefully remaining vulnerable to missile attack.

How to Stop Ballistic Missiles

For all the bad news about the ballistic missile threat to the U.S., there is the good news that missile defense is well within our technological capabilities. As far back as 1962, a test missile fired from the Vandenberg Air Force Base was intercepted (within 500 yards) by an anti-ballistic missile launched from Kwajaleen Atoll. The idea at the time was to use a small nuclear warhead in the upper atmosphere to destroy incoming enemy warheads. But it was deemed politically incorrect—as it is still today—to use a nuclear explosion to destroy a nuclear warhead, even if that warhead is racing toward an American city. (Again, only we seem to be squeamish in this regard: Russia's aforementioned 9,000 interceptors bear nuclear warheads.) So U.S. research since President Reagan reintroduced the idea of missile defense in 1983 has been aimed primarily at developing the means to destroy enemy missiles through direct impact or "hit-to-kill" methods.

American missile defense research has included ground-based, sea-based, and space-based interceptors, and air-based and space-based lasers. Each of these systems has undergone successful, if limited, testing. The space-based systems are especially effective since they seek to destroy enemy missiles in their first minutes of flight, known also as the boost phase. During this phase, missiles are easily detectible, have yet to deploy any so-called decoys or countermeasures, and are especially vulnerable to space-based interceptors and lasers.

The best near-term option for ballistic missile defense, recommended by former Reagan administration defense strategist Frank Gaffney, is to place a new generation of interceptors, currently in research, aboard U.S. Navy Aegis Cruisers. These ships could then provide at least some missile defense while more effective systems are built. Also under consideration is a ground-based system in the strategically important state of Alaska, at Fort Greely and Kodiak Island. This would represent another key component in a comprehensive "layered" missile defense that will include land, sea, air, and space.

Arguments Against Missile Defense

Opponents of missile defense present four basic arguments. The first is that ABM systems are technologically unrealistic, since "hitting bullets with bullets" leaves no room for error. They point to recent tests of ground-based interceptors that have had mixed results. Two things are important to note about these tests: First, many of the problems stem from the fact that the tests are being conducted under ABM Treaty restrictions on the speed of interceptors, and on their interface with satellites and radar. Second, some recent test failures involve science and technology that the U.S. perfected thirty years ago, such as rocket separation. But putting all this aside, as President Reagan's former science advisor William Graham points out, the difficulty of "hitting bullets with bullets" could be simply overcome by placing small nuclear charges on "hit-to-kill" vehicles as a "fail safe" for when they miss their targets. This would result in small nuclear explosions in space, but that is surely more acceptable than the alternative of enemy warheads detonating over American cities.

The second argument against missile defense is that no enemy would dare launch a missile attack at the U.S., for fear of swift retaliation. But as the CIA pointed out two years ago—and as Secretary of Defense Rumsfeld reiterated recently in Russia—an enemy could launch a ballistic missile from a ship off our coasts, scuttle the ship, and leave us wondering, as on September 11, who was responsible.

The third argument is that missile defense can't work against ship-launched missiles. But over a decade ago U.S. nuclear laboratories, with the help of scientists like Greg Canavan and Lowell Wood, conducted successful tests on space-based interceptors that could stop ballistic missiles in their boost phase from whatever location they were launched.

Finally, missile defense opponents argue that building a defense will ignite an expensive arms race. But the production cost of a space-based interceptor is roughly one to two million dollars. A constellation of 5,000 such interceptors might then cost ten billion dollars, a fraction of America's defense budget. By contrast, a single Russian SS-18 costs approximately $100 million, a North Korean Taepo Dong II missile close to $10 million, and an Iraqi Scud B missile about $2 million. In other words, if we get into an arms race, our enemies will go broke. The Soviet Union found it could not compete with us in such a race in the 1980s. Nor will the Russians or the Chinese or their proxies be able to compete today.

Time For Leadership

Building a missile defense is not possible as long as the U.S. remains bound by the ABM Treaty of 1972. President Bush has said that he will give the Russian government notice of our withdrawal from that treaty when his testing program comes into conflict with it. But given the severity of the ballistic missile threat, it is cause for concern that we have not done so already.

Our greatest near-term potential attacker, Iraq, is expected to have ballistic missile capability in the next three years. Only direct military intervention will prevent it from deploying this capability before the U.S. can deploy a missile defense. This should be undertaken as soon as possible.

Our longer-term potential attackers, Russia and China, possess today the means to destroy us. We must work and hope for peaceful relations, but we must also be mindful of the possibility that they have other plans. Secretary Powell has invited Russia and China to join the coalition to defeat terrorism. This is ironic, since both countries have been active supporters of the regimes that sponsor terrorism. And one wonders what they might demand in exchange. Might they ask us to delay building a missile defense? Or to renegotiate the ABM Treaty?

So far the Bush administration has not demonstrated the urgency that the ballistic missile threat warrants. It is also troublesome that the president's newly appointed director of Homeland Security, Pennsylvania Governor Tom Ridge, has consistently opposed missile defense—a fact surely noted with approval in Moscow and Beijing. On the other hand, President Bush has consistently supported missile defense, both in the 2000 campaign and since taking office, and he has the power to carry through with his promises.

Had the September 11 attack been visited by ballistic missiles, resulting in the deaths of three to six million Americans, a massive effort would have immediately been launched to build and deploy a ballistic missile defense. America, thankfully, has a window of opportunity—however narrow—to do so now, before it is too late.

Let us begin in earnest.

❏ ❏ ❏

BRIAN T. KENNEDY is the president of the Claremont Institute. Formerly the Institute's vice president and director of its Golden State Center for Policy Studies, he directed a project to inform state lawmakers on missile defense issues and edited the webpage <www.missilethreat.com>. A graduate of Claremont McKenna College with degrees in political science and history, he has written extensively for newspapers and magazines, including the *Orange County Register*, the *Washington Times*, *Investor's Business Daily*, and *National Review*.

Emerging Threats to United States National Security

Jesse Helms

January 2002

Senator Helms delivered the following speech at the second annual Hillsdale College Churchill Dinner in Washington, D.C.

❏ ❏ ❏

America is the only nation in history founded on an idea: the proposition that all men are created equal, and are endowed by their Creator with inalienable rights to life, liberty, and the pursuit of happiness. No other nation can make such a claim. This is what makes us unique. It is why, for more than two centuries, America has been a beacon of liberty for all who aspire to live in freedom. It is also why America was so brutally attacked on September 11.

The terrorists who struck the Pentagon and the World Trade Towers despise what America stands for: freedom, religious toleration, and individual liberty. They hate the success with which the American idea has spread around the world. And they want to terrorize us into retreat and inaction, so that we will be afraid to defend freedom abroad and live as free people at home. They will not succeed.

A Revived Sense of Vigilance

The terrorists we fight today are not the first aggressors of their kind to challenge us. Indeed, at this moment of trial, it is altogether fitting that we

319

gather to honor the memory of Sir Winston Churchill, whose courage, conviction, and steely resolve led the Allies to victory over fascism, and who went on then to warn us about the danger of the emerging communist threat and the Iron Curtain then descending across Europe. Today we face a new and different enemy—one who hides in caves, and who strikes in new and unexpected ways. Yet in a larger respect, this new enemy is no different from the enemy Churchill faced sixty years ago. And as shocking as September 11 was, it should have come as no surprise that our nation was once again challenged by aggressors bent on her destruction.

Jefferson warned that "the price of liberty is eternal vigilance." And since our founding, Jefferson has been proven right, time and time again. New enemies have constantly emerged to threaten us. The lesson of history is that to secure our liberty, America must be constantly on guard, preparing to defend our nation against tomorrow's adversaries even as we vanquish the enemies of today.

Over the past decade, America let down her guard. With the collapse of the Soviet Union, our leaders assumed that the post-Cold War world would be one of unlimited peace and prosperity, and that our greatest security challenges would be invading Haiti, or stopping wars in places like Bosnia and Kosovo. The Clinton people slashed our defense budget in search of a "peace dividend," while sending our forces all over the world on a plethora of missions that drained America's military readiness. They put off investments needed to prepare for the real emerging threats to U.S. national security. Instead of focusing on new dangers, they spent their time and energy forging ridiculous new treaties—like the Kyoto Protocol and the International Criminal Court—while fighting desperately to preserve antiquated ones, like the ABM Treaty!

In light of America's new war, it is almost humorous to look back on some of the foreign policy debates of the 1990s. Can anyone imagine Kofi Annan today declaring, as he did two years ago, that the United Nations Security Council is the "sole source of legitimacy for the use of force in the world"? Or former Deputy Secretary of State Strobe Talbott repeating his ridiculous assertion that all countries, "no matter how permanent or even sacred [they] may seem," are in fact "artificial and temporary"?

"Within the next hundred years," Talbott went on to say, "nationhood as we know it will be obsolete; all states will recognize a single global authority." Let him tell that to the policemen and firemen at the World Trade Towers. Let him tell it to all the millions of Americans flying flags from their homes and cars. Let him tell it to the thousands of brave Americans in uniform, who at this very moment are voluntarily risking their lives to defend our country.

In the wake of September 11, a measure of sanity has been restored to debates over U.S. foreign policy. Awakened to new dangers, our challenge is now twofold. First, we must win the war on terrorism that took our nation by surprise. And second, we must prepare now for the threats that could emerge to surprise us in the decades ahead.

Beyond Afghanistan

Thanks to the outstanding leadership of President Bush, the Taliban is in retreat and Osama bin Laden is on the run. But the war on terrorism is far from over. Indeed, one could argue that the most difficult challenge comes now, as the Afghan campaign moves from the taking of cities, to a cave-by-cave hunt for bin Laden and his terrorist network. Ripping that network out by its roots will be long, difficult, and dangerous work. Moreover, President Bush's greatest challenge may come *after* the Afghan phase of the war is over.

The bin Laden terrorist network operates in dozens of countries. Nor is it the only one that threatens America and her allies. Terrorist networks operate across the world, with the support of dozens of states. President Bush has made clear that this war will not end until every terrorist network with global reach is decisively defeated. He has also made clear that the United States will no longer tolerate states that support or provide safe haven to these terrorists. That means, I am convinced, that the war on terrorism cannot and will not end until Saddam Hussein suffers the same fate as the Taliban.

While we do not yet know that Saddam was directly involved with the tragic events of September 11, there is a mountain of evidence linking him to international terrorism generally, and to bin Laden's terrorist network specifically. We know for a fact that Saddam attempted to assassinate former President Bush. We know with certainty that he has chemical and biological agents, and is pursuing nuclear weapons. We know for certain that, days before coming to the U.S., one of the September 11 hijackers met with an Iraqi agent in Prague—and that soon after that meeting, this same bin Laden operative was in the United States inquiring how one goes about renting a crop duster. So the obvious next step in the war on terrorism is the elimination of Saddam Hussein's tyrannical terrorist regime.

Just as the United States teamed up with determined Afghans who were ready, willing, and able to overthrow the Taliban with American support, there are Iraqis ready to overthrow Saddam. But taking the war to Saddam will be no easy task. We must accept the probability that many of the nations rallying around us today will be nowhere to be found. Indeed, some are likely to scream and yell and stomp their feet, demanding "evidence" of Iraq's involvement in the September 11 attacks. It is then that President Bush must patiently remind them that the war on terrorism is a war against *all* terrorists who threaten America, regardless of whether they bombed the World Trade Towers, sought to murder a former President of the United States, or threaten our people with nuclear, chemical, and biological weapons of mass destruction.

We must proceed against Saddam with the same resolve with which we have proceeded against the Taliban in Afghanistan. Once the world sees *two* terrorist regimes in rubble, I suspect that support for international terrorism will dry up pretty quickly. Dictators will begin to understand that waging a war by proxy against the United States carries deadly consequences.

While we prosecute the war on terrorism to its logical conclusion, we must, at the same time, begin preparing for the *next* threats to America—threats which could be quite different from those we face today. The next challenge we face may come from a rogue state armed with ballistic missiles capable of reaching New York or Los Angeles. It may come from cyberterrorists who seek to cripple our nation and our economy by attacking our vital information networks. It may come from a country that has developed small "killer satellites" capable of attacking our space infrastructure, on which both our defense and our economy depend. Or it may come from a traditional state-on-state war, such as a Chinese invasion of Taiwan. In any event, it is essential that we begin preparing *now* for *all* of these possibilities, by developing defenses against a wide range of asymmetric threats.

Distinguishing Friends From Enemies

We must also look realistically at who our potential adversaries could be in the decades ahead. For example, Communist China—a nation with no respect for human rights, for religious freedom, or for the rule of law— remains both a present and an emerging threat to the United States. Its annual double-digit increases in military spending, its virulent anti-American propaganda, and its aggressive arms acquisitions are all very clear indications that China fully intends to become a superpower—and, when it is able, to seek regional hegemony in Asia and threaten our democratic friends on Taiwan. Moreover, China has for years exported dangerous missile technology to Pakistan—support that, according to the Director of Central Intelligence, continues today unabated. China has also supplied chemical weapons-related equipment and technology to Iran. And earlier this year, U.S. and British war planes had to destroy fiber-optic cables that had been laid by Chinese firms in Iraq, as part of Saddam Hussein's ever-improving air defense infrastructure.

Today, China is a thorn in our side. We must make sure that as China rises it does not become a dagger at our throat. Nor is China by any means the only nation that could one day threaten us. Countries like Iran, Syria, Sudan, North Korea, and Cuba continue to provide aid, comfort, and refuge to terrorist elements that wish to harm the United States, and several of them are seeking weapons of mass destruction and the means to deliver them.

In times of war, the enemy of our enemy is often our friend. During World War II, Churchill explained his wartime alliance with Stalin this way: "If Hitler invaded Hell," Churchill said, "I would make at least a favorable reference to the Devil in the House of Commons." But let us not forget what happened in the *aftermath* of World War II, when the Soviet Union went from wartime ally to Cold War adversary. We must be careful that, in our zeal to build the coalition against terrorism, we do not mistakenly turn a blind eye to the true nature of certain regimes whose long-term interests and intentions remain contrary to ours.

Of course we must, and should, take the opportunity to reach out to nations that are willing to step up and take concrete steps to help us in the fight against terror. Not for several generations has the geopolitical map of the world been so much in flux, as a variety of countries decide how to respond to the events of September 11 and to President Bush's ultimatum that "either you are with *us* or you are with the terrorists." President Bush is certainly to be commended for the rapid transformation of our relationship with Russia, whose long-term interests clearly lie with the West. President Putin seems to have seized September 11 as an opportunity to align Russia more closely with the United States, and he should be encouraged in this regard. But we must proceed with care. For example: The idea of giving Russia a decisionmaking role within NATO—including a veto over certain Alliance decisions (as NATO Secretary General Lord Robertson suggested the other day)—is absurd. Russia still has much to prove before being given *de facto* membership in the Atlantic Alliance.

We must make clear—as President Bush has made clear—that we want closer cooperation with Russia and a new relationship that puts Cold War animosities behind us. But in building that relationship, we must stand firmly behind our intention to build and deploy ballistic missile defenses. If the United States and Russia are to establish a new strategic relationship based on trust, cooperation, and mutual interests, then Russia must recognize that such missile defenses, in protecting the United States and our allies from mutual adversaries, will enhance the security of both nations in today's new and dangerous world.

Moral Foundations of Security

America is indeed the greatest nation on the face of the earth, a beacon of freedom for the entire world. We have met tremendous challenges to our freedom before September 11 and defeated them. We will do so again. But in the long run, the greatest emerging threat to America may not come from without, but rather from within. As I have said often during my years in public life, we will not long survive as a nation unless and until we restore the moral and spiritual principles that made America great in the first place.

On September 11, 4,000 innocent Americans were killed by a foreign enemy. The American people responded with shock, sadness, and a deep and righteous anger—and rightly so. Yet let us not forget that *every passing day* in our country almost 4,000 innocent Americans are killed at the hands of so-called doctors, who rip those little ones from their mothers' wombs. These are the most innocent Americans of all—small, helpless, defenseless babies. For *unborn* Americans, every day is September 11.

America was attacked by terrorists on September 11 because of what America stands for—our dedication to life, liberty, and justice under God. As we defend those principles abroad, let us also renew them here at home. As we go after the terrorists who committed those unspeakable acts against our people, let us, at the same time, get about the task of restoring our nation's moral and spiritual foundations. No matter how successfully we prosecute the war against terrorism—no matter how brilliantly we prepare for the threats of the future—we will *never* be truly secure if we do not return to the principles on which America was founded, and which made America great.

This is already taking place. In the wake of September 11, flags are flying and church pews are overflowing. This great patriotic and spiritual outpouring is proof that the terrorists' plans have backfired. They thought that their attacks would frighten and divide us; instead they have drawn us closer to God—and to each other. We must encourage this spiritual rebirth, and nurture it so that it becomes another Great Awakening. We must instill in our young people an understanding that theirs is a nation founded by Providence to serve as a shining city on a hill—a light to the nations, spreading the good news of God's gift of human freedom.

Thank you, God bless you, and, as Ronald Reagan always said, *God bless America!*

❏ ❏ ❏

JESSE HELMS was born in Monroe, North Carolina, and served in the U.S. Navy during World War II. After the war, he became the city editor of *The Raleigh Times*, and later, director of news and programs for the Tobacco Radio Network and radio station WRAL in Raleigh. After serving as an assistant to two U.S. senators and as executive director of the North Carolina Bankers Association, he ran successfully for the U.S. Senate in 1972 and was re-elected four times. He is former chairman, now ranking Republican member, of the Committee on Foreign Relations. Among his many awards are the Gold Medal of Merit from the Veterans of Foreign Wars and the Guardian of Small Business Award from the National Federation of Independent Business.